ORPHEUS AND POWER

ORPHEUS AND POWER

THE *MOVIMENTO NEGRO* OF
RIO DE JANEIRO AND SÃO PAULO,
BRAZIL, 1945–1988

Michael George Hanchard

PRINCETON UNIVERSITY PRESS

PRINCETON, NEW JERSEY

COPYRIGHT © 1994 BY PRINCETON UNIVERSITY PRESS
PUBLISHED BY PRINCETON UNIVERSITY PRESS, 41 WILLIAM STREET,
PRINCETON, NEW JERSEY 08540
IN THE UNITED KINGDOM: PRINCETON UNIVERSITY PRESS,
CHICHESTER, WEST SUSSEX
ALL RIGHTS RESERVED

LIBRARY OF CONGRESS CATALOGING-IN-PUBLICATION DATA

HANCHARD, MICHAEL GEORGE
ORPHEUS AND POWER:
THE MOVIMENTO NEGRO OF RIO DE JANEIRO AND
SÃO PAULO, BRAZIL, 1945–1988 / MICHAEL GEORGE HANCHARD.
P.   CM.
INCLUDES BIBLIOGRAPHICAL REFERENCES AND INDEX.
ISBN 0-691-03292-0
F2659.A1H36   1994
305.8'00981—DC20   93-38137 CIP

THIS BOOK HAS BEEN COMPOSED IN GALLIARD

PRINCETON UNIVERSITY PRESS BOOKS ARE PRINTED
ON ACID-FREE PAPER, AND MEET THE GUIDELINES FOR
PERMANENCE AND DURABILITY OF THE COMMITTEE ON
PRODUCTION GUIDELINES FOR BOOK LONGEVITY
OF THE COUNCIL ON LIBRARY RESOURCES

PRINTED IN THE UNITED STATES OF AMERICA

1   3   5   7   9   10   8   6   4   2

For Constance Farquhar

MY GRANDMOTHER IN BOTH

GOOD TIMES AND BAD

CONTENTS

ACKNOWLEDGMENTS

SEVERAL PEOPLE both in Brazil and the United States greatly aided me in understanding the similarities and dissimilarities of Brazil. My dissertation committee, which consisted of professors Henry Bienen, Kay Warren, and Emilia Viotti da Costa, provided invaluable guidance in helping me develop both the form and content of my research. Each in his or her own way, helped me avoid historical and conceptual errors, in addition to giving moral support. Much thanks to my gang of three.

Discussions with Forrest Colburn, Michael Jimenez, Peter Johnson, Ben Ross Schneider, Stanley Stein, and members of the MacArthur interdisciplinary seminar on national conflict also helped sophisticate my thinking about the intersections of race, gender, and national identity. Their comments on my written work also helped me become a more conscientious scholar than I might have been otherwise. I also gained valuable insights from Frank Rosengarten, who led me through the intricacies of Antonio Gramsci's ethico-political stances.

Thanks also to Anani Dzidzienyo, Thomas Skidmore, and the anonymous reviewers for Princeton. As rigorous but encouraging readers, their painstaking critiques of earlier drafts spared me errors of conceptualization and historical fact. An entire paragraph belongs to my principal interlocutor, Howard Winant, with whom I have discussed issues of racial theory in general and Brazilian race relations in particular over the past five years. A ruthless critic as well as a source of inspiration, Howard, more than any single person, has made me realize that most scholarship is the implicit result of a collective effort.

In Austin, Texas, I received constructive criticism from Richard Graham, who made incisive comments on an earlier version of this manuscript, which I subsequently incorporated. Amalia Pallares and Shannan Mattiace, my research assistants, helped in the final phases of manuscript revision, as did Suzanne Colwell. Thanks to all three.

In Rio, Januario Garcia generously allowed me to use the library and other resources at the Instituto de Pesquisa das Culturas Negras, and provided key contacts for me within the black movement, as did Julio Cesar de Tavares. It was Paola Alves Vieira who actually introduced me to the numerous worlds of the Carioca during my first trip to Brazil in 1985 and subsequently in 1988, when she helped me find that apartment in Flamengo. She also frequently challenged my interpretations of Rio's racial "harmony." Gisele Mills was quite helpful as a research assistant in 1988, especially in sharing with me her vast knowledge of Afro-Brazilian women's groups in the two cities. Olivia Lopes Galvão, Luis Claudio de Barcelos, Denise Ferriera, and Juarez Pinheiro Coqueiro were instrumental in my navigation of the library and archives of the Centro de Estudos de Afro-Asiaticos (CEAA) of the Conjunto Universitario Candido Mendes in downtown Rio. Carlos Hasenbalg provided me with a place to work at the CEAA in 1988 and 1989, read numerous rough drafts of my manuscript, and gave cautious but energetic enthusiasm along the way. It is without exaggeration that I can say that much of my fieldwork in Rio de Janeiro would not have been possible without his assistance. Many thanks to *minha familia* in Rio, including those whose help I received but did not mention.

São Paulo is considered a cold and distant metropolis in comparison to Rio, but I found numerous people there who took me into their confidences, homes, and lives. Francisco Marco Dias and Luis Paulo de Lima assumed from our first encounter that I was their brother in both senses of the word, and provided the type of support that only some close friends and family members give. I can only hope that this book and my friendship has not disappointed them. Deborah Silvia Santos is another person whose counsel and insights into Afro-Brazilian social history enriched my experiences in São Paulo. Together, they composed my second and perhaps most important family in Brazil, for they assumed the importance of my intellectual and personal tasks on this subject as their own. There is simply no way to repay such a debt.

Rafael Pinto, Hamilton Cardoso, the late Vanderlei Jose Maria, Ivair Alves Santos, Milton Barbosa, and Antonio Carlos Arruda led me through the complexities of internal debates within the *movimento negro* and *movimento estudantil* during the 1970s, and made helpful suggestions for additional interviewees and sources of information. To struggle against personal vissicitudes and racial discrimination with a sense of humor and generosity is an admirable quality fully displayed by each, particularly Vanderlei Jose Maria, who succumbed to the AIDS virus in 1990.

Most of my gratitude is reserved for my wife, Nancy, and Jenna, my daughter. Thanks for putting up with me all of these years, especially when I was off doing research on this project.

ORPHEUS AND POWER

INTRODUCTION

MY FIRST real introduction to the politics of racial difference in Brazil occurred in neither a classroom nor a library but on the streets of Rio de Janeiro during my first week there to conduct field research in September 1988. After securing an apartment and settling in Flamengo, one of the older parts of the city, I walked to Catete, a nearby neighborhood, to buy a week's worth of vittles at the *supermercado* Disco. I spent about forty minutes in the store collecting my supplies, marveling at all the known and unknown goods I could mispronounce in Portuguese. I headed for the main exit after making my purchases, proceeding directly from the check-out register, when I was stopped by a clerk who asked me if I had purchased the items that were in the bags that I was carrying.

I told him that I had and was ready to furnish a receipt when he spoke in a whisper to a nearby manager. The manager gave a quick glance from his work, then waved me on. Angry and confused, I headed to my apartment. "Perhaps I walked through the wrong exit?" I thought to myself as I returned to my apartment. That could not be, because there were several others alongside and ahead of me who made their way through that exit, undisturbed. Why did the clerk desist so easily if he thought I had committed a crime? Maybe it was my accent that ended the scene and preempted the possibility of another, more contentious one. "Maybe I was mistaken for someone else?" I thought as I neared my apartment building. It was then that I reminded myself just who that someone else might be, which led me to the core problematic of my dissertation and now, this book.

My then-halting Portuguese made me painfully aware of the fact that I was in Brazil, not the United States, so any judgments about racism in the former country could not be simply based upon the norms, experiences, practices—the history—of the latter. As a student of comparative racial politics, I knew that Brazil was not a racial democracy, despite claims to the contrary. I was also told by U.S. African-Americans, however, that Brazil was quite unlike the United States because the interaction between whites and nonwhites was much freer, less burdened by the stark indicators of racial discrimination: race-rooted violence and discrimination, anxieties over racial mixture. The result, I was assured by U.S. and later Brazilian African-Americans, was a more subtle form of racism in Brazil. "Then how could something so unsubtle happen to me in Brazil?" I thought.

I then reminded myself that people of African descent, scattered about the Earth like all other diasporic peoples, had been subjected to a peculiar form of *racial* slavery and were members of a subordinated group in every nation-state they resided, even when they governed themselves. Moreover, this enslavement was part of a more comprehensive process of racial domination that had cultural, epistemological, and ideological consequences as well. One facet of these consequences has been the attachment of negative stereotypes to African-derived peoples, so that their skin color (phenotype) triggered an ensemble of meanings, often pejorative, in the minds of others and sometimes even among themselves. This in turn, often led to social practices that were (and are) considered racially discriminatory. For me, the above incident captured in real life something I had come to assume through my study of racial theory over the past several years: "race" operates as a shuttle between socially constructed meanings and practices, between subjective interpretation and lived, material reality. It has a paradoxical, simultaneous importance, for it *is* and *is not* about skin color. Race does not, and could not, have any social significance by itself. It was then that I realized that Brazilian society could not be immune to the forms of prejudice, discrimination, and exploitation on racial grounds present in similarly constituted societies. As a student of racial politics, the incident at the supermarket strongly suggested that I had come to the right place.

It is possible that the Disco store clerk may have mistaken me for someone else. Yet it is more than likely that he had mistaken me in another way, through an interpretive scheme that constantly equates the skin color of people of African descent with the most negative denotations available in a given society, in multiracial polities both in and outside the West. For people of African descent, cases of mistaken identity nearly always have a dual connotation, both personal and impersonal. In this sense, the "someone else" the clerk may have mistaken me for was, in fact, me. And yet I was in Brazil, not the United States or any other nation-state, so although the above incident could have occurred in numerous other places, the historical and contextual circumstances were distinct. Thus it was not enough to merely assert that racism did exist in Brazil, but how.

Students who explore the "how" in Brazilian racial politics will find circumstances both like and unlike those to be found in other multiracial polities where people of African descent reside. To those unfamiliar with the literature on Brazilian race relations, this may appear as a very basic, even rudimentary assumption. Yet only over the past twenty years or so have social scientists investigated racial interactions in Brazil with the assumption that discrimination does exist in this nation.

After years of neglect, there is now a rich, emergent literature that provides a quantitative assessment of the empirical evidence of racial inequality. Building upon this literature but also attempting to push the study of

Brazilian racial inequality into more qualitative areas, I would like to demonstrate the cultural and political forms of inequality that have impeded the development of racially specific, Afro-Brazilian modes of consciousness and mobilization. While I was told by both white and Afro-Brazilians that the supermarket incident was a common form of racial discrimination in Brazil, those same people told me that the majority of whites and Afro-Brazilians would not recognize it as such. Based upon my personal experiences with whites, Afro-Brazilians, and nonwhites in Brazil, I have assumed that the interpretation of my Brazilian friends was true. The more interesting problematic for me, however, was why. This final question is the point of departure for this book. It is a question that no single book can answer, but I have attempted to do so only in the hope that my answer will lead to other answers, and to other questions as well.

Why has there been no sustained Afro-Brazilian social movement in Brazil comparable to the civil rights movement in the United States or nationalist insurgencies in sub-Saharan Africa and parts of the New World during the post–World War II period? Even though there have been attempts great and small to coalesce a divergent array of people into a racially based movement for social change during this period, there has been no national movement within civil society against racial inequalities and subordinations in Brazil.

Brazilians of African descent represent nearly 44 percent of the total Brazilian population of 138 million people according to the 1980 census. They are the single largest population of people of African descent outside of Nigeria.[1] The disparities in health, education, welfare, and employment between whites and nonwhites in Brazil suggest, at the very least, bleak social conditions that rival or surpass those experienced by U.S. blacks in the 1950s and 1960s or colonized peoples of color in the Caribbean and elsewhere. In contrast to the sustained mobilization of blacks in sub-Saharan Africa and the New World after 1945, an Afro-Brazilian social movement has operated only intermittently within the same epoch.

We know from several accounts of rebellion and revolution that horrible living conditions do not, in themselves, explain why resistance to dominant social structures emerges during certain historical moments and not others. The work of Theda Skocpol (1979), Eric Wolf (1969), and others has attempted explanations of tumultuous moments that encapsulate the dissent, response, conflict, and aftermath of mass struggles for social transformation.

Equally important, however, and in some respects more difficult to chart are situations of inequality that do not crystallize in "historical moments" but grind on with seemingly little change or with shifts too subtle to immediately discern. In such cases, mechanisms of dominance and subordination are encased in the "everyday." They are reproduced in part by political economies, but also, perhaps more profoundly, via processes of socialization and value orientation.

Unfortunately, when juxtaposed against fully articulated conflict (the rebellion, strike, war, or sit-in), quotidian forms of resistance and acquiescence have all the glamor of an unpolished stone. Consequently, in the quest to observe and explain the spectacular, social scientists have often neglected situations of inequality that are not highlighted by obvious ruptures. In these contexts it is the social construction of the normal that suggests intergroup struggles lurking below everyday surfaces, requiring as much—if not more—scrutiny as the lucid political drama of anti-apartheid struggle in South Africa, or the clash of Chinese students and troops in Tiananmen Square, Beijing.

This juxtaposition of the spectacular "historical moment" against more mundane situations of inequality produced the opening question that motivates this book: Why has there been no social movement generated by Afro-Brazilians in the post–World War II period that corresponds to social movements in the United States, sub-Saharan Africa, and the Caribbean? In response, I will argue that a process of racial hegemony has effectively neutralized racial identification among nonwhites to a large degree, making it an improbable point of mass mobilization among Afro-Brazilians in Rio de Janeiro and São Paulo.

This form of hegemony, articulated through processes of socialization that promote racial discrimination while simultaneously denying its existence, assists in the reproduction of social inequalities between whites and nonwhites while simultaneously promoting a false premise of racial equality between them. The specific consequences for blacks, I will argue, are the overall inability of Afro-Brazilian activists to mobilize people on the basis of racial identity, due in large part to the general inability of Brazilians to identify patterns of violence and discrimination that are racially specific. These consequences flow into a paradox, for activists, of attempting to subvert dominant political and cultural practices for counterhegemonic purposes without being subsumed by the ambiguities and contradictions that dominant ideological and social practices produce.

Drawing from archival materials and interviews previously untapped in Brazilian race relations scholarship, along with existing sociological and historical literatures of Brazilian race relations, I will argue that the absence of the historical moment for Afro-Brazilian activists, along with the sustained depoliticization of Brazilian race relations by white elites, manifests the ongoing struggle over racial hegemony in the Brazilian polity. While the racial hegemony of white elites has done much to defer the prospect of major upheaval, their dominance has not been total. Afro-Brazilian activists have increasingly made explicit the political implications of Brazilian race relations, and have made some inroads toward undermining racialized patterns of dominance and subordination.

Possible explanations for the absent "historical moment" in Brazilian race relations have been neglected in political and comparative analysis by Brazilian as well as non-Brazilian (principally U.S.) scholars. Several historical and sociological studies consider the structural marginalization of blacks in Brazilian society (Fernandes 1969; Hasenbalg 1979; 1985), but there has been little research on or theorizing about the political and cultural implications of their marginalization outside of the marketplace.

There have been some works on black political candidates, organizations, and their place within municipal electoral processes (Pereira 1982; Valente 1986) as well as the location of blacks in religious and popular culture (Da Matta 1984; Brown and Bick 1987), but none have attempted to situate the material conditions of black Brazilians within broader political, cultural processes of dominance and subordination. In conceptual terms, the absence of works linking Brazilian race relations to questions of power and dominance has resulted in a theoretical void in scholarship on Brazilian race relations. This is due, in large part, to the preoccupation of Brazilian social scientists with the study and analysis of races or ethnic groups in society and not the *relations* among them. This distinction, so brilliantly perceived by Roberto Da Matta (1984), has had the following repercussions for the study of Brazilian race relations.

First, at the empirical level, there are few works that situate the cultural and material interaction of whites and blacks within a normative, political totality, although the literature is replete with what could be called prefix studies, namely, works on topics narrowly defined by such phrases as *black politics* or *black culture*. As a consequence, macrolevel theorizing about the power relations between white and black Brazilians is notably absent.

The consequence has been a paucity of interpretive works that attempt to situate Brazilian "race relations" within a more comparative perspective of racial politics; the issues of power, influence, policy, and strategy found in the interaction of two or more "races." Given the absence of interpretive scholarship on Brazilian race relations, this book has two broad aims. First, the presentation of primary materials on Brazilian race relations in history and contemporary society—materials that heretofore have been absent from Brazilian race relations scholarship—will, I hope, lead readers to the conclusion that Brazil must not be exempted from critical scrutiny of its racial politics. This empirical base will lead to the second purpose, a theoretically informed analysis that links the historical and contemporary elements of Brazilian racial politics to wider debates about race, class, and culture.

While the concept of hegemony has, in one form or another, been generally applied to issues of Latin American politics, from corporatism in Peru (A. Stepan 1978), to even broader considerations of Gramsci's influence upon the political transformations in Latin America (Coutinho and Nogueira 1985), it has not been used to situate racial or ethnic tensions within analyses of national political cultures. As a result, this study of the implications of racial hegemony for an Afro-Brazilian resistance movement departs from the restricted application of the concept by Latin Americanist scholars, as well as the overall neglect of the topic of race in this region more generally.

Ironically, the whole issue of racial politics in Brazil is never mentioned in an entire volume devoted to Brazil's current phase of democratization (A. Stepan 1989). However, Brazil is an ideal polity in which to apply the concept of racial hegemony. The premise of racial equality and the attendant denial of contemporary, ongoing racist practices in society influences not only how people perceive race relations, but their very definition of democracy at a time when the crisis of Brazilian civil society also constitutes a crisis of the meaning of the word *citizen*: who gets to be considered a citizen, and who does not. The most crippling effects of racial democracy upon nonwhite Brazilians who are not activists, I will argue, are the multiple difficulties they have in distinguishing racist acts from other forms of oppression in a society that distinguishes whites from nonwhites while enforcing patterns of repression throughout society as a whole.

What distinguishes Brazil from any other plural society in the New World is that no other nation has had such an elaborate "solution" to the "problem" of racial and cultural pluralism. Racial democracy and its attendant racist ideology of whitening was "the result of the elite's struggle to reconcile Brazil's actual social relations—the absence of a clear line between white and nonwhite—with the doctrines of scientific racism that had penetrated Brazil from abroad,"[2] and greatly influenced the course of Brazilian history, race relations and national identity. Cuba and Peru have ideologies of whitening dating back to the nineteenth century, but nothing as developed or sophisticated.[3]

Chapter 1 provides an explanation of the terms, theoretical constructs, and methodology used in this study. Latin American studies have not incorporated recent conceptual innovations in the study of racial and ethnic politics, which have enriched regional investigations of Southeast Asia, Western Europe, and Africa. An array of recent theoretical approaches will be outlined in this chapter for their usefulness in the study of Brazilian racial politics. This chapter also situates the cities of Rio de Janeiro and São Paulo in comparative perspective to examine the socioeconomic and demographic differences between the two cities that made for distinct patterns of race relations.

Chapter 2 reviews past and present debates about Brazilian race relations and their implications for an understanding of the intersection of race, class, and culture in Brazil. The prevailing explanations of racial politics and inequality will then be juxtaposed against the theoretical formulations and synthesized within this alternative approach of racial hegemony.

The historical underpinnings of racial exceptionalism, the myth of racial democracy, and the development of Brazilian racial hegemony will be presented in Chapter 3. The myth of racial democracy emerged from the ideology of racial exceptionalism, the belief that Brazil was free of the racial tensions plaguing other polities such as the United States. Although the myth of racial democracy has been greatly undermined by several national critiques that emerged during the 1988 centennial commemoration of *Abolição* (abolition), significant elements of racially exceptionalist discourses and practices, and thus racial hegemony, remain intact. Chapter 3 will also present quantitative data and analysis of racial inequalities in labor markets, educational, and other institutions in civil society. This will enable us to chart the evolution of this racially hegemonic process in conjunction with the Brazilian political economy, as a means of explicating the interlocking mechanisms of ideological, cultural, and material oppression grounded therein.

Since the early 1930s in Rio de Janeiro and São Paulo, there have been several attempts to develop Afro-Brazilian social movements that would evolve into national organizations. Although there have been significant intensifications of Afro-Brazilian politics in other parts of the country, such as in Salvador, Bahia, Rio de Janeiro and São Paulo have been the principal sites for Afro-Brazilian political mobilization.

The infusion of politics into Afro-Brazilian racial identity was a significant phenomena within the Afro-Brazilian movement in the 1970s, one that would resonate in the agendas of Afro-Brazilian activists and politicians in the 1980s. Chapter 4 provides excerpts and analysis of sixty interviews with Afro-Brazilian activists in Rio de Janeiro and São Paulo, interwoven with portions of eighteen local and regional debates, conferences and organizational meetings which I attended in 1988 and 1989 as a participant-observer.[4] The material and information gathered at various events during this two-year period forged the experiential link between activism and theory. It also lent insight into possible shifts and emergent tensions within the racially hegemonic process.

Chapter 5 contains the historical coordinates of Afro-Brazilian social movements in Rio de Janeiro and São Paulo after 1945. One of the major themes in this chapter will be the flowering of strong culturalist tendencies within the movimento negro in the 1970s, showing Brazilian as well as Pan-Africanist influences. While culturalism, the excessive valorization and reification of cultural production, is a recurrent theme in this study, it will be fully developed here.

This chapter will also demonstrate how activists and organizations within the black movement have refracted some of the dominant cultural assumptions about black Brazilians, even while groping to ameliorate conditions for blacks in the two cities. This will be confirmed through the unveiling of primary materials—journals, speeches and essays written by Afro-Brazilian activists and activist collectives—which reveal the preoccupations and problems activists experienced with culturalist politics.

Most of the primary materials presented in this chapter, particularly from the 1970s, have never before been presented in Brazilian race relations scholarship. Internal debates over distinctions between negroes and mulattoes, ideology and praxis are three of several dilemmas to be examined in this chapter.

National commemorative celebrations in multiracial polities often reveal disjunctures of race and class that are rarely exposed or discussed otherwise. Issues of national and racial identity, oppression, and crossed loyalties figure prominently in commemorations that seek to project an image of popular unity and national cohesiveness.

The dialectic between racial inequality and the myth of racial democracy was manifested in the 1988 centennial celebration of Abolição and will be considered in Chapter 6. The year-long event brought forth several contradictions of Brazilian racial politics. At a macrolevel, tensions existed between the desire and strategy of white elites to "manage" the tone and force of the commemorations, and Afro-Brazilian activists who sought to disrupt them. In terms of micropolitics, tensions also existed within the black movement in Brazil, as it attempted to define itself in relation to Brazilian society writ large, and more fundamentally, in relation to itself.

Finally, Chapter 7 concludes this study of racial hegemony in Brazil with a chapter overview, a reconsideration of the concept of hegemony, and the recurrent tendencies of culturalism within the movimento negro.

The overall purpose for this study is to reinsert Brazil into studies of comparative racial politics, to redirect debates about hegemony's utility as an applicable concept to a textual analysis of Gramsci's oeuvre, rather than the literatures about Gramsci. The second point has ramifications for the students of political culture and comparative racial politics since recent quantitative data on Brazilian race relations suggests, among other things, that Brazil should no longer be considered a "special" case. Ultimately, I hope that this work will help generate new debates and scholarship about Brazilian race relations, scholarship that fuses theoretical concerns with empirical ones.

PART ONE

RACIAL HEGEMONY

ONE

RACIAL POLITICS: TERMS, THEORY,

METHODOLOGY

Race and Racial Politics

In order to explain people's perceptions of racial patterns one
would have to look outside the narrow frame of race
relations.[1]

THE EPIGRAPH above cautions students of Brazilian race relations against accepting "race relations" in Brazil on its own terms,
thereby restricting their investigations to events and dynamics that
display racism, inequality, and prejudice. More broadly, Viotti's (1985)
commentary implicitly locates theoretical lacunae within "race relations"
scholarship in general.

In some crucial respects, Latin American studies—unlike regional-stud-
ies literatures of Southeast Asia, Eastern and Western Europe, and Africa—have not incorporated recent developments in conceptualizing racial and ethnic politics. Unlike a previous generation of scholarship, which
tended to conflate race with ethnicity, more recent theoretical understandings of the formation of racial identities distinguishes between the
two in contexts where phenotype (what we define as race) becomes a
more salient issue than language, culture, or religion. The work of Paul
Gilroy and Stuart Hall on Great Britain, Michael Burleigh and Wolfgang
Wipperman on Germany (1992), and the Subaltern Studies project on
Southeast Asia (1988) all point to significant shifts in the ways in which
scholars view race and ethnicity. Such works highlight the continuing divide of phenotypical difference for certain groups when other "ethnic"
groups, because of "racial" congruence with the dominant group, are as-
similated into the dominant group over epochal time.

These changing conceptualizations could have a profound impact
upon Latin Americanist scholars' interpretations of the African diaspora in
Latin America, as well as for indigenous groups. Given the increasing
"transnationalization" of indigenous movements in Latin America, Brazil
and Guatemala being just two examples, many indigenous movements
have found it politically expedient to forge coalitions with other indigenous groups.

This has had conceptual implications as well. Groups that are now positively referring to themselves as "Indian" have assumed, at least for political purposes, a pan-ethnic or racial identity vis-à-vis the state and white or ladino elites. For both "Indians" and "blacks," external and internal factors have led to increasing racial identification with other phenotypically similar groups who have experienced racial slavery and other forms of oppression in relationships with *criollo*, European-derived elites. This identification of community outside the boundaries of nation-state underscores the entanglements of racial, national, and cultural identity. Thus, we cannot look only to phenotypical differences to understand politics of racial difference.

The term *race*, as it is used in this study, refers to the employment of phenotypical differences as symbols of social distinction. Racial meanings, and categories are socially, not biologically, constructed. These symbols, meanings and material practices distinguish dominant and subordinate subjects according to their racial categorizations. Race in this regard is not only a marker for phenotypical difference, but of status, class, and political power. In this respect, race relations are also power relations. Being black in Brazilian society, for example, generally signifies having a lower standard of living and less access to quality health care and education than whites, but also signifies criminality, licentiousness, and other negative attributes that are considered essential to people of African descent.

As a result of power relations between "racial" groups, modes of racial consciousness emerge. Racial consciousness is defined here as the dialectical result of antagonisms between two or more groups defined as "races" in a given society. Out of this dialectic emerges the collective and individual recognition of power relations between socially defined "racial" groups. These power relations are grounded in cultural and structural processes that correlate and distribute meanings and practices, which are then manifested in asymmetrical relationships between groups and individuals. Racial consciousness represents the thought and practice of those individuals and groups who respond to their subordination with individual or collective action designed to counterbalance, transpose, or transform situations of racial asymmetry.[2]

Gilroy (1987) suggests that race functions as a conduit between culture and social structure, between the meanings and values that groups place upon racial differences, and the selection, imposition, and reinforcement of those meanings and values in labor markets, the state apparatus, political, social, and cultural institutions. In this conception of race there is the conjunction of ideological and material dimensions, avoiding both the reductionism of so-called materialist explications of race as well as the positioning of race as a "transcendentalist" variable that operates independently of material or ideological considerations. It will be used in this manner to disassociate race from any suggestions of biological determinism or class reductionism that limits race to an ideological, epiphenomenal function. This conceptualization of race will have its implications borne out particularly in Chapters 4 and 5, where racially discriminatory practices of individuals and groups manifest themselves structurally and ideologically as coercive and preemptive acts by the state apparatus and in civil society.

In a country such as Brazil, where the construction of racial identities are as important as the social interaction within "race relations" itself, any approach that automatically presumes the existence of two or more phenotypically distinct "races" would severely limit a researcher's efforts to empirically and theoretically account for the "race" in question. As the voluminous literature on Brazilian racial democracy attests, there is much greater confusion over the phenotypical category of *negro* in Brazil than in other multiracial polities with African or African-derived populations. This is not to imply that unlike Brazil, polities such as the United States, Great Britain, or South Africa have a certain essentialist quality to their racial interactions. It is merely to emphasize that contrary to Geertz's notion of "primordial sentiments" (1970), there are no "givens" to ethnic or racial affiliations in virtually any national context. The meaning and interpretation of racial categories are always subject to revision, change, negotiation. Most importantly, racial constructs are dynamic and fluid, insofar as "racial" groups are not categorized in isolation, but in relation to other groups who have their own attendant norms and values of class, status, and power.

In Brazil, the absence of racial or ethnic "givens" is more profound than in other polities, but this is a matter of the *degree* of instability with regard to racial or ethnic identification, rather than the case of one polity containing "timeless" features of racial inequalities and antagonisms, with another polity—in contrast—having no identifiable patterns of dominance and subordination informed by race. The instability of racial categories, coupled with the limitations of race relations approaches, has theoretical and comparative implications.

Theoretically, the need to broaden the parameters of "race relations" warrants an alternative term, as well as an alternative methodology to extant "race relations" approaches. In his seminal, comparative assessment of race, politics, and migration in the United States and Great Britain, Katznelson (1973) noted:

> By themselves, the physical facts of race are of little or no analytical interest. Racial-physical characteristics assume meaning only when they become criteria of stratification. Thus studies of race inescapably put politics—which, fundamentally, is about organized inequality—at the core of their concern. . . . The subject matter of race which deals with questions of subordination and superordination provides the opportunity to ask not only who gets what and how, but who gets left out and how.[3]

In addition to affirming—at a conceptual level—Viotti's critique of "race relations" approaches, Katznelson foregrounded the development of the term—and field—of racial politics within the lexicon of political science. It is important to note that Katznelson's study, which focused upon the politics of race in two societies with largely dichotomous racial categories, avoided the even more misleading term of *Black Politics*, still widely used in U.S. social science jargon.[4]

The term *racial politics* provides more of a sense of the dynamics of social exchanges between "racially distinct" groups. Rather than compartmentalize the practices of one "racial" group as if it represented a distinct political species, the term *racial politics* lends a sense of the dynamics of power, identity, and mobilization both within and between racial groups.

A racial politics perspective, then, involves more than just a shift in terms. It also entails an approach that posits that in multiracial polities, nearly all politics involve racial difference, antagonism, and inequality. This is not to say that all politics in these societies can be defined in terms of race, but that nearly all dimensions of political life—at the level of the state, civil society, cultural, and material formations—reverberate within the power relations between and within racially defined groups in ways that cannot be reduced to the "variables" of class and nation.

Several innovative works in the realm of racial theory have made the case for increasing focus upon the "politics"—and not the "relations"—of race, for reasons connected to the dialectics of class and racial formation. Omi and Winant (1986) and subsequently Gilroy (1987) have utilized a racial formation approach that "underscores the definition of 'race' as an open political category, for it is struggle that determines which definition of 'race' will prevail and the conditions under which they will endure or wither away."[5]

An even earlier work that contains elements of this perspective is *Caribbean Race Relations* by Harold Hoetink (1967). In his comparison of the influences of Iberian and northwest European colonialism upon race relations in the Caribbean, Hoetink includes Brazil as an empirical referent under the Iberian paradigm. In deconstructing the alleged differences between racial interactions in former Iberian and northwest European colonies, Hoetink argues that contrary to both popular and academic belief, somatic norm-images (race) are a crucial factor for racial distinction in Iberian-influenced societies, despite the allegedly more "supple"[6] character of master-slave relationships that numerous scholars of comparative slavery and race relations refer to. Hoetink suggests that a prejudice of both mark *and* origin is operative against the "pure Negro" in both the United States and Brazil, even though the role of genealogy is different in Brazil than in the United States.[7]

Thus, inextricably connected to the process of whitening and passing in both race relations paradigms is the fact that there is a stigma attached to blackness, along with the differences between multiracial and biracial categorizations within these two patterns. Therefore, while the category "white" may actually contain a more varied set of actual phenotypes and somatic norm-images in Iberian-influenced cultures (along with the positive normative attributes normally attached to whiteness), the category "black" does not.

While Hoetink does not develop this observation, it contains powerful implications for a critical perspective on the role of racial difference for communities of the African diaspora in the New World, across regional, linguistic, national, and cultural boundaries. Besides making the point that race informs social structure, since racial type and social advancement are inextricably linked in both the northwest European and Iberian variants, Hoetink's analysis also suggests overarching similarities of oppression for African-Americans.[8] In the shift from nation to race as a unit of analysis, the exceptionalist discourse for Brazilian as well as Latin American race relations becomes less exceptional indeed.

The historical and sociological literatures (briefly discussed below) have made clear how patterns of racial discrimination and inequality in Brazil have shifted along with changes in social structure. Hasenbalg (1985) has noted, for example, how in the transformation from a slave-holding to wage-earning economy new logics of race prejudice and exclusion appeared in conjunction with capitalist relations of production. As freed blacks appeared in skilled, wage-earning functions, the state helped create and enforce immigration and market practices to effectively *disqualify* blacks from open market competition in the "new" socioeconomic order. Therefore, forms of racism under the previous socioeconomic order could not be rationalized under the newly emergent one, lending credence to the assertion within a racial politics approach that the very meanings and definitions of race and racism are historically and culturally situated in Brazil, and not simply transferred from one epoch to the next. Changes in material and cultural forms of racial oppression require political interventions.

This perspective allows for a conjunctural analysis of individual and collective identities organized upon the axis of racial differences, with an investigation of their effects in processes of social-structural interaction. On this point, Gilroy suggests, "Rather than talking about racism in the singular, analysts should therefore be talking about racisms in the plural. These are not just different over historical time but may vary within the same social formation or historical conjuncture."[9]

Katznelson focused upon the structural and institutional features of racial politics in the United States and Great Britain, playing little attention to behavioral or cultural dimensions of racial politics.[10] This emphasis on the former and dismissal of the latter is understandable given two distinct but related phenomena at the time Katznelson's research was conducted and published: (a) the abundance of so-called cultural analyses of the politics of racial inequality that included, among other propositions, the "culture of poverty" thesis expounded by Oscar Lewis (1966); (b) dichotomous race relations processes in both polities under study.

Rather than explore the "culture of poverty" or other pseudo-anthropological distortions here, suffice to say that explorations into the role of culture in political life has developed significantly since the 1970s, to the extent that "culture," in the scholarship of James Scott (1985; 1990), David Laitin (1986), and others is not a "spigot variable" as aptly described by Schmitter,[11] but a *process* that undergirds political life, giving shape not only to ideas and beliefs, but to modes of consciousness as well as social and material practices. A racial politics perspective that underestimates the importance of cultural and behavioral features risks a misunderstanding of the lived context in which institutions and markets are situated in relation to the politics of race itself. One can decry the use of "spigot variable" approaches without eliminating cultural analysis entirely, and thereby retain a more sophisticated explication of cultural processes. As will be evidenced below in the sections that detail the methodological and conceptual issues of this study, I seek to emphasize the cultural dimension of racial politics in Rio de Janeiro and São Paulo without succumbing to "spigot variable" explanations; identifying and analyzing structural and institutional features of Brazilian racial politics, ever mindful of their interaction with normative issues and patterns.

Still, a pertinent question at this stage of inquiry remains. Why emphasize the cultural dimension of racial politics in these two cities? In comparative terms, this question leads us to the second justification for the predominance of structural-institutional factors in Katznelson's comparative study. In Great Britain, de facto segregation forced the creation of parallel institutions by minority groups, who were often relegated to poorer districts and received lesser municipal and federal services.[12] In the United States, de facto and de jure segregation led to the development of parallel institutions as well as institutions, such as the church, that had multiple, often ambiguous purposes. The black church was no mere corollary to its white counterpart; it served political and cultural aims white churches rarely provided for their own congregations.

Afro-Brazilians, in contrast, did not develop parallel institutions in the same manner. There are no Afro-Brazilian hospitals nor institutions of higher learning, although there are strong traditions of self-help in communities throughout Brazil where medical, educational, and other services are performed by community members, activists, and specific-service professionals. One could point to individual Catholic churches, Candomble or Umbanda houses of religious worship as examples of such activity. But this does not constitute a *network* of Afro-Brazilian cultural politics stemming from a *national* alliance of churches and houses of worship.

Another limitation is the absence of racially delineated constituencies in electoral politics. As of 1992, there were only three black governors in the entire Brazilian federation. The absence of collective racial consciousness among Afro-Brazilians has political implications, as black political candidates with "black" platforms do not have strong constituencies to support them at voting booths.

As will be seen shortly, this difference highlights the major peculiarity of Brazilian racial politics and indeed, its hegemonic processes when juxtaposed against other much-studied polities such as the United States and Great Britain. Simply stated, an institutionalist-structuralist perspective such as Katznelson's would be incongruent with the realities of racial politics in Brazil, given the lack of parallel institutions or national resource networks. Since much of Afro-Brazilian activism has centered around a politics of culture, it makes sense to utilize a mode of analysis appropriate for such a politics.

Hegemony

Although the concept is primarily associated with Gramsci's explication of hegemony in *The Prison Notebooks*, its initial formulation precedes him. Its origins, in fact, are in the Russian Social-Democratic movement beginning in the 1890s. Perry Anderson's assessment of the concept's genealogy suggests that G. V. Plekhanov, the so-called father of Russian Marxism, was the first advocate of *gegemoniya* or hegemony, a political struggle against tsarism coupled with economic and military advances against its dominant, feudalist class.[13] Plekhanov and the Social-Democratic movement's emphasis on the political embellishment of the proletarian agenda greatly influenced Lenin, a contemporary of Plekhanov, and other key intellectuals of the Bolshevik Revolution.

Gramsci's explication of hegemony derives from the original formulation a distinction between dominance, namely the use of force, and rule, the pervasive extension of a dominant group's power into political, bureaucratic, and cultural realms of civil society. It is clear from Gramsci's discussion of Piedmontese leadership during the Italian Risorgimento in "Notes on Italian History" that leadership, not coercion, is a prerequisite for political rule. Once a dominant group assumes leadership—that is, the development of political, intellectual, and cultural influences that correlate with their economic and coercive powers—the principal tasks become those of compromise and brokerage, the ability to influence and persuade recalcitrant or even oppositional groups under a new political rubric. In this way a dominant group can effect a "passive revolution" in civil society, the universalizing of their agenda and interests without the need for a constant expression of physical or economic force.[14] A dominant social group may compromise in certain dimensions of struggle between subordinate groups in order to maintain overall dominance, or emphasize certain facets of its interaction with subordinate groups in order to maintain situations of inequality in another.

For Gramsci, the working classes represented a paradox for Italian communists and for Marxist theory in general. They were not attracted to the Communist party's call to international worker solidarity but to those of national identity and chauvinism, corporatism, and racialism, which characterized the Fascist movement in Italy and elsewhere. The "philosophy of praxis" was Gramsci's attempt to develop an ethico-political strategy that could critique, reform, and ultimately transform Italian society and culture from within. Many Marxist theorists had merely *assumed* the inevitability of proletarian revolution arising from capitalism's presumed demise, and neglected the obvious need for the development of an emergent political culture that would give shape to collective, revolutionary consciousness among subaltern peoples.

While maintaining a Marxist position with regard to the primacy of material conditions, Gramsci recognized that mere analysis of capitalist economies would not sufficiently explain the driving forces of bourgeois rule. As Gramsci persuasively explicated in his innovations upon the concept of hegemony, it is not the economic ordering of capitalism, but its embellishments—cultural, political, and ideological—that establish the normative legitimations of bourgeois rule and leadership. For Gramsci, economistic explanations simply could not provide clues to the appropriation of political power and subsequent processing of proletarian rule if workers were to, in either fact or theory, seize the levers of societal leadership.

The overarching question then, for the two predicaments that Gramsci sought to address, was the following: how do subordinate individuals (groups) forge counterhegemonic values out of existing, reactionary ones without reproducing the latter in new forms? This question is found in most struggles over domination on a national scale, and obtains in the struggles between Afro-Brazilian activists and a racist Brazilian society that has historically denied the existence of racial discrimination in its polity. As will be seen in a consideration of the existing literature on Brazilian race relations below, this question and the predicaments from which this question emerged have neither been posed nor theorized by students of Brazilian race relations.

A similar question has persisted throughout the modern history of Afro-Brazilian social movements: how could black Brazilians strive for racial equality in a nation without democratic commitment to its citizens as a whole, while at the same time struggle against an ideology that claims there is no need for such strivings in the first place? This has been the crucial and unique predicament for Afro-Brazilian activists since the 1930s.

In the process of Brazilian racial hegemony, activists have, with varying degrees of success, attempted to both undermine racist practices in Brazilian social structures and undertake the task of political education of white and nonwhite Brazilians about racial inequalities in their country. Cultural practices, for both Gramsci and for Afro-Brazilian activists engaged in a critique of Brazilian race relations, have been the key site for political mobilization. For Afro-Brazilian activists, however, I will argue that culturalist (as opposed to cultural) practices have also been an impediment to certain types of counterhegemonic political activities because of their reproduction of culturalist tendencies found in the ideology of racial democracy and in Brazilian society more generally. Culturalism is defined as the equation of cultural practices with the material, expressive, artifactual elements of cultural production, and the neglect of normative and political aspects of a cultural process. Within culturalist politics, cultural practices operate as ends in themselves rather than as a means to more comprehensive, heterogenous set of ethico-political activities. In culturalist practices, Afro-Brazilian and Afro-Diasporic symbols and artifacts become reified and commodified; culture becomes a thing, not a deeply political process.[15]

Culturalism freezes or hypostatizes cultural practices, divorcing them from their histories and the attendant modes of consciousness that brought them into being. This obviously limits the range of alternative articulation and movement by Afro-Brazilian peoples. Peter Fry (1982) has noted that Afro-Brazilian artifacts and cultural practices consistently have been transformed into national cultural symbols. In the process, they are divorced from the cultural and political contexts from which they originated. This is a process, I will argue, that both white and nonwhite Brazilians, activists, and advocates of the status quo alike have engaged in. I will also argue, though, that Afro-Brazilian activists who have attempted to subvert this process have been ignored and sanctioned as part of efforts to maintain the racial "harmony" of Brazil.

This is not to suggest, however, that the aforementioned paradoxes and contradictions of the movimento negro are representative of a false consciousness. Nor should the false premise of racial equality be construed as a variant of false consciousness. The consequences of the ideology of racial democracy are quite real: no affirmative action programs for nonwhites, the open ridicule of national activists and politicians who take up racially specific causes, and the lack of self-esteem evidenced by many blacks that is linked to a negation of their identity. There is nothing fake about this.

Nor does it suffice to say, as Gramsci does, that these features of a particular working-class identity typify "contradictory consciousness." I will argue through the presentation of interview data and a neo-Gramscian analysis of racial hegemony that *most* forms of consciousness in a given social totality are contradictory, in that they are complicated by multiple allegiances and forms of identification based on race, gender, region, and other variables that are not determined, in the last instance, by materiality.

In contrast, many Gramsci-inspired readings of ideology, politics, and cultural praxis have concocted what has been termed "the dominant ideology thesis" (Scott 1990). Although there are several forms of this thesis, from crude to nuanced, their articulation resembles the following: to achieve the desired effect of ideological congruence and subsequent political acquiescence, *the* dominant class simply hurls an ideological pellet upon the stage of civil society. An impenetrable mist arises, enshrouds *the* dominant class, and obscures its movements before a captive audience (*the* masses), who reel back in their collective seats, transfixed, spellbound.

This influence of this tendency is found in even the most sophisticated writings on hegemony. Stuart Hall's improvisations upon hegemony for studies of race and ethnicity suggests that it can become the conceptual backdrop for examining "the most common, least understood features of 'racism': the 'subjection' of the victims of racism to the mystifications of the very racist ideologies which imprison and define them."[16]

Yet if racist ideologies are "mystifications," should we infer that by a mere removal of the veil of ideology that the more "objective" circumstances of a racialized working class would become clear to that class? This is but one of several problems with "dominant ideology" formulations of any kind that have their pedigree in the notion of false consciousness, even in those as subtle as Stuart Hall's. If racist ideologies of everyday experience and the material forms that they assume are false (i.e., non-real), then subordinated racial groups could not possibly use commonsense understandings of everyday experience to subvert that experience and make it "real," or more "objective."

This would entirely negate and contradict Gramsci's broader claims for counterhegemonic forms of praxis that evolve from the everyday.[17] The major consequence of these distortions of Gramsci's position have been an adverse equation of the entire concept of hegemony with the singular position of "false consciousness" or "mystification," as noted above.

James Scott (1990) uses a totalizing interpretation of false consciousness as the basis for a dismissal of the entire concept of hegemony.

Unlike those who suggest that there is *one* single dominant or subordinate ideology recurring in group interaction, I will argue that a dominant ideology, if such a single entity exists, is multivalent, contradictory in itself. This will be evidenced in the distinction between racial exceptionalism and racial democracy in Chapter 3.

There is no single dominant ideology but in fact, ideologies that complement each other at certain instances to form a cluster of beliefs, which could be characterized as dominant, while at other moments produce tensions as competing visions of social life during other moments. As a result, groups and individuals are neither wholly dominant nor wholly subordinate, at levels of both ideology and practice. They represent a variety of normative assumptions about the everyday world in which they live, and their social practices may reflect both acceptance of and resistance to "common sense" understandings of race relations and their location within them.

With race and ethnicity as dimensions of a hegemonic process, there exists the possibility of contradictory elements within a single consciousness in the following forms: an expressed belief in social equality while harboring and manifesting racist sentiments; a position of material comfort derived from professional status, coupled with personal insecurity in social spheres where this status is subjectively diminished because of one's color; or the expressed belief by members of a subordinate group of the superiority of a more powerful one.

These are just some of the possibilities of contradictory consciousness to be found in multiracial polities like Brazil, where race and color are salient variables. Only under these conditions are prospects for counterhegemony possible through the subversion of political, cultural, and economic instruments of dominance that structure and inform *common sense.* Counterhegemony, in this regard, is the process by which dominant meanings become undermined to the extent that they lose their common-sense value, and new meanings (in this case interpretations of Brazilian race relations) emerge with new values of their own. Yet attempts at subversion hold new contradictions, as those who seek change may reconstitute certain ideological subsets of the dominant group even while contesting a social whole.

As will be explored in the chapters to follow, many activist groups and individuals have been self-conscious of both intended and unintended contradictions within the *movimento negro,* and have attempted to reverse their pull. Their struggles, debates, and concerns expose a two-tiered discourse within the movement that has rarely been acknowledged:

a discourse of internal criticism within the movimento negro as well as a critique of Brazilian society and politics as a whole. The tensions between inertia and resistance, macro- and microlevel politics, will be addressed in the history of the *Carioca* and *Paulista* movements in Chapter 5.

A mixture of "domination" and "leadership," that is, the intermittent use of coercion and persuasion by Brazilian whites in their relations with nonwhites has made their hegemony possible, to the extent that while state-generated violence against Afro-Brazilians does occur, systematic coercive practices are unnecessary. This, I would argue, is the best employment of the concept of hegemony, connoting the push and pull of group interaction, not a mere imposition of one group's ideals, beliefs and values upon another.

The Afro-Brazilian

The term *Afro-Brazilian* used in this study reflects two phenomena that emerged from the black movement in the 1970s. The first reflects the increase in levels of racial consciousness among blacks and thus the formulation of an Afro-Brazilian identity linked to racial identification with blacks elsewhere. While such identification among Afro-Brazilians did exist prior to the 1970s, it became more intensely political and internationalized in that decade.

The international dimension of Afro-Brazilian racial consciousness, analyzed in Chapter 4, is evidenced in Afro-Brazilian identification with the cultural and political practices of the African diaspora. Diasporai have existed in history far longer than nation-states, yet confound most social scientists because they are neither spatially nor temporally fixed. For Afro-Brazilian activists who have developed racial consciousness, Africa and its diaspora have been a crucial foundation for racial identification on a national, international, and transnational scale, utilizing forms of protest and commonality exercised by "black" peoples elsewhere in both the Old World and the New.

As reflective of this intensification of racial consciousness, the term *Afro-Brazilian*, and to a lesser extent *Negro*, marked a new phase of social struggle for the movimento negro. Most activists in Rio de Janeiro and São Paulo, from lighterskinned mulatto types to those who are actually considered negro (black) refer to themselves with one or both of these terms.

Their usage of these terms as points of self-reference warranted their employment in this study. In addition to the two phenomena noted above, the use of these particular terms also suggest a recognition of the increasing bipolarity of Brazilian racial politics, which, the folklore of Brazilian racial harmony notwithstanding, has come to resemble the racial politics of countries like the United States or South Africa.

Activists

Activists are defined as those who devoted at least ten hours per week on a consistent basis to the black movement.[18] Those activities included leadership-participation in community organizations, research institutions devoted to Afro-Brazilian issues, political parties, labor unions, and centers for education. While the degree of leadership responsibility varied, the criteria for inclusion was involvement in issues with disproportionate impact for Afro-Brazilians (race-related violence, job discrimination, community education, abandoned children).

In the process of interviewing and meeting with various activists and students of Brazilian racial politics, several people were identified as important subjects for this study. Their roles within the movement were subsequently confirmed by my personal attendance at meetings, conferences, debates and internal discussions (see appendix) and through discussions with Brazilian journalists and public officials with knowledge of the black movement. In some instances, interviewees were easily identifiable through their documented experiences with the state apparatus (interrogation, surveillance, torture). The life experiences of Thereza Santos, Abdias do Nascimento, and Joel Rufino dos Santos, all interviewees, exemplify this type of identification.

Methods

A combination of approaches from political science and anthropology was employed for this study, since much of Brazilian racial politics occurs outside the channels of representative democracy, and because so much of Afro-Brazilian politics occurs within the realm of culture. The concept of culture, as it is utilized here, refers to the beliefs, values and artifacts of a distinct social collectivity. Since Afro-Brazilian culture is both a distinct element of Brazilian society as well as a feature of national culture, there is an inherent dynamic between local and general, racial and national forms of identification and representation.

Balandier (1970), in his discussion of methodologies in political anthropology, posits that the most comprehensive approach within this field is dynamist, as opposed to functionalist or structuralist. For Balandier, it is an approach employing dialectics to consider how custom and conflict, rebellion and order are ritualized in symbolic forms and in political practices—state formation, the articulation of dissent, and other contestations for power.

For Balandier, power relations generate asymmetries in group interaction. Rituals and symbols, as expressions of politics, embody the asymmetries between groups. Rituals not only embody conflict but, when generated by either dominant or dominated groups, work to present a transcendentalist image of societal unity. That false premise of racial equality known as Brazilian racial democracy is paradigmatic of the transcendentalist image of societal unity.

The articulation of dissent by Afro-Brazilians suggests rituals of dominance and subordination that activists seek to disrupt. In this way a dialectic is forged between the conflicting rituals of Brazilian racial politics and the attempts, by civil and state elites, to present and maintain representations of racial harmony.

Popular newspapers, school textbooks, and other mass media were obvious sources for the examination of this dialectic at a macrosocial level. They were also sources for more microfocused tensions within groups on either side of the racial dynamic.

Gramsci's own methodology was quite similar, as evidenced in his preoccupation with mass media, political rhetoric, and the Italian educational system as tools and mechanisms of bourgeois and Fascist socialization.[19] In addition, participation in and observation of conflicts, coalitions, events, and nonevents of Brazilian racial politics provided the opportunity for "thick description" (Geertz 1973) of the symbolic implications of gestures, movements, ideas and artifacts of that politics. The artifacts of the black movement itself—plastic arts, newspapers, political and quasi-academic journals—provided ample resources as well.

This approach involves not only the attempt at an understanding of the political motivations, beliefs, and values of activists as they relate to themselves and other activists, but as they interact within a social totality. The last part entails a largely public interaction with various groups and institutions, but also "private" institutions within and between activist communities.

Interviews

Activists and other participants were interviewed (twice, in some instances) for periods ranging from forty-five minutes to two hours. The interviews themselves were divided into two sections, personal and political. While this is neither a neat nor an entirely accurate distinction, it served to highlight the interventions of private, personal experiences into public political life. The personally grounded experiences of racial discrimination motivated those interviewed toward either political action or self-denial. Without detailed accounts of their personal experiences, it would have been impossible to examine the confluence of personal and political moments or distinguish these activist-oriented individuals from other Afro-Brazilians in daily life.

Since each individual subject—due to socioeconomic, regional, chronological, gender or even color-based variables—was introduced to forms of Brazilian racism at different points on a social continuum, there was a diversity of responses alongside the persistence and recurrence of certain features endemic to white-Afro-Brazilian relations. A more qualitative interviewing method helped in this regard, since points of commonality could be subsequently distinguished from more personal justifications for political heterogeneity among activists.

In contrast, most survey studies of political behavior with an interview component are concerned with political preferences at moments of choice (elections, referendums, etc.) rather than with the more critical task of attempting to locate conscious *attitudes* about politics based upon personal experiences. This is a crucial prerequisite for a comprehensive understanding of racial politics and political cultures in multiethnic polities.[20]

The combination of approaches from the disciplines of political science and anthropology will enable me to demonstrate both the centrality and frustrations of cultural politics for Afro-Brazilian activists, as well as the constant barriers placed before them and their constituencies in daily societal interaction. This political-anthropological approach will also demonstrate its usefulness as a mode of inquiry when juxtaposed against the approaches and methods of other students of Brazilian race relations in the next chapter.

Rio de Janeiro and São Paulo in Comparative Perspective

While cross-national comparisons are useful for highlighting general patterns of similarity and difference in racial interaction, they can also obscure internal variations of racial politics within nations. A country like Brazil, with vast demographic variation from region to region, has manifold patterns of racial interaction. Increasing urbanization and industrial development has led to migratory shifts of various racial groups and social classes, particularly the working poor, over the past twenty years. It can no longer hold (assuming that it ever could) that studies of race and racism in a particular part of the country can account for all of the variations and idiosyncracies in race relations nationally, as it was assumed by both Florestan Fernandes and Gilberto Freyre, whose research was confined to the states of São Paulo and Recife, respectively.

Both Rio de Janeiro and São Paulo exemplify the changes in Brazilian demographics, and as a result, a transformation of racial dynamics in different parts of the country. Both cities are in many ways quite unlike the rest of the country. According to the statistics of the 1980 census of the Instituto Brasileiro de Geografia e Estatistica (IGBE), São Paulo is approximately 30 percent nonwhite (*negro e pardo*) of nearly 28 million people. Rio de Janeiro is 40 percent nonwhite of just over 12 million people.

São Paulo and Rio de Janeiro have historically been the industrial capitals of Brazil. Unlike the state of Bahia, where Afro-Brazilians are in the majority, Carioca and Paulista blacks are in the numerical minority. In both cities there is evidence of the whitening process at work, insofar as the mulatto percentage of the population has increased in the past thirty years, in direct proportion to the decrease in the black population during the same period. It is not that the black population has disappeared, but that more and more blacks have come to define themselves as mulatto (Wood 1991).

Rare is the study of residential segregation in Brazil, but there are some. Working from 1980 census data, Telles (1992) shows that São Paulo is the third most segregated area of the country, after, surprisingly, northeastern and southern Brazil. In one of the few comparative studies on racial segregation and demarcation in the two cities, Rolnik notes that while "black" areas of the two cities were never entirely black (blacks resided alongside Italians in São Paulo, Portuguese in Rio) there are spaces within both cities that were and are clearly demarcated along racial-cultural lines. She asserts that the "history of Rio and São Paulo is marked by the marginalization and stigmatization of black territory,"[21] Samba schools, football (soccer) teams, dance halls, and spaces of religious worship are architectural and spatial coordinates of the physical existence of black communities. At the same time, in keeping with the denial of racial exclusion in Brazil, there is a general lack of recognition that racially specific areas of these cities exist. Rolnik (1989) chronicles the distinct spaces for slaves, free blacks, and subsequently middle-class blacks in response to the specific conditions of racial exclusion in urban Brazil, and the utilization of these spaces as sites of community and resistance. In both cities, gentrification projects undertaken at the turn of the century forcibly removed blacks and mulattoes from the centers of the city. Its most visible impact was in Rio de Janeiro, where by the 1940s blacks had moved to the north zone (Zona Norte), and the favelas that now outline the choicest real estate in the southern portion of the city—Copacabana, Leblon, and Ipanema (Perlman 1976).

The city of São Paulo has historically been the principal site for Afro-Brazilian mobilization. Though other cities like Salvador and Recife have now become loci of activism since the 1970s, São Paulo was the place of gestation for several key organizations that ultimately had national impact for the movimento negro since the 1920s, the Black Brazilian Front (FNB or Frente Negra Brazileira) and the Unified Black Movement (MNU or Movimento Negro Unificado) among them. Fernandes (1969) cites the effects of proletarianization upon skilled black laborers, the anonymity of the city, and the intensity of racism within the context of market competition as reasons for the early efforts at political cohesion in the city, points echoed by Moura (1988) and Bastide (1965). Black residential nuclei emerged in boroughs such as Barra Funda, Bixiga, Lavapes, and Saracura in São Paulo, both in response to and as a consequence of the racial exclusion mentioned by Rolnik. Collective houses and semirural enclaves also developed in the periphery of the city, in addition to predominantly Afro-Brazilian churches and *terreiros* (houses of worship).

Unlike São Paulo, Rio de Janeiro did not have a massive, subsidized influx of European immigrants after abolition. Rio, up until the period of capitalist expansion in Brazil, was a much more important city than São Paulo. In 1872, blacks were almost half of the city's population. By 1887 blacks were 37 percent of the population, a decrease that Rolnik attributes to the decline of coffee production during this period. This led to intense migration of freed blacks from the periphery to the city of Rio in search of work.

By the 1940s, increased urbanization in Brazil led to migration, mostly nonwhite, from more agriculturally and artesanally productive states such as Bahia, Pernambuco, and Minas Gerais, to Brazil's two major urban centers, Rio de Janeiro and São Paulo. In São Paulo, the migration of these populations from the northern states has led to intense antinorthern sentiment in the state. This sentiment is also racialized, since the immigrant population is, as already stated, predominantly nonwhite,[22] while those criticizing the immigrants are white Paulistas.[23]

This issue raises the intense overlapping of race, economics, and regionalism in Brazil, which has been a constant feature of Afro-Brazilian life. It also underscores the pervasiveness of racialist, antiwhite discourse in Brazilian society affecting not only Afro-Brazilians but Jews, Asians, and other groups. As will be explored in Chapter 3, much of the language of racial purity and impure blood that recurs in the criticism against Brazilians from the Northeast is identical to the negrophobic and anti-Semitic discourse prevalent in Brazilian culture since at least the eighteenth century, as part of the philosophical sediment of racial prejudices of the Spanish and Portuguese that was transplanted in Brazil (Tucci Carneiro 1983).

The responses to whitening, the myth of racial democracy, and blunter forms of racism in Rio de Janeiro and São Paulo have been informed by the differences, as well as the similarities, of racial oppression in these two locations. The intensity of market and racial competition in São Paulo appears to have greatly influenced the formation of racial consciousness and race-specific institutions at an earlier period there than in Rio de Janeiro (Chapter 5). It has also led to greater inclusion of labor-related agendas along the race-class axis by Afro-Brazilian activists than in Rio, where there has historically been less coordination between white labor and Afro-Brazilian groups. In both places, however, the alliance between the left and Afro-Brazilians has been uneasy, since only recently have Afro-Brazilian activists addressed the class dimensions of racial oppression, while many white union and labor party militants have considered racial issues "particularist" concerns (also in Chapter 5).

TWO

BRAZILIAN RACIAL POLITICS: AN OVERVIEW

AND RECONCEPTUALIZATION

TO UNDERSTAND contemporary racial politics in Brazil in terms of both its scholarly and political debates, it is important to place present circumstances in some historical context. This chapter serves to orient readers toward the significance of a racial politics perspective in light of the extant empirical literature on Brazilian race relations. It will provide a countervailing interpretation of the history of Brazilian race relations as well as a critique of the race versus class paradigm that is prevalent in both scholarly and activist treatment of the problematics of race.

Debates over the relative importance of class or race in structuring oppression has yielded innovative approaches to the study of linkages between race, modes of production, and social inequality. The work of Oliver Cox (1948), Stanley Greenberg (1980), and others in the post–World War II period have provided ample evidence to suggest, at the least, that race does play a role in the structuring of social inequality. Whether its role is epiphenomenal (superstructural) or at the core of relations of production (structural) has been a major source of tension between class- and race-based perspectives on the role of race in plural societies.

Similar debates have occurred and are occurring in Brazil along these lines, as the following review will attest. At stake in these debates is not only a recognition of the role of racial prejudice, discrimination, and exploitation in Brazilian society but also the suitability of Marx-inspired analysis for their study.

The existing literature on Brazilian race relations can be separated into two areas, class-based and structuralist. While there are distinctions from these two broad categories, as well as distinctions within, they have overshadowed all other approaches to the study of Brazilian race relations. They have done so, in large part, because most of the work on Brazilian race relations has focused on slavery and the shift from slave to wage-labor, two epochs of Brazilian history that highlight the intersection of race and class. Rather than attempt a complete review of the literatures of these two approaches, I will assess principal texts and their relation to this study.

While both schools have significantly advanced study and debate about racism in Brazilian society, I want to demonstrate their conceptual limitations for further theorizing on the politics of race in Brazil. The most renowned and unarguably the most important exponent of the determinist school is Florestan Fernandes.

Economic Determinism: The São Paulo School of Sociology

In *The Negro in Brazilian Society*, a classic study of Brazilian race relations, Florestan Fernandes succinctly characterizes the hegemonic position of white elites in Brazilian society, who limit themselves to "treating the Negro with tolerance, maintaining the old ceremonial politeness in interracial relationships, and excluding from this tolerance any truly egalitarian feeling or content."[1] He was alluding to the ideology of racial democracy; the premise of racial equality in a society where there was none. First written in Portuguese nearly thirty years ago, it provided the first systematic critique of an ideology greatly at odds with the social relations that spawned it.

Fernandes based his analysis of Brazilian race relations on the unequal patterns of racial interaction that emerged in the state of São Paulo during a crucial period in Brazilian economic development, 1880–1920. The state of São Paulo remains the industrial capital of Brazil and was the site for the first organized Afro-Brazilian movement of the modern era, the Black Brazilian Front. For these two reasons alone, Fernandes's work remains of seminal importance, since it is the first of its kind to analyze the nexus of race and class within the process of Brazilian socioeconomic development.

His deconstruction of *democracia racial*—through interviews with Afro-Brazilian activists, "elites," and everyday people white, nonwhite, and black—represented a genuine advance in the study of Brazilian race relations, particularly when read against the backdrop of charitable explanations by Gilberto Freyre, Charles Wagley (1963) and Donald Pierson (1967). It was the first sociology of Brazilian race relations to openly question Brazil's "unique case" status in comparative studies of race, class, and social mobility. Fernandes presented Brazilian blacks as exploited, both during and after slavery, by uncaring whites who occasionally extended a paternalistic hand to their darker-skinned compatriots, only to withdraw it when blacks such as members of the FNB made assertions about the need for a *real* racial democracy and self-help organizations within Afro-Brazilian communities (Fernandes 1969).

The irony of Fernandes's conclusions was that he, along with other scholars, had been commissioned by UNESCO to study Brazilian race relations because it had been assumed by the organization that Brazil was indeed an anomaly among multiracial polities. Fernandes went further, however. He drew a sociological portrait of Afro-Brazilians that resembled Daniel Patrick Moynihan's assessment of the African-American family in the 1960s: dysfunctional, suffering from anomie, hopelessness, and immorality.

While highlighting the processes of racial discrimination, Fernandes reproduced some of the prevailing assumptions about Afro-Brazilians' lack of preparation for the emergent capitalist marketplace. Basing his analysis on interviews, first-hand observation, as well as secondary sources, Fernandes argued that newly freed Afro-Brazilians, especially those from rural-agricultural occupations, "lacked the self-discipline and the sense of responsibility of the free laborer, which were the only attributes that could spontaneously endow the laborer with regularity and efficiency under the new juridical-economic order."[2]

Thus, Afro-Brazilians, because of their lack of gradual proletarianization and preparation for the new socioeconomic order, were no match for Italian immigrants and other wage-laborers competing for gainful employment in the state of São Paulo. Yet Fernandes' assessment, aside from the normative assumptions about the absence of patrifocal families and attendant "family values" within the lower socioeconomic segments of Afro-Brazilian communities, neglects an important dimension in the structuring of race relations: the role of the state in promoting both capitalist development and racial-social formation.

While Fernandes notes that slaveholders provided virtually no assistance to Afro-Brazilians to make a successful shift from slavery to freedom, he ignores the intervention of big landowners and government officials to bias the new marketplace in favor of southern European immigrants. Historians concentrating on the same period have highlighted the efforts of São Paulo *fazenderos* (farmers) to exclude blacks from entering the wage-labor workforce by subsidizing European immigration in the waning years of slavery (Dean 1976; Toplin 1974), to ensure that the new proletariat would not be former slaves.

But it is the work of George Reid Andrews, *Blacks and Whites in São Paulo, Brazil, 1888–1988*, that systematically refutes Fernandes's explanation for the marginalization of Afro-Brazilians after 1888. Using Stanley Greenberg's *Race, State and Capitalist Development* as a model to analyze the nexus of institutionalized racism and state policy, Andrews underscores the collusion between state government and landowning planters to foster economic development, subsidize European immigration and further impede occupational diversity among newly freed Afro-Brazilians. For Andrews, slavery is but one of several explanatory variables to consider in determining why Afro-Brazilian workers were displaced from "objective" market competition in São Paulo by 1889, just one year after abolition. In providing his assessment of the outcome of subsidized southern European immigration and preferential treatment for these new immigrants relative to Afro-Brazilians, Andrews states that São Paulo's labor market in the years immediately following the abolition of slavery was one shaped by an unusual degree of state direction and intervention. "This was intervention seemingly devoid of any racial content, but in fact by choosing to invest funds in European workers, and refusing to make comparable investments in Brazilians, the province's planters, and the state apparatus which they controlled, had made their ethnic and racial preferences in workers crystal clear."[3]

Andrews also explores the impact of elite ideology and racial "common sense" upon whites and Afro-Brazilians across the continuum of class positions. He juxtaposes the assumptions about lazy and incompetent Afro-Brazilians inherent in Fernandes's perspective against an analysis of two major employers in São Paulo in the 1920s, the Jafet Textile Factory and the São Paulo Tramway, Light and Power company.

By comparing the personnel records of the two companies—hiring, resignations, promotions, and suspensions—Andrews notes that black men were more likely to be suspended than whites and that *preto* (black) and *pardo* (brown) men were fired without cause to reduce the work force, while white males were promoted more quickly. Thus, not only were black and brown Brazilians discriminated against before entering the industrial workforce, they were systematically disqualified from objective market competition both during and after their entrance.

Andrews's analysis is gendered as well, exploring the emergence of occupational differentiation between Afro-Brazilian women and men. Andrews emphasizes that Afro-Brazilian women had relatively greater employment opportunities than men, which helps explain the higher unemployment rates for Afro-Brazilian males during this period. Moreover, Andrews's survey of popular newspaper and other accounts of the working classes during the early part of the twentieth century provides a counterargument to Fernandes's assertions of a peculiar moral laxity among the poorest Afro-Brazilians,[4] for there were similar characterizations and stereotypes of Italian and other immigrants.

Andrews's historiographic rebuttal of the Fernandes thesis concerning Afro-Brazilians' lack of preparedness during this period resonates with some conceptual tensions within the race-class debate. The planters, in both their discussions and material practices, expressed their racial and economic interests *simultaneously* through state implementation of racially and economically specific policies.

In this sense, the subordination and marginalization of newly freed slaves was overdetermined in the new marketplace, limiting their prospects regardless of occupational differentiation within Afro-Brazilian communities, as many Afro-Brazilians were skilled laborers at the time of abolition. In fact, there were more free mulattoes and blacks than slaves in the state of São Paulo in this period.[5] Race clearly had a material dimension. It structured life choices and possibilities for both Afro-Brazilians and Italian immigrants, and also structured occupational differences and inequalities within the proletarian class.

Given this historical reality, it should become clear that the structural versus superstructural distinctions presumed by class-based advocates are problematic not only in their theoretical formulation, but also in their limited utility in helping us understand how race and class are often inseparable in historical processes. This problem, manifest in many class-based readings of racism and racial slavery, is the consequence of a more general problematic within Marxist thought, in which "base" and "superstructure" are treated as abstract, sequential categories rather than products of historical relationships involving real people.[6] As Williams noted, many "real Marxists" have come to "think of the 'base' and the 'superstructure' as if they were separable concrete entities. In doing so they lost sight of the very processes—not abstract relations but constitutive processes—which it should have been the function of historical materialism to emphasize."[7] This limitation is not peculiar to Fernandes, nor merely to academic discussions of race and class. It has had repercussions in the white Brazilian left's considerations of racial inequality and politics, which will be explored in Chapter 5.

Nowhere is this limitation clearer than in Fernandes critique of the FNB. To Fernandes, the front was a self-doomed project because of its preoccupation with racial uplift, integration, and Afro-Brazilian social advancement within the parameters of capitalist development, rather than a critique of capitalism itself. In discussing Negro social movements in general in São Paulo in the 1920s, Fernandes stated that these movements did not "struggle against the established economic, social and political order, but against a kind of racial despoliation that it has harbored owing to the prevailing relationship between Negroes and whites."[8]

While the FNB did not seek to overturn an entire social system, its critique of racial democracy and promotion of black self-help was a contestation, however limited, of white hegemony. It set a historical precedent for black political activity in twentieth-century Brazil. Mitchell (1977) and Andrews (1991) detail the Black Brazilian Front's efforts during its six-year life span (1931–1937) to develop "buy black" campaigns, employment opportunities, schools, and political and even paramilitary organizations within Afro-Brazilian communities before being shut down by Getulio Vargas's Estado Novo (1937–1945). Given these efforts, and the reconceptualizations of "race" in Chapter 1, it must be asked if the activities of the front both their successes and limitations, can be perceived as a "struggle against the existing economic, social and political order?" How could it not be, when the very "racial despoliation" the front was responding to grew out of Brazilian society, the economic, social, and political order in question? At the very least, the Black Brazilian Front epitomized the possibility that Afro-Brazilians could refer to their racial and cultural identity as a positive organizing principle within the context of capitalist development.

Such an alternative formulation, however, was beyond the narrowly economistic scope of the Fernandes and the São Paulo school. Though Fernandes was sensitive to the role of race as a relatively autonomous variable, he nevertheless categorized race as contingent upon class conflict, without an independent role in the construction and reproduction of social inequalities and more generally, power relations. Although his work did represent a more sophisticated explication of the sociology of race relations, race was a central issue for Fernandes only insofar as it helped explain mechanisms of exploitation in dependent capitalist development.

Winant proffers a cogent analysis and rebuttal of the theoretical assumptions of Fernandes and the São Paulo cadre:

> As a consequence of centuries of inscription in the social order, racial dynamics inevitably acquire their own autonomous logic, penetrating the fabric of social life and the cultural system at every level. Thus they can not be fully understood, in the manner of Fernandes, as survivals of a plantation slavocracy in which capitalist social relationships had not yet developed. Such a perspective ultimately denies the linkage between racial phenomena and post-slavery society.[9]

Similarly, Hasenbalg (1985) argues that Fernandes provides little explanation for the persistence of racially discriminatory practices within the process of dependent capitalist development, an evident weakness in Fernandes's argument given the fact that Fernandes considers twentieth-century racism in Brazil to be an archaic holdover from the previous century. Here, Fernandes echoes Marx's broader assertions regarding the eventual dissolution of racism and national chauvinism with the advent of world capitalism.

Andrews concludes that neither Fernandes's Marxism nor Gilberto Freyre's racial democracy in Brazil can account for the persistence of racial discrimination in labor markets and in state policy long after slavery's demise. To underscore his point, Andrews argues that despite their intellectual and political differences, both Gilberto Freyre and Florestan Fernandes attribute contemporary racial inequality to the legacy of slavery and the inability of Afro-Brazilians to make the adjustment from slave to wage labor, ignoring both persistence and change in the structure and process of racial discrimination, and treating slavery as a world unto itself. These criticisms lead to two insights for a reevaluation of the role of race and class in Brazil. First, racism in Brazil has assumed new forms in the twentieth century, in conjunction with the shift from slave to wage labor. Much like the evolution of Jim Crow laws in the United States after Reconstruction, new laws and social practices were devised within the process of industrialization to maintain patterns of racial inequality, but these patterns were not identical to those from the previous epoch of slavery. Both the ideological and material constructions of race had changed.[10]

Second, both Fernandes and Freyre, though on distinct sides of the race-class chasm, have presented analyses of racial dynamics in Brazil that have been limited by a paternalistic vision and economic reductionism; the market economy in the case of Fernandes, the domestic economy in the case of Freyre. Ironically, the role of race and gender are underdeveloped within their respective analytic frames and as a result are understudied.

Structuralists

In the 1970s, the third generation of race relations literature emerged from Brazil. Written mostly by Brazilian scholars working from census data and quantitative studies, this most recent tendency represented the desire to debunk the racial democracy myth perpetrated by the first wave of scholars of Brazilian race relations, as well as the reductionist conceptualization of racism as a residual "pathology" to be resolved by integration.

The two most important scholars of this tendency are Carlos Hasenbalg and Nelson do Valle Silva. Through joint and independent research, both have presented the most sustained critiques of the reductionist literature, forever changing the methodological presuppositions about the sources of racial inequality in Brazil.

Rather than treat race and class as oppositional categories, Hasenbalg and Silva situate racial inequality at the core of economic relations in Brazil. It serves a necessary function for Brazilian capitalism (Hasenbalg 1979; Hasenbalg and Silva 1988). Using demographic data from the 1976 and 1980 Brazilian censuses to buttress their claims, Hasenbalg and Silva's interpretations of the race-class conundrum in Brazil also represent a significant advance from the work of Marvin Harris (1964) and Thales de Azevedo (1966), which also treated race epiphenomenally.

In this sense, they should not be viewed as structuralists due to economic reductionism or determinism, but because of their preoccupation with what is commonly referred to as the "social-structural" or material conditions of racial dynamics. Hasenbalg contends that not only does racial discrimination play a central role in the perpetuation of socioeconomic inequalities between whites and blacks, but that it functionally complements labor markets of the Brazilian capitalist economy (1979; 1985). Racism then, was not an "archaic" ideology summoned on occasions of intergroup conflict as Fernandes suggests, but an ever-present reality in Brazilian society, a significant indicator in assessing levels of education, employment opportunities, health, even marriage choices.

Conversely, Silva, through his analysis of the 1960 and 1976 census data, refutes a key assumption in the race relations literature, the purported existence of an "escape hatch" for mulattoes; "Mulattoes do not behave differently from Blacks [*sic*], nor does race play a negligible role in the process of income attainment. In fact it was found that Blacks and mulattoes are almost equally discriminated against. . . . This clearly contradicts the idea of a 'mulatto escape-hatch' being the essence of Brazilian race relations."[11]

Silva refers to the well-known mulatto "escape hatch" thesis of Degler (1971), who suggests that mulattoes, the results of miscegenation, escape the stigma of racial difference and are sociologically better off than their darker-skinned counterparts. In asserting that the Degler thesis was not borne out in actual social relations, Silva provided "hard" evidence for a point raised by Thomas Skidmore in the same 1985 volume, that while the escape hatch thesis might be plausible in theory, there is no evidence to suggest that the "whitening" process had material benefits for mulattoes, "that the person of mixed blood got preferential treatment."[12] As a result, Silva uses the categories of white and nonwhite in his quantitative methodology for assessing Brazilian racial inequality, rather than the black, white mulatto categories that are commonly used.

Furthermore, even if the mulatto "escape hatch" thesis had some validity for the colonial or postabolition period, it would not distinguish Brazil from other multiracial polities since at least the 1960s, for the following reasons. First, within U.S. African-American communities there have always been debates and controversies over lighter-skinned blacks, whose existence betrayed at least one miscegenating moment within the black community. Film criticism has a far more developed literature on the role of the mulatto within the U.S. African-American community, in response to a movie corpus that has used the mulatto and the phenomena of "passing for white" as a central theme.[13]

More general demographic changes within the country also problematize the biracial categorization of the United States. As Skidmore has remarked, the increasing Latino population in the United States since the 1960s has meant that there are demographically significant sectors of the U.S. population that do not fit into white or black categories, which has made the biracial definition of racial classification there less valid (Skidmore 1992). As Mintz (1964) notes, laws designed to prohibit certain activities within African-American populations and between African-

American and white populations in the New World also confirm that these activities had already been in practice. Miscegenation is such an activity and has occurred in every society where whites and blacks have resided together.

Still, there are far-reaching political implications within Silva's conclusions that remain unexplored. There are always issues in any given society for which presumptions do not match realities, so the disjunction between the ideology and reality of the whitening process is not particularly surprising. The absence of material benefits for mulattoes relative to black Brazilians does not explain why many people in Brazil, blacks and mulattoes included, believe that there are. Secondly, if black and brown Brazilians do perceive differences in their respective positions in Brazilian society, it could partially explain the difficulties of joint social and political mobilization of negros and *pardos*. Conversely, it would also highlight the difficult tasks of black and brown activists who consider themselves Afro-Brazilian to convince their phenotypical cohort of common cause, as well as provide insight into the peculiar circumstances that make lighter-skinned Afro-Brazilians consider themselves, well, Afro-Brazilians.

These problems of racial inequality, Afro-Brazilian identity and social mobilization are rooted in politics as well as economics. While Silva and Hasenbalg do provide ample evidence of the socioeconomic basis of racial inequality, there is relatively little discussion of how racial inequality is politically constructed, or contested.

This is exemplified by Hasenbalg's brief mention of "the smooth maintenance of racial inequalities" (Hasenbalg 1985) by white elites who dominate the state and civil society, and the lack of sustained political opposition by Afro-Brazilians. Hasenbalg's notion of smooth maintenance obscures what has, in fact, been smoothed over—the attempts by Afro-Brazilian activists to politicize discussions of racial inequality in Brazil. However limited, the attempts by Afro-Brazilians to disrupt the "smooth maintenance" of racial inequality would have to be accounted for if observers of Brazilian racial politics are to have any indication of the extent to which white elites within the state apparatus and in civil society repress Afro-Brazilian dissent.

To be fair, Hasenbalg's cryptic notion of "smooth maintenance" to characterize white dominance and Afro-Brazilians subordination can be partially justified by the relative absence of racial upheaval in Brazilian history. Similarly, Dzidzienyo (1971) referred to the relatively tensionless maintenance of the structures of racial dominance in Brazil when contrasted with other multiracial polities such as the United States. In his critique of the power-laden underpinnings of the ideology of racial democracy, Dzidzienyo argued that its grasp on Brazilian culture was "pervasive," serving as "the cornerstone of the closely-observed 'etiquette' of race relations in Brazil."[14] The etiquette to which he refers, oddly enough, brings us back to Fernandes' observations about the "ceremonial politeness" of white Paulistas, which were cited at the start of this chapter.

From a racial politics perspective, however, the "smoothness" or "pervasiveness" of Afro-Brazilian subordination is but a description, not an explanation, of one outcome of white dominance. Part of the problem, it seems, stems from the presumption that the ideology of racial democracy and its related sociopolitical practices are "givens," ideological and material conformities that are not subject to change or contestation. Another dimension of the problem may be disciplinary; the majority of scholars investigating race-related problems have been sociologists, historians, and anthropologists, not political scientists.

For whatever the reasons, the "ceremonial politeness" of Fernandes, the "smooth maintenance" characterized by Hasenbalg, and Dzidzienyo's "etiquette of race relations" in Brazil are not presented as elements of contestable, or contested terrain, but the consequence of the "victory" of white domination in the course of a struggle that was "settled" some time ago.

Forms of protest by subaltern groups, however minimal, give an indication of the limits of domination. If the dominance of white Brazilian elites is not total, then what—and where—are its limits? While there is considerable treatment of how white elite dominance was attained, there is virtually no development of how it is maintained or challenged. Fontaine (1985) briefly examines the role of power in the interchange of whites and blacks in Brazil, but largely treats power and powerlessness as separate realms. He suggests that Afro-Brazilians have "interstitial" and "residual" power, that is, power to affect existing patron-client relationships between local leaders and white politicians through the extraction of promises for goods and services for their constituency. Though he advances his earlier position, white-black relations are treated as fairly distinct spheres, not as part of a dynamic process.[15]

Winant offers useful commentary on the structuralist approaches: "They did not seek to explain how racism had survived in a supposed 'racial democracy,' nor how true integration might be achieved. Rather they looked at the way the Brazilian social order had maintained racial inequalities without encountering significant opposition and conflict."[16] Although racial discrimination was not characterized as purely epiphenomenal, the structuralist approach suggested that the "smooth maintenance of racial inequalities" was predicated upon elite manipulation of class conflict. Their notion of elite manipulation was not unlike dual or segmented labor market theories that attempt to make Marxist theory applicable to studies of race and class interfaces.[17] While there are accounts of such elite manipulation in Brazilian history, it is also true that even labor-based movements with clearly articulated challenges to both capitalism and the state have at best neglected problems of ethnic diversity within their rank and file (Maram 1977; Andrews 1991). At worst, they have reproduced them in new forms, as will be explained in Chapter 5.

Thus, for students of contemporary racial politics in Brazil, several questions remain: What are the reactions of Afro-Brazilians to the "tolerance" and "ceremonial politeness" of white Brazilians? How do Afro-Brazilians, who perceive a complex of discriminatory practices behind the simulacrum of racial democracy, respond to the "normal conditions" of their social and political realities? Moreover, with the challenges to the notion of a racial democracy in Brazil posed by activists and scholars alike, have there been shifts in the relations between whites and nonwhites in Brazil over time?

Missing from the depictions of white elites' relatively smooth racial dominance in both the determinist and structuralist literatures are two other key elements of racial politics—power and culture. Like protagonists on both sides of the race-versus-class divide, the forms of power largely recognized and investigated are those that are economic and formal-institutional. Culture—as an arena in which the tensions of dominanance and subordination, appropriation and resistance are manifest—has largely been ignored. Presumably, this is due in part to the ubiquitous role that expressive culture plays, in both national and Afro-Brazilian life, as a unifier of distinct cultural and racial identities under the banner of nation, and as a suppressor of a distinctly Afro-Brazilian identity.

Despite the conceptual differences between the reductionists and structuralists, both tendencies seemed to concur about one crucial dimension of Brazilian race relations, a dimension that seemed to distinguish Afro-Brazilians from their U.S. counterparts: a lack a collective awareness of themselves as a subordinated racial group, due to the myth of racial democracy and the vagaries of dependent capitalism.[18] And yet aside from Fernandes's ambiguous interpretations of individual and collective behavior among blacks in São Paulo, there is little in either literature that addresses issues concerning the formation of political identities and behaviors; the existence of racially conscious individuals and organizations in Brazil throughout its history, despite the discouragement and denial of their existence. As Fontaine has noted in one of the few review essays concerning research of Afro-Latin America, the literature of Afro-Brazilian studies does not "deal with political institutions, behavior or attitudes, or with elections, electoral behavior, or political parties, or even public policy."[19]

What is sorely needed is a conceptual framework to enable scholars to move from microfocused issues such as individual and collective identity and forms of resistance, to macro-oriented ones such as socioeconomic inequalities and national political discourse relating to race. If we accept Winant's contention that racial power dynamics are suffused throughout cultural, political, and material practices in Brazil, then we recognize that any structural analysis of race relations that neglects cultural and ideological factors, or treats them as secondary, provides an incomplete explanation of the full ramifications of racial inequality articulated in social interaction. Only then can one trace the forward and backward linkages between endogenous and exogenous spheres of racial dynamics in Brazil. The concept of racial hegemony, briefly presented above, is an attempt to generate analysis and debate on these linkages. These linkages, which are embedded in contemporary racial politics in Brazil, will be outlined in the following chapter.

THREE

RACIAL DEMOCRACY: HEGEMONY,

BRAZILIAN STYLE

What was once called a time of peace was only the moment
before the victim cried out.[1]

To be sure the social distance between masters and slaves was
an enormous one, the whites being really or officially the masters and the blacks really or officially the slaves. The Portuguese, however, were a people who had experienced the rule of
the Moor's, a dark-skinned race but one that was superior to
the white race in various aspects of its moral and material culture; and accordingly though they themselves might be white
and even of a pronounced blond type, they had long since
formed the habit of discovering in colored peoples . . . persons,
human beings, who were brothers, creatures and children
of God with whom it was possible to fraternize and all this
from the very first years of colonization tended to
mitigate the system.[2]

THE LONG QUOTATION above, taken from Gilberto Freyre's
classic *The Masters and the Slaves* (1946), highlights the Brazilian
variant of the Iberian model of racial exceptionalism,[3] which has
been long ignored by Brazilianists and Latin Americanists alike. The Brazilian variant, punctuated by the myth of racial democracy, appears in its
most elaborate form in Freyre's *The Masters and the Slaves, Sobrados and
Mocambos* (1951), and other works.

Freyre's vision was crucial for the development of the racial democracy
myth. Racial exceptionalism, however, as a broader ideological construct
of slaveholding and Republican elites, has outlived racial democracy as an
ideological form. The formation of an ideology of racial exceptionalism is
a prerequisite for comprehension of racial politics in Brazil.

My conceptualization of racial exceptionalism reflects an attempt to
explain the subtle ideological shift from the commonsense belief that Brazil is a country without racial antagonisms to a qualified recognition of
racial prejudice, discrimination, and subordination as a feature of Brazilian life, while maintaining the belief that relative to other multiracial polities Brazil is indeed a more racially and culturally accommodating society.

The importance of this shift will be made obvious in Chapter 6 in an analysis of the 1988 centennial commemoration of abolition, when there was an open refutation of the myth of racial democracy coupled with the public repression of Afro-Brazilian dissent during the commemorative events.

This chapter has four broad aims. Its first is to highlight Brazilian racial exceptionalism as the precursor and grounding of racial democracy. Second, the historical antecedents for Brazilian racial democracy will be assessed for their influence upon the historiography of Brazilian race relations. The third task is a critical reading of the elaboration of the racial democracy myth by Gilberto Freyre, to demonstrate the legitimation and rootedness of an exceptionalist credo in both "high" and "low" culture in Brazil by the 1930s, in spite of the asymmetrical racial dynamics that were evolving simultaneously.

The final objective of this chapter is to show the linkage between the myth of racial democracy, the logic of racial exceptionalism, and the social consequences for black Brazilians; the disjuncture between an ideology of conservative liberalism and the lived reality of symbolic and material oppression of blacks by whites. Both racial exceptionalism and racial democracy will then be situated within the context of racial inequality in Rio de Janeiro and São Paulo. While much has been written about racial democracy as the peculiar barrier to discussion and resolution of racial discrimination in Brazil, there has been virtually no theoretical development of the implications *democracia racial* contains for more contemporary racial politics, in which the racial democracy myth itself has been refuted by even white elites at the level of the state and in civil society (see Chapter 6).

This last task is an attempt to underscore the interconnectedness and interdependence of cultural and structural forms of inequality. Racial ideologies in Brazil in general, and in Rio de Janeiro and São Paulo in particular, are not mere reflections of unequal relations between wage earners and wage givers but an integral cog in the wheels of a hegemonic process that distributes economic, political, and cultural privileges according to race. While class and gender are critical factors in this distribution of privilege, racial differences will be emphasized in order to highlight its previously neglected role as the arbiter of cultural and material forms of marginalization.

Iberian Exceptionalism: Racialism and Racism by Another Name

One of the most enduring myths regarding Iberian colonialism in Latin America has been the supposed recognition of the humanity of African-derived peoples under Spanish and Portuguese rule, which helped contribute to less harsh patterns of racial interaction in the nation-states that had once been part of these empires. When compared to the United States, racial dynamics in other parts of the New World have seemed tame. In many parts of Latin America, Central America, and the Caribbean, myths exist of harmonious race relations between European, African-derived, and indigenous peoples.

In much of the literature on race relations in these regions, Iberian colonialism (Hoetink 1967; Tannenbaum 1946; 1947) has been cited as a major factor in mitigating the harsh relationships between master and slave during the eighteenth and nineteenth centuries. Degler (1971) and other Latin Americanist scholars of a previous generation have cited the incorporating tendencies of Catholicism, the presence of the Moors in Iberian history and culture, and the higher rates of manumission of enslaved Africans as factors that contributed to the relative lack of racial animosity between whites and nonwhites or, more specifically, the absence of racial hatred of former slaves.

In turn, many Latin American intellectuals and statesmen argued that U.S. patterns of race relations were unique to the Anglo-dominated culture of the north. Latin American nationalisms, in contrast, had successfully fused racial and national identities to the extent that nationalism superseded racialism or racism. This virtually wiped out the possibility that presumed racial differences would be the basis for discrimination or organization, marriage or any social mechanism in which race could be used as an organizing principle.

For these reasons, the United States was viewed as the exception to processes of racial amalgamation and assimilation in the rest of America. This dubious exception was a source of national pride for several important Latin American intellectuals like José Marti of Cuba, José Vasconcelos of Mexico and Gilberto Freyre of Brazil, who saw the possibility of a third path between European feudalism and U.S. racial segregation, societies that utilized racial miscegenation as a biological basis for social harmony between the races.

By the late nineteenth and early twentieth century, many Latin American intellectuals grappled with the profound impact of positivist thought upon academic and political discourses in their nations in an attempt to discredit theories concerning the inferiority of black and brown races, which, if true, would have relegated every Latin American nation to second-tier status; nations of mixed races, mongrels. Both Vasconcelos and Freyre engaged in what Nancy Stepan characterizes as "constructive miscegenation" (N. Stepan 1991), an attempt to subvert the negative rendering of racial mixing in positivist thought into attributes of nation building. Freyre envisioned a meta-race *(alem-raça)* evolving out of racial mixture that would be superior to those produced in the Old World. Vasconcelos articulated a vision of a cosmic race (*raza cósmica*) with a similar outcome—the creation of a race of people that combined the intellect of the European with the sensuality and adaptability of the African and native American.

By the 1940s, Mexico had become a model for the rest of Latin America for "resolving" tensions and prejudices with respect to indigenous populations (Knight 1990; Diaz-Polanco 1987). No other nation was as successful in celebrating and integrating Indigenismo into national popular culture, even though others, such as Peru, had tried. Conversely, Marti emphasized the role of revolutionary struggle during the Independence War (1868–1878) to fuse whites and blacks into one superior race, a "Cuban" race (Marti 1979).

Yet in each of these countries, there is historical evidence of strong racist sentiments and discriminatory practices not only against people of African descent, but against indigenous, Asian, Jewish, and other peoples as well. In Mexico, these practices ranged from the upholding of certain standards of beauty and aesthetics to anti-Chinese immigration policies (Knight 1990). In Cuba, the 1912 race war in Oriente province gives evidence of simmering racial tensions that ultimately erupted into violent conflict, "national unity" notwithstanding.[4] In Brazil, as we shall see below, the chasm between the rhetoric and reality of racial interaction was just as wide.

In short, racially exceptionalist discourses bear little resemblance to the realities of racially based inequalities in the region, but this disjuncture is not what is most important about them. Their importance lies in their resonance within popular, common sense and in elite discussion, rhetoric, and social policy. They are replete with the prejudices, biases, and predeterminations about the location and role of various racial and ethnic groups.

A glance at the sparse literature on people of African descent in Latin America gives evidence of racially exceptionalist discourses prevalent in Venezuela (Wright 1990), Argentina (Andrews 1980), and other nations. Given this study's focus, the broader implications of racial exceptionalism for Latin America will not be examined here. The conceptual implications, however, for studying the evolution of racial exceptionalism in Brazil is exemplified in the common assumption held by Brazilians and non-Brazilians alike that because Brazil, even if it can no longer be considered a racial democracy, was not a racist nation because its racial problems were not identical to those in the United States. The putatively more benign form of Brazilian slavery, coupled with the alleged psychic intimacy of Portuguese colonizers with their African slaves, contributed to the relative absence of racial discrimination and conflict. This relative absence was something Gilberto Freyre and other Brazilians would look to with pride.

As a consequence, the manifold forms that racism assumed in Brazil were either denied or considered idiosyncratic. While the pronounced celebration of "Africanness" in Brazil distinguished the country from all others in Latin America, Brazil's treatment of its African-derived population was similar in many respects. First, there was the institutionalization of racially discriminatory practices in immigration and national education policies, the diffusion of negative depictions of people of African descent, and the imposition of Latin American aesthetics and popular culture that idealized European intellectual and cultural traditions. Both explicitly and implicitly, these discursive and nondiscursive practices denigrated and essentialized Afro-Brazilians. Both elite and popular discourses disseminated an ideology of racial harmony and exceptionalism as integral components of national identity. At the level of the state, social polices sought to mask or downplay racial differences. The most damaging consequence, though, is the inability of many Brazilian citizens to identify problems of race at all, and the lack of recognition that particular problems of racial discrimination, violence, and inequality exist in Brazil.

Historical Antecedents: Slavery, Democracy and Cultural Rationale

The ideology of Brazilian racial democracy that emerged from Brazil's version of racial exceptionalism was spawned in the early part of the nineteenth century, in response to the abolitionist wave that gradually surged across slaveholding societies in the New World. Brazil, as both colony and republic, had the longest-lasting slave system in the New World, from the fifteenth century until 1888. It was harshly criticized by Britain, the United States, and other republics for its reluctant termination of the institution of slavery and its related commerce, trading in slaves.

Brazilian elites, though eager to respond to criticism, did not want to do away with the peculiar institution so easily, for even by the mid-nineteenth century, a new mode of production was not firmly in place. Conrad, in his valuable documentary history of black slavery in Brazil notes: "As the anti-slavery movements of the United States and Britain began to call the world's attention to the horrors of their own domestic and colonial slave systems in the decades after the American Revolution . . . the Luso-Brazilian world began to wage its own systematic campaign both at home and abroad to defend and exonerate slavery and the slave trade."[5]

Anti-abolitionist Brazilian elites, including the bishop of the Brazilian Catholic church, began concocting favorable representations of Brazilian slavery for foreign consumption, especially for British audiences (*para ingles ver*). This tactic was applied at home as well by influential Brazilian historians and people of letters, all of whom suggested at one point or another that slavery was less harsh than in Brazil than in other slaveholding societies. Some went so far as to suggest that the living conditions of Brazilian slaves were superior to those of the working classes in some European countries.

Elite depictions of slavery as beneficial and abolition unnecessary had great success outside of Brazil. As early as 1850, the British minister to Brazil, one William Christie, noted that "the *'Brazilian agents'* have, I believe, succeeded in establishing a general impression that slaves are very well treated in Brazil. The general English public have, for many years past, had little or nothing before them but *the flattering pictures of Brazilian agents.*"[6]

Christie's conspiratorial tone (agents!) aside, the above quote provides an indication of early efforts by Brazilian elites to foster a more benign image of Brazil than its actual social relations would warrant. Thus, the diffusion of the image of a racial paradise in Brazil effectively internationalized the myth of racial democracy and provided Brazil with an "escape clause" from a race relations critique until the 1950s.

For slave trade advocates in Brazil, this logic was attractive because of its contradictions, not in spite of them. It offered a confluence of penury and paternalism, a cultural rationale for their material interests, which kept abolition at bay until another mode of production, complete with another subaltern class, could take is place. So despite their claims regarding Brazilian slave society, the elites who first set forth the idea that Brazil was an exception to the harsh, unmitigated penury of slave society marked an important precedent, one that would characterize academic and societal discourses about racial inequality in Brazil until the 1950s. Proslavery elites successfully disseminated an image of Brazilian society and culture, which, although untrue, had become a part of both a national and international folklore.

This was, to be sure, propaganda, especially when juxtaposed against the revisionist historiography of Conrad (1972; 1983), Degler (1971), Graham (1990), Moura (1987), and others. These scholars have convincingly refuted earlier scholarship that laid claim to a less harsh slave society in Brazil and a natural affinity for darker-skinned peoples. The "fraternization" alluded to by Freyre can be accounted for by the paucity of Portuguese women in the colony (Russell-Wood 1982). Elite abeyance of abolition can be attributed not to the idyllic conditions under which Brazilian slaves toiled, but to the relatively late start Brazil had in capitalist, liberal-democratic development in comparison to the United States or Britain.

Through comparative assessment of slave systems in the United States and Brazil, Degler, Davis, and Viotti (1985) argue that Brazilian slavery was actually harsher than the U.S. system. Slave mortality rates were higher in Brazil than in the U.S. Slaveholders found it less expensive to import more Africans than to provide the necessary means for the slave population to reproduce itself, and as a result there was less incentive to provide for slaves in Brazil. Steps taken toward abolition, for example, were ambiguous at best. While the 1871 Free Womb Law, for example, freed children of slave mothers born into the empire after that date, it allowed slaveholders to keep these children until age twenty-one as payment for the cost of their upkeep. All those born before the date remained slaves.[7]

There were other ambiguities to racial slavery in Brazil. By 1871, seventeen years before abolition, there were more free blacks than slaves in the state of São Paulo (Fernandes 1969; Andrews 1991). Brazilian slaves were manumitted in greater numbers than those in the United States. Yet even during the colonial period in Brazil, skilled free blacks (*homens de ganho*) were discouraged from developing consistent trade routes and business relationships through laws and informal practices devised by the Portuguese to discourage them from objectively participating in labor and trade competition with whites (Russell-Wood 1982).

Moreover, preoccupations with "purity of blood" (*pureza de sangue*) belie assumptions that the Portuguese were devoid of racist sentiments as Brazilian statesmen and intellectuals led others to believe. Tucci Carneiro's study of Jewish converts to Catholicism in Brazil documents the existence of anti-Semitic and anti-Moor prejudices in Spain and Portugal as early as the fifteenth century. These sentiments, which evolved into edicts and covenants against Jews, Africans, and other people of "impure blood" were subsequently extended to the New World as part of the process of Spanish and Portuguese colonial expansion. Tucci Carneiro notes that discriminatory laws against Moors and Jews existed in Portuguese legislation until 1774,[8] while legislation specifically discriminating against negros and mulattoes first appeared in 1671 and lasted until the nineteenth century. Most interestingly, Tucci Carneiro traces the first appearance of anti-Jewish sentiments in Portugal to the Portuguese adoption of a policy of forced conversion of Jews into "new Christians" not long after the Spanish Inquisition. These prejudices and consequently, colonial legislation that institutionalized such prejudices, were transferred to Brazil with the arrival of the Portuguese.

In this respect, neither Portugal nor Spain were fundamentally different from their central and northern European counterparts in the dissemination of racist sentiments and practices in their colonies of the New World. Most importantly, Tucci Carneiro asserts that Jews, New Christians, Moors, mulattoes, indigenous as well as other racial and ethnic groups "faced a series of barriers that impeded social ascension, making them be considered veritable pariahs. . . . The social separation of those of "pure blood" from the "infected" gave the political system the means to create a lexicon that, when applied within a discourse, gave Portuguese Legislation a racist character [translation mine]."[9]

This provides ample evidence to suggest that the Iberian cultural experience was not vastly different from other European civilizations with respect to tolerance of religious, racial, and ethnic differences. What distinguished Spain and Portugal was their inability to stay in the big leagues, along with France and Britain, of imperialist sophistication and competition, and their culturally conservative response to the Enlightment. Neither could successfully make the transition from mercantile to industrial capitalism, an impediment that would relegate them, along with Italy, to roles as bit players in the process of global, industrial expansion.

The history of Portuguese colonialism in Brazil and in Lusophone Africa suggests that its own underdevelopment, the backward state of its private sector and "an inability to meet the costs of the administrative and military infrastructures of colonial expansion"[10] led to the necessity of more direct interaction between colonizer and colonized. As Perry Anderson (1962) notes, the Portuguese, unlike the other major colonial powers, did not have charter companies to do their bidding outside the metropole, and had to rely heavily upon military might to maintain their dominance.

As a consequence of this aberrant colonialism, the countries of Lusophone Africa were among the last to be decolonized, as Portugal fought dearly for its imperial life, long after other imperial powers had either fostered or were pushed into granting independence. As McCulloch (1983) notes, Portugal simply could not *afford* to relinquish its African colonies. The cost of decolonization was greater than the marginal profits colonialism provided. Given their peripheral status within the international political economy, there was no profitable scheme, either nationally or internationally, to replace the colonial relationship.

Uniting these two distinct epochs and modes of dominance, however, is the predominance of "cultural" explanations to justify the postponement of abolition and national independence. The relative lack of economic and geopolitical strength required greater human interaction between colonizer and colonized. The form that this interaction assumed depended upon the historical circumstances. In the case of Angola, Guinea-Bissau, and Mozambique, arguments about the softer nature of the Portuguese exploded in the brutality of independence wars (Bender 1978). In Brazil, the shift from monarchy to republic was not nearly as tumultuous, with power remaining in the hands of large landowners, who in effect became the "new" elite (Viotti 1985).

The reason for presenting this countervailing portrait of Portuguese colonialism is to suggest that there are *structural* factors that can help explain the peculiarities of Portuguese colonialism and cultural residue in

Brazil, peculiarities that assumed more personal, less mediated forms than in other colonial contexts during the era of Western expansion into Africa and Latin America. While the distinctive modes of racial interaction within Lusophone societies can be explained in terms of culture, these patterns of racial interaction grew out of certain material limitations.

Contemporary, scholarly refutations of racial democracy and exceptionalism are one thing; however, the popularity of the racial democracy myth is quite another. The internationalization of the racial democracy myth reached African-derived peoples in other parts of the hemisphere as well as early as the 1920s. For African-Americans with a hemispheric perspective, Brazil represented the ideal point of comparison for race relations scholars, a large New World country with a significant African-derived population that had better race relations than the United States. Black U.S. historians attempting to relate the experience of other blacks in the New World noted this purported difference in the treatment of Afro-Brazilians. In a comparative analysis of Brazilian and U.S. racial slavery, Mary Wilhelmine Williams wrote in 1930 that

> the broad hospitality of the Brazilians which ameliorated the conditions of the Negroes in slavery, and saved them from becoming a menace when free, also permitted Brazil to escape a permanent Negro problem—with its hatreds and discriminations; its riots and its lynching—such as troubles her northern neighbor. In Brazil, the blood of Negros and whites mingles freely, and no attempt is made to prevent the fusion. Meanwhile the two blending peoples are peacefully cooperating to work out the destiny of the Republic, each individual making the contribution his abilities permit, unrestrained by the *accident* [emphasis mine] of race.[11]

U.S. African-Americans who had the opportunity to visit Brazil (and who did so on the basis of the nation's reputation), helped propagate the myth of a racial paradise. In a study of "Afro North-American Views of Race Relations in Brazil,"[12] Hellwig (1990; 1992) notes the predominance of favorable reviews of Brazil within this segment of the African-American population. They traveled to Brazil and returned with glowing praise, which was duly reported by the black press. From the turn of the century until the 1940s, noted black leaders such as Booker T. Washington and W. E. B. DuBois wrote positively of the black experience in Brazil, in contrast to the United States. Black nationalist Henry McNeal Turner and radical journalist Cyril Biggs in the United States advocated emigration to Brazil as a refuge from oppression in their own country.[13]

These positive depictions of Brazilian race relations greatly influenced North American scholars such as Frank Tannenbaum, who would later broaden the racial paradise thesis in his classic work *Slave and Citizen*. It is no exaggeration to suggest that an entire generation of scholars, and those who read their works, ascribed to some variation of the racial democracy theme, so much that countervailing perspectives on this racial nirvana were often met with skepticism and fierce rebuttal, both in academic scholarship and in more popular discourse (Ramos 1957).

Gilberto Freyre was greatly influenced by this popular discourse, which emerged forcefully during the years of the First Republic (1889–1930) and sought to emphasize the regional variations within Brazilian culture, especially in the Northeast. This emphasis was in contrast to the efforts of Brazilian modernists like Mario Andrade de Andrade, who saw Brazilian modernism as an attempt to deregionalize Brazil through a common language—colloquial, baroque-inflected Portuguese. He also rejected the eugenicist explanations of Nina Rodrigues and sought instead a cultural trajectory for the possible evolution of a Brazilian society consisting of indigenous, African-born and white European peoples. Freyre took the "facts of Brazilian social life" namely, the shortage of white women and the controlled abundance of African-born ones, and reconstituted them in a scenario that suggested that the slavemaster's "big house" was the theater for a racially egalitarian polity unknown to the New World:

> The scarcity of white women created zones of fraternization between conquerors and conquered, between masters and slaves. While these relations between white men and colored women did not cease to be those of "superiors" with "inferiors," and in the majority of cases those of disillusioned and sadistic gentleman with passive slave girls, they were mitigated by the need that was felt by many colonists of founding a family. . . . A widely practiced miscegenation here tended to modify the enormous social distance that otherwise would have been preserved between big house and slave hut. What a latifundiary monoculture based upon slavery accomplished in the way of creating an aristocracy by dividing Brazilian society into two extremes of gentry and slaves, with a thin and insignificant remnant of free men sandwiched in between, was in good part offset by the social effects of miscegenation . . . the indian woman . . . or the negro woman and later the mulatto, the quadroon and the octoroon becoming domestics, concubines and even the lawful wives of the white masters, exerted a powerful influence for social democracy in Brazil.[14]

If anywhere, these "zones of fraternization" were charted in the realm of eros, specifically in the desires of white, male slaveowners. Black, or dark-skinned males, as well as white females are absent from this scenario. Absent too is any possibility that so-called fraternal zones were spaces of brutal intimacy, where relations between landowner and servant were structured by a relative freedom of choice for the landowner, and the relative absence of choice for the female servant. Servant, in this vein, has a double connotation, related to a laboring as well as a sexual function.[15]

Whether in the voice of the Boaz-influenced anthropologist or that of the privileged male child of Pernambucan plantocrats, Freyre's racial mélange is no free-flowing historical accident but an orchestrated intermingling generated by males of the dominant social group. In Freyre's reconstruction of preindustrial Brazil, miscegenation first occurs between white, landowning males and females from indigenous and enslaved social groups only, not between enslaved men and white women. Therefore, regardless of the degree of humanity that Freyre infers from these relations, they were, objectively, relations of dominance and subordination between owners and owned in which racial and gender roles were commodified in accordance with the preferences and choices of slaveowners.

Yet Freyre pushes his selective miscegenation even further, by connecting it, at the end of the passage, to the rise of social democracy in Brazil. This gives the notion of a "trickle down effect" in economic and philosophical liberalism a novel resonance, for this is precisely what Freyre is suggesting by the passage's end; sexual union between white males and nonwhite females had a socializing effect for the composition of families, the inheritance of estates, the very redistribution of land, property, and capital in Brazil. Where blacks and other people would normally have been excluded from such interaction and sharing with white owners in other slave societies, in Brazil they were *integrated* into the domestic economy, indeed a vital component of the pattern of human relations on the colonial estate.

Actually, the racial composition of Brazil brought consternation to many Brazilian elites. Skidmore (1974), Levine (1970) and Viotti (1985) note that Comtean positivists and eugenicists, partners in social alchemy, confronted Brazilian elites with racialist formulations of its own. If Brazil was to be modern, with the nonwhite hue of its people, it could not possibly be like Europe. National intellectuals like Nina Rodrigues saw the African presence in Brazil as an impediment to national development and warned Brazilians of the dangers race-mixing posed for the nation's progress (Graham 1990).

Brazilian politicians and policymakers responded to this concern. The national immigration decree of 1890 contained a clause excluding Africans and Asians from freely entering the country, to ensure that Brazil, with its economy bolstered by coffee production, would not lure nonwhites.[16] The clause was enforced until 1902. Baron Rio Branco, Brazilian foreign minister from 1902 to 1912, sought to enhance a whiter image of Brazil abroad by stocking his diplomatic corps "with white men whom foreigners would consider civilized and sophisticated—to reinforce the image of a Europeanized country growing whiter and whiter."[17]

These political acts were manifestations of what has been termed "the whitening ideal" (*branqueamento*), found in several Latin American and

Caribbean countries, but nowhere so explicitly as in Brazil. A new, mulatto race of people would be formed by the conjunction of African and European descendants, combining the best attributes of both to create an intellectually sophisticated but sensualized race of people, neither black nor white but Brazilian. Of course, the intellectual attributes would derive from those of European blood; the sensual would of course be African. Indigenous people would serve to ameliorate the process.

At the same, there was the recognition that those of African descent would not disappear entirely. The normative correlation of social ascension and whiteness was a recognition of the impossibility of any wholesale exclusion of blacks and mulattoes to positions of power and status. Blacks too could be white, if they were of sufficient wealth or social status. Examples of this attitude, along with a disdain for nonwhite people, abound in historical accounts of life in colonial, monarchial, and Republican Brazil.[18]

Historical reality notwithstanding, Freyre's pastoral scene became the basis for Brazil's self-portrait for the latter half of the twentieth century (Skidmore 1974). In this regard, Freyre's vision should be seen not merely as one about race and racial difference, but as a subset of a national project of conservative liberalism, complete with the paternalism and patron-client relations that have marked Brazilian society and culture from colonial times to the present.

Brazil would not be weakened by its racial plurality, Freyre's Luso-Tropicalism suggested, but strengthened by it. As Emilia Viotti da Costa has observed, advocates of Luso-Tropicalism "discarded two of the European racist theories main assumptions; the innateness of racial differences and the degeneracy of mixed bloods."[19] In this respect, Freyre must be considered revolutionary; rather than being repulsed by the prospect of a country of half-breeds, he celebrated its possibility. At the same time, Freyre's thorough critique of the monolithic "African" race that Rodrigues and others disparaged set off an entire generation of scholarship and popular interest in the diversity of African cultural practices and residuals in Brazil. The genealogical inquiries into Angolan, Nago, Bantusan, and other African peoples in Brazil gave proof that Africans were not a single "race." It was a continent with some civilizations that were more advanced than the Portuguese in terms of mining and metalworking, for example, two areas that enabled the Portuguese to amass fortunes in Brazil at their slaves' expense.

All the while, however, there was an implicit acceptance of the terms of the debate set by Brazilian eugenicists and Positivists. As noted in Chapter 1, the eugenicist's preoccupation with racial types and categories, and not racial groups and their interactions, carried over into Freyre's *democracia racial*. Freyre's cataloging of the various racial mixtures in Brazil, the mulatto in particular, has more phenotypical than social implications. *Mulatos, caboclos, cafusos, zambos,* and other racial phenotypes appear as individual offspring, not as members of groups interacting with other groups.

This too, however, fits within the scheme of racial exceptionalism. Without the analysis of group exchanges, there can be no claims made for group inequalities. Discrimination against a dark-skinned woman on the basis of her color, for example, can only be conceived of at the level of the individual or isolated phenomena. Conversely, the social ascension of a handful of blacks, mulattoes, and *pardos* to positions of high social status is viewed by adherents to the doctrine of racial exceptionalism as confirmation of Brazilian racial democracy. Even an astute historian of racial slavery like Eugene Genovese has accepted this thesis to a large extent, as evidenced in his comparative analysis of slave societies in the New World.[20]

From the first position to the second there is a transposition of logic; when racism appears it is treated as an aberration that does not undermine the broader social premise. The logic is transposed when considering instances of social mobility; the elevation in status of a few individuals bodes well for racial democracy as a whole.

On its own terms, racial democracy was rife with contradictions. The mulatta came to be a sexual ideal; the mulatto or negro was not. Whites of course, males in particular, were. Like Surrealist and Fauvist movements in Europe during the early twentieth century, Freyre's Luso-Tropicalism reconfigured middle-class whites alienated by Eurocentricism at the center of an alternative cultural pantheon. Even though Freyre saw Luso-Tropicalism as a regionalist, traditionalist response to modernization and industrialization, his movement still reflected Brazilian elites' historical anxiety about their European ideals and Afro-Brazilian realities.

Freyre's vision, and the rearticulation of this vision in Brazilian society by its citizens, represents the second antecedent for racial exceptionalism. Like the first moment involving proslavery advocates, the second provides a highly normative explanation for patterns of social inequality, an explanation based upon specific group interests and desires. What distinguishes the second instance, though, is the elevation of a cultural rationale to the level of social science and, ultimately, its reentry into the contradictory belief systems and social practices of everyday life in a different epoch and mode of production. The new Brazilian intelligentsia, as intellectuals of the dominant class, was able to commandeer the terms of racial discourse so that their interpretations and preoccupations as a group were considered to be those of Brazilian society writ large. This transformation from the specific to the general is what Gramsci termed "universality," the process by which the intelligentsia, as the political and ideological vanguard of the dominant classes, assures their political-cultural legitimacy in civil society.

From the first publication of *The Masters and the Slaves* and well into the late 1970s, racial exceptionalism and racial democracy were grounded in social science discourse and in commonsense understandings of race relations in Brazil. This occurred in spite of evidence suggesting patterns of dominance and subordination that were irreducible to the "social problem," that is, the consequences of being poor.

From Myth to Consequence: The Emergence of Racial Hegemony

The path from racial exceptionalism and racial democracy to social consequence was cleared by the emergence of racial democracy discourse in everyday life. It became, in Gramsci's terms, the philosophical sediment for colloquial interpretations of Brazilian race relations. In "The Study of Philosophy" section of *The Prison Notebooks* Gramsci declared:

> Every philosophical current leaves behind a sedimentation of 'common sense'; *this is the document of its historical effectiveness* [emphasis mine]. Common sense is not something rigid and immobile, but is continually transforming itself, enriching itself, with scientific ideas and with philosophical opinions which have entered ordinary life. 'Common sense' is the folklore of philosophy. . . . Common sense creates the folklore of the future, that is a relatively rigid phase of popular knowledge at a given place and time.[21]

Racial exceptionalism, as the principal commonsense explanation of Brazilian racial reality, has become the document of the historical effectiveness of the Brazilian intelligentsia at the turn of the century in keeping racial difference from becoming a politically charged issue, and more specifically, in deterring the abolition of slavery until a new, profitable mode of production for them was in place. Racial democracy represents a phase in the historical development of racial exceptionalism. Now superseded, the initial formulation of racial exceptionalism has been reinterpreted, negotiated, and finally altered over social time, so that it no longer pertains to the unqualified absence of racialism in monarchial and early republican Brazil but a *qualified* acceptance of racism in contemporary Brazil, albeit on an individual rather than a systemic basis.

What remains from the previous belief system of racial democracy and earlier notions of racial exceptionalism is the denial of the existence of *ongoing* racial oppression of Afro-Brazilians. While the era of racial slavery and its attendant ideologies and discourses has been rendered obsolete, its philosophical sediment has been rearticulated in new, distinct forms of racial oppression. Most importantly, the discussion of race has yet to fully enter the domain of formal, institutional politics and has largely remained within the spheres of expressive culture for both whites and nonwhites.

This, I will argue, is the most profound consequence of racial democracy. When combined with racially discriminatory practices in education, labor markets, and popular culture, Brazilian blacks have been locked in an elliptical pattern of racial oppression, where claims against discriminatory practices are rarely heard and hardly ever addressed by Brazilian elites.

The key elements to the nonpoliticization of race and the discouragement of group identification among blacks are the following: (*a*) the assumption, mainly by white elites, that due to racial democracy, racial discrimination does not exist in Brazil or at least not on the level of countries such as South Africa and the United States; (*b*) the continuous reproduction and dissemination of stereotypes denigrating blacks and valorizing whites, which results in low, distorted self-images and an aversion to collective action among the former; and (*c*) coercive sanctions and the preemption of dissent imposed by whites upon blacks who question or threaten the fundamentally asymmetrical patterns of racial interaction.

The interplay of these elements, as belief systems and social practices, has come over time to situate racial difference within an arena of noncontestation, where the dominant and subordinate social roles of blacks and whites are assumed to be the natural order of social relations. In the few instances where racial conflict is clear and unambiguous, debates over the existence of racism in Brazil overtake any discussion of specific racist acts. The acts themselves go unresolved.

Two important cautionary points must be considered in light of this disjuncture of belief and social practice, and its significance for the discussion of racial hegemony in Brazil. First, while racial exceptionalism and racial democracy were first generated by white elites in Brazil, they are not their sole propagators. Once generated, these beliefs and practices assume forms radically distinct from the first utterance of racial exceptionalism as a proslavery ploy.

There is the temptation, present in studies of power in human interaction, to demonstrate a causal relationship between these more normative aspects of racial discrimination and its extension into the workplace, where the beliefs of a white shopkeeper or industrialist has a direct impact on those he or she chooses to hire. This type of investigation into the role of causation in human relationships invariably is a search for single determinants. In this study, the conscious intentions of white elites would not suffice as a comprehensive explanation of dominance and subordination.

For one, those intentions would not explain the actions of black Brazilians, intragroup conflict or diversity of opinion. Consequences then, not intentions, are the focus of this study.

Second, with the sediments of a discourse of racial democracy embedded in the concrete relations of Brazilians, people have exchanged, responded and reacted to these presumptions about Brazilian race relations. In theory, this could be characterized as a process of "social rubbing," where people come, as representative individuals, into contact with other individuals and groups in Brazilian society. When framed in power relations between whites and blacks, these sediments can be described as the scrapings from a soft collision between relatively mobile whites and relatively immobile blacks, with each leaving a mark upon the other. As in a collision between two automobiles, one parked, one not, it is the mobile vehicle that inflicts the most damage, but not without some external or internal impression of the encounter.

This is a useful metaphor for the discussion of racial hegemony. It captures the relative mobility of whites in relation to blacks, the undeniable influence of Afro-Brazilian culture upon whites and blacks alike, and the widespread inequalities between whites and blacks, which are manifested symbolically, materially, and culturally. Attempts at explaining and analyzing hegemonic processes with terms like *instilling beliefs* and *false consciousness* are misleading not only because they imply that expressed beliefs or observed behavior, studied in isolation, represent the *entire* consciousness of a social group, but also because they are abstractions from the realm of the social, in that they remove groups from the rubs or collisions which occur in social contexts.

We can now operationalize the three key normative elements of racial hegemony in Brazil noted above, to demonstrate the socially forged circumstances that make the conditions for racial hegemony possible.

(A) Racial discrimination does not exist in Brazil, or at least not on the level that it occurs in the United States.

Due to a lack of data, there are few scientifically derived indicators on the effects of race upon political and sociological behavior. Most available information has been anecdotal or ethnographic, both useful sources in their own right but ones that only provide a fragmented picture of the attitudes, opinions, and dispositions of whites and non-whites toward each other.

Pierre Van den Berghe and Roger Bastide's study of the white middle class in São Paulo in the 1970s provides an image of white elites who ascribe to the credo of racial democracy without actually practicing it. Ninety-two percent of those surveyed believed in equal opportunities for mulattoes and blacks; the subjects surveyed accepted at least 75 percent (23) of the forty-one stereotypes against blacks and mulattoes presented in the questionnaire. The stereotypes pertained to, among other concerns, the inherent sexual promiscuity of blacks and mulattoes and their aversion to thrift, work, and trustworthiness. Mulattoes fared better than blacks overall, but with minor percentage differences. For example, 95 percent of the whites surveyed would not marry a black, while 87 percent would not marry a mulatto. Two hundred sixty-nine out of 580 subjects judged blacks and mulattoes as equally inferior. Two hundred sixty-eight viewed mulattoes more favorably, while forty-three stated blacks were superior to mulattoes.[22]

While admitting that their sample was neither random nor proportional, Van den Berghe and Bastide argued more generally that attitudes such as those surveyed infer "an extreme form of racial prejudice rather than a milder aesthetic preference of 'physical appearance' which has been propounded by certain students of Brazilian race relations."[23] Like more dichotomous race relations contexts like South Africa, Britain, or the United States, the survey revealed an association of racial prejudice with sexuality by its subjects that would be "incomprehensible if there were only a class prejudice."[24] Their conclusions provide a glimpse of the fundamental paradox of racial exceptionalism, the simultaneous denial of—and contribution to—racial prejudice and discrimination in Brazil.

Central to the denial and promotion of racial discrimination in Brazil is the evasion of blackness at the most basic level—phenotype. In an analysis of the normative constructions of color in everyday discourse, anthropologist Yvonne Maggie (1988) found that both whites and nonwhites rarely refer to pretos or pardos as black, for fear of insulting someone. It examined just who, in fact, is referred to as negro (black). According to Maggie, Brazilians prefer to use descriptions that emphasize the numerous, often arbitrary gradations on the Brazilian color continuum, such as *escurinho* (very dark) or *clarinho* (a little light-skinned), rather than oppositional categories like *branco e preto* or *negro e branco* (white and black). The latter categories are reserved for strangers, people once-removed in a social setting. They are never used to refer to friends or those one directly interacts with.[25]

Maggie's findings are in keeping with the broader anthropological interpretation of the extensive use of the diminutive phrase in Brazil as a means of mitigating hierarchical distance between people of different social status (Holanda Barbosa 1988). This discursive device does not erase the *actual* social distinction, however. Instead, it softens the potentially negative impact of encounters between members of dominant and subordinate groups, the "soft collision" referred to previously. The hierarchical distinctions, though, are ever present. The silence regarding the use of *negro* or *preto* obviates the negative connotations attached to these terms, as well as the uneasiness experienced by Afro-Brazilians when referring to themselves in this manner.[26]

(B) The continuous reproduction and dissemination of stereotypes denigrating blacks and valorizing whites, resulting in low, negative self-images and aversion to collective action among Afro-Brazilians.

The negative socialization of black Brazilians begins at the earliest stages of educational development, persisting throughout the course of adult life. From the first years of formal education, blacks are confronted by a panoply of images and representations of themselves, which can only be characterized as negative. Numerous studies of children's primary school textbooks depict blacks as more sexually promiscuous and aggressive, intellectually inferior to whites, and rarely in positions of power. Specifically, black males are often represented as brawny types, long on stamina and physical strength, short on intellect. Black women are portrayed as a form of "superwoman," an image found in evocations of women of African descent throughout Western literature.[27] In a content analysis of forty-eight lesson books used by the secretary of education for the state of São Paulo between 1941–1975,[28] Pinto (1981) explored the manner in which an "unequal and divided society, but one that articulates a discourse of equality"[29] reproduces the inequalities symbolically through textbooks. Working by percentage distribution, Pinto found that 34.9 percent of whites represented in school texts were in the highest professional positions, as opposed to 6.9 percent of blacks and 22.2 percent of mulattoes.[30] Conversely, blacks led as representatives of nonspecialized manual labor, at 82.9 percent, in contrast to 8.7 percent and 27.8 percent for white and mulattoes respectively.

In addition to the racialist symbolism of textbooks and their illustrations, black school children are negatively socialized through subtle forms of discrimination in primary schools. Cunha's (1987) study of *velhos negroes* (old blacks) in the city of São Carlos, 230 kilometers from the capital of São Paulo, displays the exclusionary practices that black children undergo. They are left out of school plays that do not require black actors, are verbally insulted with racist epithets by their white classmates, and face other forms of racial differentiation and segregation. Puzzled by this response, and without any prior knowledge of racial prejudice and discrimination, these children turn to their parents for assistance. According to Cunha, working-class parents who have had little formal education were indecisive because they believed in the ideology of racial democracy and viewed schools to be value-free institutions. As a consequence, they mistrusted the insights and observations of their children. In contrast, Cunha also observed the tendency of Afro-Brazilian children from more edu-cated and economically stable families to anticipate and be better prepared to deal with forms of racial discrimination in their schools.[31] According to Cunha, parents with experiential knowledge of racial discrimination in schools were not only cognitively aware of its problems and dynamics, but were strategically prepared to impart this knowledge to their children.

The results from Figueira's (1988) study of Rio de Janeiro school-age children and adolescents, most of whom were black, reversed the premise that generated the study: that class, rather than race, distinguished poor from rich. Of 309 students interviewed, 82.9 percent responded by iden-tifying black figures as stupid, as for only 17.1 percent who linked a white figure with stupidity. Only 14.3 percent considered white figures ugly, while 85 percent labeled black figures as such; 5.8 percent identified black figures as people of wealth, whereas 94.2 percent of white figures were identified this way.[32]

This study provided further evidence of the comprehensiveness of ra-cially discriminatory practices within educational institutions in Rio de Janeiro. First, the inculcation of black students in situations of negative socialization can result in the internalization of negative self-images pro-jected in the classroom. The process of inculcation becomes even more acute when one considers the reproduction of these negative-self images in Afro-Brazilian homes and communities. This underscores the fact that Afro-Brazilians, in the areas of mass media, education, and technology, invariably occupy the role of consumer in the relations of production. They lack the media and technology to create textbooks and literature, positions and occupations (teachers, professors, etc.) that oversee the dis-semination and distribution of textbooks and literature. As a conse-quence, they are subject to those whose commodities reify Afro-Brazilian stereotypes captured in the imaginations of white Brazilians.

Figueira's more recent study of racial discrimination in Rio de Janeiro municipal schools illuminates the paradoxes of racial democracy in a ra-cially discriminatory environment. White professors interviewed admitted they had no pedagogical training on racial questions. When confronted with racial conflicts in the classroom or school, they relied on "good sense, in everyday practice, independent of any pedagogical basis."[33]

The professors also admitted that most schools do not have any special classroom projects or programs on Afro-Brazilian history. The few initia-tives in this vein are schools that have projects on blacks in candomble, rhythm, and culinary arts,[34] another example of the culturalist tendency in Brazil. This identification of the lack of pedagogy and educational materi-als about racial-ethnic differences in Brazil is particularly telling in light of the fact that the research for this study was undertaken during the 1988 centennial celebration of abolition.

Another form of racial subordination within the realm of education is "steering," which many activists interviewed for this study have experienced. Blacks are often discouraged by teachers from pursuing vocations of power and status, that is, liberal professions and military careers, and were encouraged instead to pursue menial trades or forms of manual labor.[35]

When compounded by the bleak circumstances under which the Brazilian poor are educated, the chances for a full, meaningful education for black Brazilians, most of whom are poor, is even worse. In addition to Nelson do Valle Silva's analysis of the 1980 census data, referred to in Chapter 1, additional statistics from that census provide us with quantitative evidence of educational disparities. Only 21 percent of blacks have nine or more years of education. In contrast, 79 percent of whites do; 50 percent of the black Brazilian population is illiterate, as opposed to 25 percent for whites.[36] Only 1.9 percent of the *pardo* population have attended college, while just 1 percent of the black population has done so. This is in contrast to 10 percent of the Asian population (*amarelo*), and 6.4 percent of whites.[37]

Their educational disadvantages have economic consequences as well. While blacks constitute just over 40 percent of the population, they account for 60 percent of those gaining the minimum monthly wage in the country. Sixty-nine percent of black women in the labor force earn the minimum wage, in comparison to 43 percent of their white counterparts. Conversely, a black doctor at the same professional level receives a lower salary. A black secretary earns 40 percent less than a white secretary.[38] This census data provides quantitative evidence of what some Afro-Brazilians have asserted for years: racial inequality exists at all socio-economic levels of Brazilian society.

The active discouragement of and exclusion from situations of objective competition in the classroom and in labor markets is directly linked to the absence of black Brazilians in attractive sectors in the workforce, in formal and informal organizations and institutions. Lovell's 1990 demographic study of the intersection of racial inequality and the Brazilian economic "miracle" of the 1970s points out that black professionals did not benefit economically from the increased rate of capital accumulation and expansion during the period of the so-called miracle. According to the Instituto Brasileiro de Geografia e Estatistica's data from the 1987 census, the median monthly salary for whites is almost two and a half times the amount of blacks, and well over 100 percent more than browns (*pardos*).[39]

When the consequences of dependent development and authoritarianism are added to an analysis of black economic and educational exclusion in Brazil, the conditions that help explain the absence of black Brazilians in positions of power and authority are apparent. Moreover, these conditions may also structure the reluctance of many black Brazilians to "compete" within formal educational and market-oriented institutions in Brazil.

One of the difficulties in assessing levels of apathy, indecision, or resistance among black Brazilians is the paucity of survey data pertaining to black self-characterization and responses to situations of inequality. One study, done in 1987 in the predominantly black, poor municipalities of Volta Redonda and Nova Iguaçu in Rio de Janeiro, revealed that 88.9 percent of survey respondents stated that racism exists in Brazil. Of the respondents, 32.7 percent acknowledged an experience with racial discrimination, while 63.7 percent said they had never experienced racism. Of those who said they experienced racism, 57.9 percent said they did nothing in response; 20.2 percent stated they reacted verbally or denounced the action in the press, and 18.9 percent said they left their jobs as a result of acts of discrimination in the workplace.[40]

While these statistics are revealing in some way, there does not seem to be any control within the data for the possibility that the majority of respondents opted for silence in situations of discrimination in order to hold onto their wages or in fear of simple coercion. This could be the not-so-hidden transcript that James Scott refers to in *Weapons of the Weak* (1985), which may not have anything to do with apathy or indecision on the part of black Brazilians, but a calculated perseverance in order to maintain their already precarious hold on employment opportunities.

Another example of helpful but ultimately inconclusive data is taken from the State Council for the Black Community in São Paulo: the sub-council on racial discrimination and racial violence has recorded approximately 230 cases of race-related violence between October 1986 and December 1988. Only one victim of the 230 became a plaintiff and actually sought to prosecute his assailants in military court (see below). The coordinator of the program stated during a 1988 interview that the overwhelming majority of cases were never actually pursued because of a fear, not directly identifiable or traceable by police, military, or public officials, but a powerful aversion of confrontations with institutions and agents of power.[41]

This may be, in fact, a plausible explanation, but it does not identify race as the determining factor in the calculus of aversion. Most cases of racial violence involved civilian or military police, which under Brazilian law at the time required hearings with military judges and tribunals. It could very well be the "shadow of the barracks,"[42] to use Rouquie's phrase, the spectre of the military hovering over civil society and the courtrooms within it. The torture and interrogation of the *ditadura* was, as we now know, indiscriminately applied, with little concern for skin color.

At the same time, however, this is paradigmatic of Brazilian racial politics. The feature that may be most peculiarly "Brazilian" is the relative absence of cognitive and practical referents for the recognition of—and reaction to—situations of racial inequality. In the case of black Paulistano parents and their children, Cunha's study suggests that for many blacks there is no precedent for publicly utilizing the experiential knowledge of discriminatory acts of the past to address situations of institutionalized racism in the continuous present. Under (*c*) we will explore the ways in which the black movement and individual activists, in the process of claims-making, are compromised by the inculcated values of racial democracy as well as the coercive measures of white elites.

(C) Coercive or preemptive sanctions await those who question or seek to overturn the fundamentally asymmetrical patterns of interaction between whites and blacks.

Antonio Arruda, a black lawyer attending a soccer match with two white friends (also lawyers) at a São Paulo stadium in 1988, was beaten by military police for not responding quickly enough to their order for personal identification. What prompted the delay and subsequent beating was a single word—why? Arruda asked the police why he, and not his two friends, was required to furnish documentation. Arruda stated that three policemen were involved, one black, two white, with the former providing most of the whipping. The beating itself was not unusual, Arruda stated. What was unusual was the subsequent decision to file a legal claim against the military police in question: "For the military police, who are mostly white, it is normal for them to commit violence against the black community. . . . they accept the stereotype that the black is marginal. Very few people, unfortunately, have the knowledge to respond to the acts of violence as I have done. The possibility of black people responding to the military police the way I did is one in a million."[43]

Yet Arruda would not attribute his actions to his professional status, for he recalled situations involving other black professionals who did not protest when faced with situations of racial inequality: "Even though they are professionals, those black professionals do not frequent the better schools, and feel a sense of inferiority from this. They are subjected to, or witness acts of violence committed against the black community, and so when they are confronted by the police and are asked for their identification they too believe that it is normal and present their documents to them."[44]

This incident contains a fundamental paradox for Afro-Brazilian activists for the following reason: while Arruda's beating was informed by the politics of Brazilian racial inequality, Afro-Brazilians do not have a monopoly on violence unleashed by the state. For Afro-Brazilians without a racial consciousness, that is, a recognition of the role that their "race" plays in the structuring of social inequality, there is an inability to distinguish a racially specific act of oppression from one that is not racially specific. This is exemplified in the incidents analyzed at the end of this chapter. In this sense, racial consciousness is not an ideologically specific "way of seeing" in the form of a coherent *response* to racial oppression, but a simpler cognitive awareness of its exsistence. Activists in Rio de Janeiro and São Paulo have identified the relative absence of racial consciousness among Afro-Brazilians as the principal impediment to sociopolitical organization around racial issues. Thus consciousness raising is a primary goal in most black Brazilian organizations with intentions of public outreach.

For activists and others with a heightened racial awareness, there is the triple task of articulating the existence of racial oppression, making other black Brazilians aware of the problems inherent in combating racial oppression while providing avenues of resistance. These activities are often compromised by the coercive and preemptive measures of white elites.

Arruda, with legal skills and indignation, decided to pursue the case in a court of law, which, as noted earlier, was a military court. Approximately six months after presenting his case before military officials, providing names of the officers involved, Arruda received a letter from the military judge informing him of a thorough investigation of the incident at the soccer stadium. Based on their investigation, the judge concluded that Arruda fabricated the entire story, because no account of this incident was taken by police officers at the stadium.

A politics of race looms at the borders of this incident. There exists the possibility that the black police officer's disproportionate participation was an expression of power in relation to the lawyer who, in sociological terms, had attained more status than he. The white officers, responding either to their own racial prejudices or their loyalty to a fellow police officer, responded in kind.[45]

Yet race, at least in this particular case, did not make itself clear. It was entangled within a skein of political fibers that includes authoritarianism, systematic police brutality, as well as indiscriminate state-generated terror. In theory and practice, a police beating could happen to Brazilians of any color, given the nature of the political regime in Brazil during the period when the incident occurred.

This conclusion, however, is too facile. From the "facts" of this incident we do know that Arruda was beaten, much in the same way we know of the unequal distribution of educational, institutional, and market-driven resources along a racial axis without the existence of legislation meant to legally regulate racial discrimination.

The act of juridical-bureaucratic denial is a preemptive strike against dissent, evidenced in the judge's conclusion that Arruda's was a fit of imagination. Under these circumstances, an attempt to redress an instance of racial violence can seem futile, if these results continue over time. The preemptive strike serves not only to quell dissent, but to transform claims about racial inequality in Brazil into isolated incidents of the imag-ination, where blacks are forced to prove their own legitimacy, rather than the legitimacy of their claim against society. This, I will argue, is a more important feature of Brazilian racial hegemony than violence, for it is through preemptive acts that coercion becomes an infrequent necessity, exercised to defend the ideological legitimacy of racial democracy rather than to confirm it. Once it is assumed that racial democracy exists, the need to define its terms becomes superfluous.

Other examples of the preemption of dissent that activists experience in Rio de Janeiro and São Paulo pertain to bureaucratic neglect, the pur-poseful malfunctioning of bureaucratic procedures that in theory, people have access to in order to vent grievances. Activists in both cities re-counted difficulties in obtaining meetings with public officials and other institutional representatives to address specific instances of racial discrimi-nation. In Rio de Janeiro, militants for the S.O.S. Racismo organization recounted numerous occasions when they were kept waiting three or four hours, or when appointments were missed entirely, by public officials or school principals who were scheduled to address an incident of racial bias.

These examples resonate with Lukes's and Gaventa's expositions of power's third face, the locus of subtler intrigues of dominance and subor-dination that are voiced outside the conventional forums of Brazilian pol-itics—congress, elections, and public policy. Yet the most common ploy of white elites to defer the management or resolution of racial inequality is to deny racism's very existence. Examples abound in the postwar period of the denial of the existence of racial discrimination in Brazil, even as racially discriminatory practices are ongoing and recurring.

Fernandes's adage that Brazilians have *o preconceito de não ter precon-ceito*, or "the prejudice of having no prejudice" (Fernandes 1969, xv) succinctly characterizes this ploy's ideological basis. This ideology of de-nial operates on two levels. On the cognitive level, the prejudice *against* prejudice serves to deny the possible existence of racism as a social mecha-nism, its norms and "rules of the game," the possibility that like the social construction of race itself, racial discrimination changes not only from one context to another but within singular contexts at local and individual levels. It is highly unlikely that an individual or social group lacking a cognitive understanding of racial discrimination would then be able to identify the winners and losers in the very "game" whose existence they deny. This practice serves to translate an indictment of society into an indictment of the very groups or individuals making social claims.

Lukes and Gaventa have argued that the inherent biases of political and cultural systems serve, over time, to mute dissident voices and produce a certain apathy among the subordinated, thereby making rare moments of state or elite-generated violence against subordinate groups.[46] There is qualified agreement here on the subsidiary role of violence in these situations of sustained, institutionalized inequality, although the degree of apathy that these situations produce is debatable and ultimately, never absolute. Individual, "Brechtian" forms of resistance (Scott 1985), as well as collective action, were witnessed and noted during field research for this study. Although they represent a small segment of the Afro-Brazilian community in São Paulo, and an even smaller segment of Brazilian society as a whole, sufficient evidence is present to argue that apathy or a low propensity toward resistance amongst blacks is perhaps predominant (admitted by activists themselves), but not total. Activists and common folk alike create acts of defiance in spite of their limitations, indeed, because of them.

At the same time, it is the relative lack of power of Afro-Brazilians that determines the forms that their resistance assumes. The manner in which they resist defines them as a subaltern group, one whose movements are necessarily "fragmented and episodic."[47]

Everyday Forms of Racial Hegemony

There's no race problem in Brazil. Take me, for instance.
My wife is a blond!
—*São Paulo cab driver, a mulatto, in 1988.*

Nowhere are the manifestations of Brazilian racial hegemony more apparent than in daily life; its rituals, proclamations, and silences contain forms of political expression and practice that go unaccounted for in formally established arenas of political disputation. The symbolic dimension[48] of social relations can serve as a refracting prism of exchanges between dominant and subordinate groups. It can expose conflicts not expressed in campaign or congressional debates, public policy, or other state-oriented processes that assume institutional forms.

The following incidents reveal the mixture of unconscious and conscious political activity on the ever-turning axis of white–Afro-Brazilian relations. At least one incident will show how both whites and Afro-Brazilians often engage in racially unconscious activity, that is, participate in modes of social interaction that are racially prejudicial, subordinating and/or discriminatory without identifying the racial import of the circumstances in which they are engaged.

The Smuggler Incident: Oppositional Realities

On 2 October 1988, an advertisement for children's clothing in *Jornal do Brasil* generated controversy in the black activist community in Rio de Janeiro. The advertisement, in anticipation of Children's Day on 12 October, showed six children, all white, tying up and muzzling a seated nurse-maid (*baba*), who was a black woman. Everyone in the advertisement, including the nursemaid, was smiling. The caption below read "conform yourself: October 12 is our day," an obvious reference, or so the advertisers believed, to a day of liberation for children.[49]

The advertisement generated considerable uproar among several black activist organizations in the city of Rio de Janeiro. Various organizations forwarded petitions and letters of protest to *Jornal do Brasil* in response to the advertisement. For the members of the community-based watch-dog agency S.O.S. Racismo as well as the nearly one hundred telephone callers to its adjoining institution, The Institute for the Study of Black Cultures (IPCN), the advertisement contained a dual message. Not only did the roping and muffling of the "baba" resonate with images of enslavement, subjugation, and imprisonment of Afro-Brazilians, but the caption suggested to many that blacks were to revert to behavior patterns that were consonant with their prior historical experience as slaves. The following comments, excerpted from the IPCN letter of complaint filed with the Board of Self-Regulating Publicity in São Paulo and the thirteenth precinct in Copacabana, provide a sense of the outrage that the advertisement generated: "In English, Smuggler (the clothing manufacturer) signifies contraband, and the image of the bandit, implying that white children and black women are the first to commit illegal crimes of racism, and of torture."[50]

The president of IPCN further commented that the depiction confirmed that "advertising was one of the vehicles that sustained racism as an ideology of domination."[51] IPCN, in filing a formal complaint with the civil police, invoked Article 5 of the newly enacted Brazilian Constitution, which states that the practice of racism constitutes a crime "unbailable and without prescription, subject to penalty of imprisonment."[52]

In contrast, the creators of the advertisement as well as the clothing manufacturer denied any bad intentions or racist content to the advertisement itself: "This photo has a feeling of love and emotion, not hate. It is dedicated to nursemaids, 90 percent of whom are people of color. All the children are smiling and playing in the photo, including the nursemaid. A message of affection, not racism. If we were mistaken, then please forgive us. The intention was pure."[53] Extending this response, one of the owners of Smuggler stated that "the idea to put a person of color in the advertisement was not because we are racists, but that the majority of nursemaids are of color. If we put a blond woman, it would not be expressing our reality and would not evoke *the idea of the nursemaid* [emphasis mine]."[54]

For the creators and promoters of the announcement, "reality" was symbolically mounted within the borders of the advertisement; for its detractors the real lurked at the borders of the picture, informing and undermining the putatively neutral, nonracial scenario. To put this another way, the promoters of the advertisement seem to suggest that the advertisement was merely *reproducing* the "reality" of white-nonwhite social relations, not their interpretation of "reality." The activists sought to problematize the contemporary social relations that the advertisement claims to represent, to enlarge the "frame" of the advertisement enough to include depictions of racial oppression and economic exploitation. In this sense, the groups and individuals involved in this controversy developed interpretive frameworks for symbolic orderings of social reality that were largely based upon their location within the power dynamic of racial and economic disjunctures in Brazil.

The "idea of the nursemaid" to which the owner referred belies his assertion of an "objective" basis for the nursemaid's socioeconomic categorization. It suggests a normative correlation between race, gender, and labor function (black female = baba) as opposed to a more occupational correlation between labor function and tasks (baba = babysitter, cook, family therapist). Therefore, "the idea of the nursemaid" expresses the conjunction of racial difference and materiality that constitutes the base of productive relations between nursemaid and employer, and more broadly, between whites and blacks. Moreover, this expression is a hegemonic ideological construct since the "idea of the nursemaid" was presented not as one among several choices, but as the only "correct" representation of social reality.

Bourdieu (1977) suggests that such outbursts of symbolic power reflect a dominant group's ability to present "the established cosmological and political order . . . not as arbitrary, i.e. as one possible order among others, but as a self-evident and natural order which goes without saying and therefore goes unquestioned."[55]

The activist's identification of racial oppression within the advertisement questioned the intrinsically *consensual* basis of symbolic power disseminated by the advertisement. Despite the varying social locations of the nursemaid, advertiser, clothing manufacturer, and consumer, there was a presumption of consensus on the meaning and arrangement of symbols within the advertisement. Otherwise there would not have been surprise when the advertisement was poorly received. Once the ideational congruence eroded, the meaning of the Smuggler advertisement was lost and had to be reconstituted through explanation.

Barthes conceives of symbolic arrangements like the Smuggler advertisement as social myths, "made of material which has been already been worked on to make it suitable for communication: it is because all the materials of myth (whether pictorial or written) *presuppose a signifying consciousness* [emphasis mine] that one can reason about them while discounting their substance."[56] In this sense, myth is an edited, streamlined version of reality that has abstracted individuals or groups from their social contexts. The final stage in the process of myth production is the fusion of myth with a "natural" social order, collapsing distinctions between the fictive tale and lived experience, relieving groups and individuals of their historical content. Barthes develops this point: "In passing from history to nature, myth acts economically; it abolishes the complexity of human acts, it gives them the simplicity of essences . . . things appear to mean something by themselves."[57]

Barthes's observations are relevant here for two reasons. The first is Barthes's recognition of the need for an ideological congruence between diverse forms of consciousness in order for symbols to contain, or be deprived of, social meanings. In this instance, social class became the site of ideological congruence between the nursemaid and her advertiser-employer, with race operating as either an unconscious or neglected feature of their relationship. Thus it can be said that an implicit compromise was reached with regard to the exclusion of racial difference from any consideration of the baba's location within the advertisement.

Consider the following response of the nursemaid herself to the debates surrounding the advertisement, for which she earned approximately $100 U.S. dollars, the equivalent of several month's salary for the average nursemaid: "I earned $20,000 cruzados. . . . these people are crazy from debating racism. Nobody was being racist. They were tying up the nursemaid in order to spray graffiti upon the walls. It was the day of children and I was allowing and adoring. . . . They (the protestors) believe that it is absurd and excessive that a black woman appears in an advertisement all tied up. It is in their minds, to see the bad side of the thing."[58]

After concurring with those who paid for her services in the advertisement, the nursemaid suggests that racism is found in the minds of the detractors, those "who see the bad side of the thing." She identifies those who dissent from the prevailing interpretation of the advertisement as the source of the problem, rather than the complex of discriminatory practices and patterns that the advertisement reproduces.

The material satisfaction of receiving $20,000 cruzados for a photographic session undeniably represents a great opportunity for a poor person and cannot be trivialized in terms of "false" consciousness. The nursemaid's declaration of the advantages of obtaining $20,000 for her services is an obvious recognition of material need and the advantages of posing for an advertisement over physical labor. Yet the congruence between nursemaid and employer, at the level of semiotics, is informed by the contradictions of their relations within both a putatively private, domestic economy, and a public economy as well. The nursemaid has entered into an arrangement of unequal relations in the household and within the advertisement, with disproportionate advantage for the employer in each instance.

It is here where the racially hegemonic relationship becomes most prevalent, as the nursemaid complies with the terms and conditions of her labor based upon a limited array of choices, taking the least painful avenue to wage-earning and subsistence. Thus she is led and constrained by her choices, not some idealized notion of her "objective" or "subjective" interests. In addition, what detractors of the concept of hegemony have misunderstood in their zeal to dismiss it is that so many of the working poor do *not* have a "hidden transcript" (Scott 1985; Scott 1990), that is to say, a strategic agenda of private, ideological interests that contradict public articulations of either consent or material compliance with dominant actors in a given society.[59] It must be stressed that this nursemaid was neither an activist nor a racially conscious Afro-Brazilian with some private leanings toward the movimento negro, as confirmed by her statements *against* critical *militants*.

Some might argue that since we do not *know* her private leanings, we cannot discern whether she, in fact, *really* meant what she said. Yet this is precisely the point. Without a confirmation of political agency, whether privately subversive or publicly confrontational, we would end up in a discussion of the nursemaids "public" versus "private," "cosmetic" versus "real" intentions, as opposed to the consequences of her choices and actions.

What we can confirm however, is that when confronted with a moment of public choice, the nursemaid opted for a critique of the activists rather than one of her employers, the advertisers, or the conditions that led to the intersection of all three. It can thus be said, without any necessary links to a false consciousness argument, that the nursemaid articulated one particular form of contradictory consciousness. As I state in Chapters 2 and 5, however, there are several forms of contradictory consciousness observable within and between racial groups in Brazil.[60]

Appearances Deceive?

In the "Espaço do Leitor" (reader's space or letter to the editor) section of the *A Tarde* daily newspaper on 31 December 1987, a reader, one Edson Ramos Vieira, recounted the following as a human interest story:

> I went to the beach, and as I parked my car a guard suddenly appeared, fat and very dark, with a doubtful appearance to the extent that it left me fearful. I trembled, and from the beach, I kept an eye on my vehicle. After relaxing for a few hours I left the beach and returned, giving a look to the guard

alongside my car. I entered the car and paid him rapidly at the same time . . . and left in the direction for the U-turn. To my surprise . . . the big black guard was in the center island whistling and gesticulating for me to stop, which I did with fear. Directing me, he said 'Doctor, your forgot your sandals'. My jaw dropped upon the discovery that within that big round body beat a tremendous heart of an honest gentle person.[61]

Was the deception to be found in the black guard's appearance or in Mr. Ramos's imagination? Totally absent from Mr. Ramos's account is any behavior from the guard that warranted Mr. Ramos's anxiety-laden reaction and ultimately, his surprise to discover that the "big black" (*negão*), after all, was only being attentive to his job. The example best epitomizes how an ideology of racial discrimination becomes embodied in real life, as the presence of the black guard triggered an ensemble of assumptions that had nothing to do whatsoever with the actual conditions of the situation or with the black guard himself. While the incident had a seemingly harmless ending, its implications are dire for people of African descent. For while the guard "redeemed" himself through an act of decency, Mr. Ramos's suspicions concerning him were entirely out of his control. Had Mr. Ramos reacted differently to his initial anxieties, the ending of the story might have been quite different. Like the Smuggler incident above, the gendered construction of racial difference informed the encounter between these two men. For Mr. Ramos, a black male equaled suspicion and danger, a thing to be avoided. It was an equation that overrode any consideration of the guard's laboring function.

The United Colors of Benetton

In 1990, another clothing advertisement generated protest and debate over Brazil's racial equilibrium. Benetton, the Italian clothing manufacturer launched the Brazilian version of their United Colors of Benetton campaign. First implemented in 1989, the campaign attacked racial intolerance on a global scale, depicting people of various racial and ethnic groups interacting in Benetton advertisements.

One particular advertisement of a black woman—shirtless, breasts exposed, nursing a white baby with her left teat—was placed on billboards throughout Brazil in June 1990. The reaction was immediate. Many activists and citizens denounced this representation as a reminder of the racial and gender-inflected subservience that Afro-Brazilians experienced under slavery.[62]

Ironically, the advertisement was rejected by black magazine publishers in the United States for the same reason that activists and others in Brazil found it offensive.[63] A representative for J. Walter Thompson, the multinational advertising agency commissioned to adapt Benetton's campaign to a Brazilian market, suggested that the advertisement would not generate racial animus, given the distinctiveness of Brazilian culture.[64]

A Benetton shop owner in Belo Horizonte suggested that the polemics surrounding the advertisement were first generated in countries where racial conflict was more palpable,[65] such as in France, where the advertisement led several white supremacy groups to threaten to bomb Benetton stores if the advertisement was not withdrawn.[66] More ambiguous opinions were documented in a random survey of responses to the advertisement. One person doubted the prospects of racial violence such as in France because "racism here is more cynical and veiled."[67] Although there were no reports of race-related violence in reaction to the advertisement as in France, members of the movimento negro in capital cities throughout the country circulated pamphlets criticizing the announcements. In some instances black activists spread graffiti across the advertisements with the words" 'Mucama' (nursemaid) never more."[68]

The different reactions to this particular advertisement in France, Brazil, and the United States highlights the variegated dynamics of racial politics within nation-states and between them. The incident is replete with what Patricia Hill Collins refers to as "controlling images," symbols that convey an authority to define people through stereotypes. For black women in particular, the stereotype of the "mammy" is pervasive.[69] Benetton's prior consultation of black magazines and eventual withdrawal of the advertisement from the U.S. market implies that for the manufacturer, racial politics was a more salient *market* factor in the United States, in contrast with France and Brazil.

Yet the United Colors of Benetton campaign sought to erase national histories of race and racialism in France and Brazil through their global projection of racial harmony. In doing so, it only exacerbated existing forms of racial conflict in these countries. At the same time, this campaign helped underscore the fact that disputes between "whites" and "blacks," or "whites" and "nonwhites" vary from one context to another, and are predicated not solely upon issues of race but upon those of nation as well.

Conclusion

In this chapter we have considered the development of racial hegemony in Brazil. First, this chapter has outlined its historical rootedness in the pervasive ideology of racial exceptionalism in Latin America and the Caribbean, which ultimately become the polemic of proslavery elites who defended the continuance of slavery. The second phase of its development was its reformulation within the ideology of racial democracy formulated by Gilberto Freyre. In the process of nation-state and industrial development, the ideology of racial democracy has become national common sense that has informed both popular folklore and social scientific research. Within the economy of racial democracy, Afro-Brazilians occupy roles as arbiters of expressive culture and sexuality, but little else. Culture appears to be the only concessionary realm where black Brazilians have relative autonomy in their relationships with whites. Meanwhile, blacks and mulattoes are being excluded from employment and educational opportunities reserved for whites, and relegated largely to positions of inferior economic and social status. Thus, the myths of racial exceptionalism and democracy proclaim the existence of racial egalitarianism in Brazil relative to other societies while producing racially discriminatory belief systems and practices at the same time. The maintenance and reproduction of this disjuncture between rhetoric, ideology, and social practice by white elites defines racial hegemony.

This chapter has identified racial hegemony as a predominant practice in both the institutions and popular culture of civil society—labor markets, schools—and in symbolic representations of daily life. Like other multiracial politics with African-derived populations, the category of blackness is either denigrated or avoided in daily discourse. Afro-Brazilian men and women are presented within the symbolic constructs of controlling images as renderers of service to the white population.

The two principal consequences are the absence of racial consciousness among Afro-Brazilians and, as a consequence, the nonpoliticization of racial inequality by those who suffer most from it, and the continued discrimination against blacks in employment and education. The discriminatory belief systems and practices of racial hegemony in Brazil have assumed more general social forms that extend well beyond the domain and intention of white elites. We do not have a conspiracy theory come to life but a convergence of beliefs and practices with intended and unintended consequences, within an ongoing process of racial subordination.

The following section will focus on the attempted formation of counterhegemonic projects by Afro-Brazilian activists in response to the dynamics of racial dominance and subordination. Chapter 4 will emphasize the politics of identity formation among Afro-Brazilian activists, with the intent of situating the process of creating an Afro-Brazilian racial identity within the realms of class conflict and cultural politics. Chapter 5 will provide an overview of Afro-Brazilian social movements in Rio de Janeiro and São Paulo between 1945 and 1988 in order to situate the tensions and contradictions of Brazilian racial hegemony in historical perspective.

PART TWO

NEGATION AND CONTESTATION

FOUR

FORMATIONS OF RACIAL CONSCIOUSNESS

JOEL RUFINO DOS SANTOS, one of the leading intellectuals of
the movimento negro and the Democratic Laborist party in Brazil,
was a member of the National Liberation Alliance in the 1970s. The
alliance was one of the left-wing organizations that emerged in response
to the "revolution" of 1964 with a commitment to armed struggle (Skidmore 1988).

After spending several years in exile after the 1964 coup, Rufino returned to Brazil, only to be captured on a train destined for Rio de Janeiro
from São Paulo. He was imprisoned from January 1972 until August
1974. He was subjected to various forms of interrogation and torture
during his confinement. Rufino was often interrogated by a three-man
team consisting of a Japanese, black, and Jewish person which, according
to Santos, was unusual for an interrogation team.

At one point near the end of his term, Rufino was told by his interroga-
tors that he would be shot to death. His death, he was told, would be
announced in the media as the result of an escape attempt. Rufino describes what followed:

> They ended by telling me I was to die the following day. I spent that entire
> night preparing myself for death. The following morning they took me from
> my cell and put me in a car. I was placed in the back seat with a person seated
> on the other side, with the white man to my right and the black person to my
> left. The white guy left the car to urinate and I was left alone with the black
> man. The black guy tapped me on the arm and then told me to remain calm,
> and that nothing was going to happen to me. It was all staged, he said, just
> to frighten me. He was being friendly. I asked him why he chose to treat me
> this way after helping to interrogate and torture me. He just looked at me
> and rubbed one of his fingers across his forearm, to show that it was because
> of my skin color.[1]

This dramatic incident exemplifies several paradoxes of racial identification and solidarity among Afro-Brazilians. The relation between captor
and captive, agent of state coercion and radical Afro-Brazilian militant was
suspended, if only momentarily, by a narrowly defined assumption of
commonality. As Rufino added, "It is always said that black Brazilians
don't have solidarity, which is true, but it is not an absolute truth."

Yet the solidarity displayed by one of Rufino's captors at a moment of
crisis warrants closer scrutiny. Was the captor ordered by his superiors to

assume the role of "brother," or was the act an autonomous one triggered by a glimmer of recognition, between captor and prisoner, of common marginalization?

Though the answer to these questions may never be fully known, their complexities extend far beyond this incident, for at stake are prospects for the development of racial consciousness among Afro-Brazilians. For whether the black captor acted on his own or at someone's behest, the captor had to assume that racial consciousness, for Rufino, was real, even if it was not a mode of consciousness that he himself assumed. However fleeting and ambiguous, it was one of the rare occurrences of conscious solidarity among Afro-Brazilians. At the level of ideology, occurrences like these signify the gap between a relative and absolute lack of racial identification, and it is precisely within this gap that the movimento operates.

This chapter will focus on the forms of racial identity as they are found among activists in Rio de Janeiro and São Paulo. Evidence culled from interviews and debates involving members of the movimento negro in those two cities suggests some degree of identification among Afro-Brazilians. Yet the relation between racial consciousness and political ideology is often unclear to both students and activists of Brazilian racial politics. Indeed, even those with strong beliefs about racial-ethnic identification have appeared unclear about the forms that their identification should assume. The absence of clarity has impeded the development of racial consciousness and the formulation of distinctive political positions that successfully combine analyses of race with those of class and culture.

Due to the indeterminacy of the term *negro* in Brazil, given that its usage is contingent upon individual self-reflection, one person's *negro* could be another person's *morenihno* (a little dark, but not black). Consequently, phenotype is an even more precarious base for collective mobilization than it is in other multiracial polities, teetering between the phenotypical hierarchies of racial democracy on one side, and Afro-Brazilian activism on the other.

This precariousness also distinguishes, but does not exempt, discussions of racial and ethnic identity in Brazil in the almost visceral, highly vertiginous lines extant in arenas of ethnic conflict like the Basque region of northern Spain or Northern Ireland. Since racial differences between and within social groups are actively discouraged by the constant emphasis on racial diffusion, race and ethnicity does not have the delimiting force it does in other cases.

Yet racial identification, consciousness and solidarity does exist between some Afro-Brazilians, as the movimento negro's existence attests to. Its existence also displays the complexities of racial affiliation in Brazil in another way, through the alliance of people within the movimento negro, who would be considered members of distinct color categories, mulattoes and negros.

While Brazil does not have all the elements of a "classic" case of ethnic or racial politics, there are moments of solidarity among activists in their attempts to mobilize Afro-Brazilians. These moments can be characterized as points of resemblance among Afro-Brazilians. Perhaps the most subtle conceptualization of ethnicity in this regard is Fischer's (1986) "family of resemblances." For Fischer, ethnicity is "something reinvented and reinterpreted in each generation by each individual. . . . ethnicity is not something that is simply passed on from generation to generation, taught and learned; it is something *dynamic* [my emphasis], often unsuccessfully repressed or avoided."[2]

While Fischer's understanding of resemblance refers to ethnicity as conventionally defined, I suggest that it holds for race and racial politics as well. It captures the dialectic of self-conscious Afro-Brazilian identity; the acknowledged resemblance among some nonwhites of their phenotypical, experiential, and locational similarities, coupled with the denial of these similarities by whites and nonwhites alike. Too often ethnic and racial identification is characterized solely by its material facets, particularly those for consumption (food, clothing, self-inscription). Instead, the emphasis here is placed upon its ideational component, an important factor in the politicization of ethnic and racial identities, and in its instrumental use in differentiating group "relatives" from strangers and enemies.

Among those interviewed in Rio de Janeiro and São Paulo, racial identity assumes the form of resemblance between individuals of similar, not necessarily identical color, through their contradistinction from white Brazilians. With the absence of dichotomous phenotypical categories in Brazil, this is of strategic importance, for it allows the few *mulatos* and *pardos* who consider themselves "black" to do so.

While this form of resemblance does occur in Rio de Janeiro and São Paulo, I will argue that this dynamic is largely apolitical in terms of Afro-Brazilian mobilization. It can be, under specific conditions, politically salient for the movimento negro. Those conditions, however, are not widespread enough to catalyze the mass of Afro-Brazilians, and is largely operative between activists and their Afro-Brazilian constituencies in those two cities and in other parts of the country where the movimento negro has relative strength. For this reason it is necessary to break Fischer's "family of resemblances" into two categories of attachment—faint and strong resemblances.

Faint Resemblances in Rio de Janeiro and São Paulo

In conceptualizing racial consciousness, three broad categories exist: (*a*) faint resemblance, (*b*) strong resemblance, and (*c*) a mixture of faint and strong resemblances. Faint resemblances are largely based upon a glance (visual memory) that prompts an instinctive notion of common origin or shared history of oppression. While not as complex as other forms of resemblance, it is the cornerstone of other patterns of identification. The criteria for membership to this family of resemblance is more emotional than critical or strategic. Broadly speaking, just about anyone who is deemed part of the group can belong. Faint resemblance, in brief, is a matter of disposition, attitude.

Luis Carlos de Souza, thirty-three, rode a bus one evening in Rio de Janeiro when a group of robbers entered from the front and rear entrances. The apparent leader of the group, a young black male, entered the bus through the front exit and pointed with his pistol to identify those who would be robbed from those who would not.

The robber singled out the few black passengers on the bus, Carlos being one of them, as those who would reach their destination with their valuables. When the robber reached Carlos and another black passenger he shouted "not them" to his accomplices and with a wave of his pistol, directed them to move along.[3]

Like the first example with dos Santos, a black has identified with another at a moment of crisis. However poignant, these examples can be thought of as apolitical (or perhaps micropolitical) in that they signify the withdrawal of imminent punishment through an ephemeral bonding. It represents an allegiance, of course, but of a circumscribed type not based on ideological, religious, or other forms of solidarity with an inclination toward affecting long-term change. It is similar in this respect to Hobsbawm's conceptualization of social banditry (1964). Much like the incident with which this chapter began, the absence of Afro-Brazilian racial solidarity is not total, but its presence is without focus or direction.

Due to its easy membership, this form of resemblance has a high propensity for breakdown with the infusion of religious, ideological, even geographic differention. In short, history complicates the patterns of faint resemblance, since group choices and options invariably segment broad-based affiliations. Once choices are made, emphasis shifts from "race first," to another issue or complex of issues that fall outside the spectrum of faint resemblance.

An example from Rio de Janeiro highlights the inner complexities of faint resemblance and the difficulty of its politicization. Januario Garcia Filho, two-time president of the Institute for the study of Black Cultures, has presented himself in debates and in personal discussions as strictly an activist in the black movement. "I'm neither left nor right. I am black," he has stated, distinguishing himself from both worker-based politics and the venerable patron-clientelist relations of traditional Brazilian politics. In justification of this "neither left nor right" position, he has argued that Afro-Brazilian struggles, from the first slave insurrection to the present, antedates sindicalist and party politics.

According to Garcia and other activists, the movimento negro deserves an autonomous position in relation to these groups, a position shared by black activist intellectuals of other communities of the African diaspora (West 1988). Garcia, within the same debate and subsequent discussion, advocated separate negotiations for black workers within the labor movement, given wage disparities between white and black workers, to accord equal pay scales for blacks.

Given the history of tenuous relations between Afro-Brazilian activists and both the Brazilian left and right, desires for political autonomy are justified. Yet neither the black movement nor any other social movement operates outside of a political context. Slave uprisings prior to abolition, the Unified Black Movement in the 1970s, and the Afro-Brazilian nuclei of political parties today in Brazil exist in relation to social structures, organizations, and institutions. Even "race first" advocates must select economic, political, and cultural modes of organization that extend beyond phenotypical categories. Like members of all other social groups and movements, activists of the movimento negro must make political choices. Indeed, Garcia has been criticized by at least one member of the movimento negro for his comments.[4]

Specific positions regarding political affiliations signal the shift from attitudes and dispositions to practices and consciousness. Political practices are an outgrowth of not only attitudinal dispositions but *ideological* predispositions as well. Therefore it becomes increasingly difficult to remain independent on the basis of faint resemblance while other "family" members are defining themselves in nonphenotypical ways. Faint resemblances can be found in the three examples presented, due to their indeterminate nature. In the incidents involving Carlos and Rufino, the political repercussions of these incidents remain unclear even though each is ripe with mobilizing potentialities. Was Rufino's captor a "race first" man, in the sense that Marcus Garvey spoke; was he acting spontaneously or at the state's behest? What would the robbers have done if the bus was filled entirely with black people? Was the robber a racial Robin Hood, stealing from whites and redistributing capital goods to blacks? The fact that we do not have answers to these types of questions makes these incidents speculative forms of micropolitics, rather than explicit modes of collective action. These micropolitical moments remain at the level of the interpersonal.

Strong Resemblances: Coloration of the Faint

Strong resemblance, the second level of identification, signifies the strategic mobilization of feelings initially nurtured on the faint level. What distinguishes the strong resemblances from weak ones is an ability to override particular differences within a social collectivity for concrete political goals, however temporal. Political differences are temporarily repressed, fissures de-emphasized, in favor of unification.

Strong resemblances operate at specific historical moments (Israeli nationalism, for example) when an interloper outside the particular group threatens its ability to have differences even within itself. At this point, groups perceive the need to protect themselves on a more existential plane, in order that they may be able to collectively flourish, despite their differences. The U.S. civil rights movement had innumerable instances of this when, for example, black voting rights drives in the U.S. South garnered the support of groups that differed significantly from each other, such as the Nation of Islam, the Student Nonviolent Coordinating Committee, and the Southern Christian Leadership Conference.[5]

Unless protracted by war (as in the case of Israel) or continuous exploitation (South African apartheid), these moments recede. The strands that constitute the fabric of a unitary identity begin to fray. In Brazil, the absence of external threats and dichotomously segregated society has precluded the existential necessity of strong resemblance in absolute, one-dimensional terms. Racial democracy, which discourages the strategic essentialism[6] intrinsic to a politicized ethnic or racial consciousness, has transformed most Afro-Brazilian markers in Brazilian culture to generic, national symbols.

Even individuals who would be free to wield a more forceful version of Afro-Brazilian identity among the masses are hesitant, for fear of alienation in a society where strong resemblances are not mutually reinforced. Franciscan friar Luis Fernando of the Black Pastoral Agents in São Paulo, for example, responded to a question about the possible creation of an alternative black church by stating that "to break with the church would cause us to be discredited by the mass of people. . . . it is better to fight within the church to create a larger space."[7] Two other Afro-Brazilian priests, the late Batista Laurindo, also from São Paulo, and Frei David, from Rio, stated during their interviews that it is more strategically efficient to work from within the Catholic church and assist the black movement than to work from outside. For both, the task begins at the level of consciousness raising. It is easier to address issues of racial inequality and identity with Afro-Brazilians already present.

Padre Batista stated simply, "The majority of (Brazilian) blacks have a Christian mentality, and we can work together with them in this way. If I put together a conference as a padre and say it will deal with black issues, I would get only one tenth of the people I would get if the conference was directly labeled as an outgrowth of the church."[8] This encapsulates the struggle of black members of the Catholic church hierarchy in Brazil to create more space within ecclesiastic institutions for discussion about racial discrimination. This also encompasses the desire of black clergy to have more Afro-Brazilian members among their ranks, and the practical difficulties involved in extending Afro-Brazilian strong resemblances to a mass public.

This is quite a different scenario from the black churches of South Africa, pre-Zimbabwe Rhodesia, and the United States, due in large part, to the dichotomous race relations patterns that brought one-race religious institutions into existence. The contrast between these phenomena and the absence of national black churches in Brazil highlights the perverse silver-lining of racial segregation, namely, the creation of self-sufficient institutions and collective projects. Although these institutions operate under greater constraints than their dominant counterparts, they persist as resources for subordinate groups and provide locations for alternative, even emergent political activities. These locations help individuals and groups make the small but noticeable leap from racial awareness to racial consciousness, that is, faint resemblances to strong resemblances.

Genovese's discussion of the role of the church in slave communities in the U.S. South resonates with the notion—and reality—of alternative resources. In his analysis of private church meetings among slaves Genovese wrote, "The meetings gave the slaves strength derived from direct communication with God and each other. . . . the meetings provide a sense of autonomy—of constituting not merely a community unto themselves but a community with leaders of their own."[9]

In contrast, Samba schools and other cultural spaces that were overwhelmingly Afro-Brazilian—Umbanda, Candomble, and other forms of spiritual worship—have attracted many white Brazilians over the past twenty years, making the content and purpose of their forums largely national, rather than racially specific. This assertion will surely draw some debate, as there are many practitioners and students of Candomble who perceive these spaces of worship as veritable hatcheries of racial consciousness (Elbein n.d.; Braga 1992; Prandi 1991). Yet these forms of racial consciousness, which generally emerge though participation in the *terreiros de Candomble*, emphasize the cultural dimensions of Afro-Brazilian identity.

As a consequence, Afro-Brazilians have precarious, often fleeting organizational reservoirs for leadership as well as collective development. In addition, strong resemblances are not absolute resemblances. That is to say resemblances within a group of like-minded individuals is not identical, even when groups form on the basis of racial or ethnic solidarity. Political fissures inhere in racially or ethnically conscious group formations, based on differences over ideology, gender, region, or strategy. These differences are always present, but often suspended in the name of community. Race and ethnicity, as political variables, merely underscore

the salience of phenotype in relation to other possible axes of organization. Racial and ethnic affiliations are choices, not imperatives.

For example, recent attempts to create an Afro-Brazilian political party
or transpartidarian organization have been frustrated by internecine conflict despite the unanimity of strong resemblance (Valente 1986). At one
important meeting of Afro-Brazilian groups and political parties in São
Paulo in 1982, the consensus among its participants was the *absence* of a
consensus between participants because of political and ideological differences. Ironically, all participants hoped for "a future harmony or understanding that will come with time."[10] Baptista suggests that hopes for
unity by a diversity of Afro-Brazilian activists is partially based upon a
racial mythology, the belief in "common ground." This racial mythology
that Baptista refers to is merely another way of conceptualizing faint resemblances turned strong. Such hopes run counter to the sentiments expressed by those interviewed for this study. No one expressed interest in
being part of a racially specific political party, church, or other institution
on a national level.

Faint and Strong Resemblances

The complications that faint and strong resemblances pose for Afro-Brazilians, when used exclusively, lead activists to employ a combination of
the two that is contextual. Social exchanges between blacks appear to contain more faint resemblances than strong. In situations that are explicitly
political, (forming community-based alliances and networks) strong resemblances overtake weaker ones. In the latter, skin color becomes less
salient, emerging as a factor only after political affiliations are formed. The
process is triggered by what can be conceived of metaphorically as the first
glance of ethnic resemblance. The second glance, confirms either "kin" or
an instance of mistaken identity, where the person first perceived has been
mistaken for someone else. It is like encountering someone on the street
who closely resembles an intimate friend, only to discover upon closer
inspection that this individual is in fact someone else.

At that instant, the image of a racial or ethnic "other" serves as the
reference for differentiation. Thus, what distinguishes faint resemblance
from strong is the practice or materialization of racial consciousness in
social exchanges. In this sense a racially conscious Afro-Brazilian could
meet another Brazilian and assume, by virtue of the latter's darkness, that
the individual assumes an Afro-Brazilian identity. When the second person responds in a manner that confirms for the first person that no such
commonality should be assumed between the two, the potential for collective consciousness and action is deflated.

Ivanir dos Santos, an activist within the Workers party (PT) and in the black movement, embodies the mix of faint and strong resemblances. During his interview, he denounced the idea of generic Afro-Brazilian solidarity, which, if assumed naively, can lead to a "schizophrenia" (his word), which separates culture or race from its political context: "Solano Trinidade (an Afro-Brazilian poet) was a member of the Communist party. Amilcar Cabral was a member of the Communist party. Augustinho Neto was a Marxist. But most people in the black movement only discuss them in terms of their blackness, their skin color, and not the significance of their political positions, and the relevance of those positions to black people. Many are concerned only with the symbolism."[11]

For Santos, racial solidarity emerges in a political context only after the criteria for ideological compatibility are met. Only then will he join in coalitions with like-minded blacks. An important point is raised in this quote about the quandary faint resemblance poses for racial identity. While it can lead to commonality, it can also lead to betrayal.

Adalberto Camargo, one of the few black politicians to serve two terms as a congressman in national politics, gives us another glimpse of mixed resemblances. In his case, the use of mixed resemblances is less pronounced. He is thought of as a political conservative by most blacks active in the movement, but his ideological position remains unclear. By his own admission, he is not concerned much with ideology. What motivates him, he has stated, is private enterprise, capitalist development and the social development of Afro-Brazilians.[12]

Camargo has founded an Afro-Brazilian chamber of commerce with entrepreneurial links to Africa, and provided academic scholarships for talented Afro-Brazilian students (including several leftists). During his interview, Camargo stated that he could not care less for the ideological stances of students he funded. For Camargo the principal issue, was that the students were talented and black.

In his politics, however, Camargo has supported black candidates with views similar to his own, suggesting, despite his comments, some ideological correlation and a narrowing of the faint resemblance. In 1968, for instance, he publicly supported Regina Ribeiro, a black woman, for the São Paulo state assembly. Like Camargo, she was a member of the formal party of opposition during this period, the MDB, which at the time was an umbrella party for various opposition groups against the military regime. It was in essence, a liberal-democratic party with no substantial links to social-democratic or other, more radical organizations.

Ribeiro was elected to office in 1968. Like many of his other undertakings, Mr. Camargo viewed his support as another extension of his racial solidarity: "If our (black) community at that moment had the political sensibilities to analyse what occurred in 1968, they would have understood that this was a demonstration that when a black rises they should extend a hand to another."[13] Camargo's comments here are meant as a countervailing reference to the prevailing sense among Afro-Brazilians that once blacks achieve a modicum of success they desert their communities. In addition, as Valente (1986) has noted in her brief study of the São Paulo state elections in 1982, Camargo's election to state and federal positions represents one of the few times in São Paulo politics that blacks have voted to elect black officials.

While the faint and strong impressions of racial solidarity are not entirely clear in Camargo's statements, they are obviated by his behavior, the support of more conservative positions and candidates, and in his support of and for Afro-Brazilians more generally. The rejoinder to his final comments, then, would be in the form of a question. If blacks, who ascend professional and socioeconomic ladders extend their hands to brethren on the lower rungs, to whom in particular should those hands be extended? This question holds the problematic of political choice, the kernel of strong resemblance.

The three examples, however, do challenge both epiphenomenal and reductionist characterizations of race in its relation to class or to political formations. On one side is the essentialism of Glazer (Glazer and Moynihan 1970), who projected in the 1960s the increasing saliency of ethnicity above all other forms of conflict. This thesis was an implicit attack upon class determinism and the inability of Marxist-oriented analyses to deal with social disjunctures that were not structurally determined, yet it was a mere substitution of one essentialism for another. Less so, but in a similar vein, was the primordialism of Geertz (1970), who depicted ethnicity as something dependable, a constant amidst changing historical conditions.

In opposition was the class reductionism of Orlando Patterson, among others. Patterson (1975), in an assessment of the market behavior of Sino-Guyanese and Sino-Jamaicans, concluded that when faced with economic constraints, the merchants of Chinese descent in Jamaica and Guyana always made their decisions based on class, not racial or ethnic factors. Cultural or racial solidarity became salient only in the absence of material constraints.

A careful reading of the evidence Patterson presented, though, provides an alternative interpretation and conclusion from the *same* empirical evidence. Both material and racial factors affected decisions about trading, hiring, and other economic activities. The Brazilian examples presented above imply—as does the evidence, which belies Patterson's own argument—that not only are ethnic identifications fluid, but they are not zero-sum. That is to say, it is a rare occurrence when an individual or group has to categorically pick ethnic affiliation over and above class affiliation, or vice versa. An Italian union leader, to use one of Patterson's examples, can make a class- and ethnic-based decision simultaneously without determining priority. There is no need to do so.[14]

The work of Kay Warren (1978) among Mayan peasants in Guatemala similarly depicts indigenous communities of highland Mayans constantly reforming their ethnic identities in light of historical circumstances, despite the constant ethno-class division between Indians and ladinos. Changes in social structures and the forms of ladino oppression have not forced Mayans to drop their ethnic affiliations so much as redefine them, and manifest them in new ways.

When brought under further examination, as done in the interview excerpts to follow, what becomes clear is how single categories of identification (individual and collective) are inherently plural. Bienen's (1985) explication of first, second, and third-person identification is useful here. In his analysis of the range of self-references and affiliations between and within ethnic groups in Nigeria, he demonstrates how ethnic affiliations are contingent upon local, regional, national, and international contexts. Thus, depending upon the scenario, a member of the Hausa tribe of over 20 million people may present himself or herself as the member of a particular family in one context, from a certain faction within the Hausas in a second, and as a national subject in encounters with foreign nationals outside of Nigeria in a third scenario.

This provides two further considerations that have conceptual as well as methodological repercussions. First, individuals can have faint and strong identifications with a particular group at the same time. I will extend the example above to draw out this possibility. The Nigerian, who is a member of the Hausa "tribe," travels to Great Britain, where there is a large African and West Indian population. Despite the objective national, regional, and linguistic differences within this collectivity, the Nigerian recognizes himself or herself to be a part of the "Third World" community in Great Britain rather than as a Hausa, a member of the Nigerian or African expatriate community.

Another way, noted by students of East Asian ethnic identification in nationalist movements (B. Anderson 1983), is through a perceived communality of historical oppression. The second consideration, then, is an outgrowth of the third, in that the claim of "family resemblance" is much broader than the first, and more tenuous. I suggest these two options, among others, because the conventional ties of language, nation, or religion are decentered according to historical necessity. Race, combined with visual memory, as Enloe (1973) suggests, are the principal ingredients of this form of consciousness.

Americanists versus Africanists: The Complexities
of Faint and Strong Resemblances

The issue of political choice (and its absence) was most apparent in the early 1970s when the emergent black movement developed tendencies and fragments, the result of in-fighting between activist clusters. During that period a chasm existed between two broadly defined factions within the black movement. The chasm emerged out of ideational struggles between Afro-Brazilian activists over the content and form of their movement. While activists in Rio de Janeiro and São Paulo (as well as throughout Brazil) found motivation and imagination in the struggles of nonwhite peoples outside of Brazil, they were not, in the last instance, defined by them. Neither a national struggle for liberation nor a civil rights struggle for racial integration occurred in Brazil. Many activists, in fact, lamented the absence of open confrontation between racial groups in the belief that clearly defined antagonisms would breed greater alliances among blacks.

With neither broad alliances nor stark, unambiguous oppression, activists tried to forge identities and strategies for a mass-based black movement in Brazil with situational templates from the United States and Africa. In Rio de Janeiro and São Paulo, many activists hoped to apply the lessons of civil rights and anticolonial struggles in Brazil.

One cadre of Afro-Brazilians in Rio de Janeiro likened their struggles to those in the United States, combining Black Power and Black Panther ideologies with the more integrationalist agenda of civil rights activists. This group, who believed that boycotts, sit-ins, and protests against specific acts of racial exclusion could work in Brazil were known as the *Americanistas*, or the Americanists. In purported contrast were the *Africanistas*, the Africanists, those who advocated a more transformative sort of black movement in Brazil, based on the anticolonial movements in Africa.

The word *purported* is used in the previous sentence because there was no clear line separating Americanistas from Africanistas. In fact, there were several individuals who had a sort of dual membership in each camp. Once again, scarce ideological lucidity made it difficult to correlate political affiliations with political language and action. Yet the chasm existed, insofar as it led to the formation of group clusters predicated upon perceived differences. There were similar divisions in São Paulo, between groups like CECAN and MNU (see Chapter 5), but not formulated along Africanist and Americanist lines.

The Africanists were in some ways more easily identifiable than the Americanists, because after an initial period of group affinity, the Africanists situated themselves in opposition to Afro-Brazilians who advocated such things as black capitalism and equal opportunity. Africanists saw themselves as part of the revolutionary wave that undulated across the African continent in the 1950s, with its ebb and flow of national liberation, then neo-colonialism. For Africanists, it was not enough to sit alongside white Brazilians in bathrooms and restaurant dining facilities (which in theory, nonwhites could always do). This would not solve, they argued, the deeply rooted problems of racial dominance in Brazil. In addition, only by the most conservative estimates were blacks a minority group in Brazil as they were in the United States. Black Brazilians, the Africanists suggested, should make demands upon the state and civil society as a majority group.

Discussions between Africanists and Americanists took place at three principal locations; Candido Mendes University, at that time in Ipanema, where the Center of Afro-Asiatic Studies (CEAA) was founded; the Institute for Study of the Black Cultures (IPCN), and at the Society for Brazil Africa Exchange (SINBA). Candido Mendes University was originally the site where people met. After differences emerged, the Americanists met at IPCN, the Africanists at SINBA.[15]

Yedo Ferreira, one of the founders of SINBA, discussed the rationale for its creation: "We were interested in the liberation movements in Africa and most of all the work of Frantz Fanon: we were observing the black movement in the United States and found black Americans also looking for an historical referent in Africa. . . . for us it was very easy to have a great cultural identification with Africa. We were returning to Africa, not the United States.[16]

Thus, Africa signified a place of origin and return, or more precisely, a site to be symbolically retrieved by members of SINBA in the quest for a political compass. Unlike IPCN and CEAA, SINBA did not receive funding from U.S.-based institutions, and considered this a sign of autonomy on its part. But with little resources, SINBA members could only manage to publish their journal, also entitled *SINBA*, and hold meetings and small conferences through the mid-1970s. IPCN and CEAA, on the other hand, used their funding to provide assistance to Afro-Brazilians in the form of small scholarships, legal advice, and institutional support. Both IPCN and CEAA exist today, while SINBA does not.

Ideological cloudiness added to SINBA's demise. Its push for an Afrocentric position alienated SINBA from some of its founding members and compounded its inability to make alliances with Americanist or other groups. Several members decided that merely assuming an oppositional stance for all things American and an attraction to the African continent would not suffice as a strategy for effecting change in Brazil. Two of its founding members cited the increasingly narrow ethnocentrism as the virus that SINBA succumbed to.[17] Ferreira, in retrospect, admitted as much about his own position when he decided, along with several others, to create the organization: "I had the desire to create an institution, but without a formulation of political struggle. . . . no one stopped to reflect on this . . . so the institution remained, just like this, without being able to advance more than where we were at the start."[18]

As will be seen shortly in a brief discussion of the Black Brazilian Front (FNB), Ferreira's observations are reminiscent of ideological predicaments within the FNB in the 1940s. Without the ideological clarity to at least sustain a fairly stable relationship between issues and praxis, these groups became susceptible to prevailing strains of political and cultural discourse. In the 1940s, the FNB succumbed to Integralism. Thirty years later, SINBA, CECAN, and numerous other groups in Rio de Janeiro and São Paulo followed the path of unchartered culturalism, in search of the elusive African essence.

The absence of demarcated ideological positions also suggests a reactive, day-to-day tendency of a social movement that has existed without a firm grounding in party or organizational politics along the left-right continuum. Also absent is any coherent version of cultural nationalism, in the Garveyite sense, with a "race-first" doctrine of separate, autonomous Afro-Brazilian institutions. While the movement's long-standing independence from political parties is the source of its vitality, it is also been the incubator for regressive tendencies. Without a competing ensemble of beliefs, values, and ideologies to mediate the relationships between leftists and conservatives, the likelihood increases for activists to employ commonsense understandings of race and politics that are congruent with dominant interpretations of these issues, which they proclaim to be against.

A most unfortunate example of this in the history of Brazilian racial politics is the Black Brazilian Front, which existed as a political party from 1936 to 1937. The broad, contradictory array of positions compressed into a single political organization brought about coalitions with socialists in some parts of the country, and fascists in another (Mitchell 1977). Aristedes Barbosa, a Frentista of the 1940s, mentioned during his interview some of the confusions during this period: "Blacks were always a bit lost on the question of political ideology. In the period of the Black Front the prevailing ideology (in the Front) was Integralism, the Nazi line. Blacks during this period fought against being discriminated on a day-to-day basis. . . . blacks were not preoccupied with future questions."[19]

The preoccupation with "future questions," a speculative trajectory, is the stuff of ideology. Here "future questions" are juxtaposed against the "day-to-day." The day-to-day, Barbosa implies, is a temporal site where blacks sought to construct more racially egalitarian positions within an existing system, and not transform the system itself. While the Black Brazilian Front made advances, it also incurred new contradictions. For Afro-Brazilian activists, (indeed, not only Brazilian ones) there exists the quandary of engaging in daily forms of resistance; appropriating dominant codes of political thought and expression while not being subsumed by them.

Racial solidarity, then, while resolving certain problems of consciousness and collective solidarity, leads to new contradictions. For the FNB, such contradictions came in the form of fighting against racism while supporting a fascistic political party.

Yet even halting articulations of strong resemblance suggest undercurrents of racial consciousness that may be worthy of more comparative, cross-spatial analysis in the future. These undercurrents, the foundations of faint and strong resemblances, will be explored in the following section. Despite a low level of Afro-Brazilian mobilization, there are experiences leading to racial consciousness not unlike those in other multiracial polities.

Racial Consciousness: From Within and Without

Among Afro-Brazilian activists there is a two-tiered form of racial identification, an internal and external dimension. Most of those interviewed expressed a global identification with blacks in other parts of the world, in spite (or because of) the lack of racial solidarity at home. Secondly, most activists articulated a home-grown process of identification filled with the peculiarities of the Brazilian case, where racial identification cannot be broadly assumed.

The second building block in evidence is the conscious recognition by activists of the linkages between racial identification and power. This recognition is not dissimilar to the emergence of racial identification among subordinated groups in places like Kenya, Ghana, and Nigeria. Note that at least in the first phase of anticolonial movements in Africa, temporary unity between various ethnic groups was attained *after* ethnic elites determined that their "otherness" relative to each other was more easily bridged than the political chasm between themselves and their colonizers. Moreover, in the clamor for national emancipation, calls for national resistance were interconnected with Pan-Africanist, Third World, and other more globalized narratives highlighting the difference between the West, as a total category, and the non-Western other. Here too, although on a much wider canvas, is the two-tiered edifice of racial identification.

Of the sixty activists interviewed for this study, forty-seven gave detailed accounts of incidents or experiences which gave shape to their racial "becoming." The thirteen who did not provide personal dimensions to interviews were people who were being interviewed for their roles in specific institutions, movements, and organizations. This is not to suggest that in those interviews people did not offer personal insights into the complexities of their relationships to those institutions, movements, or organizations. The remaining forty-seven interviews contained specific details about individuals whose family and childhood experiences nurtured the seeds of racial identity.

Several patterns emerged from the interviews that suggest an interplay of racial consciousness and political activism that stemmed from personal experience. That is to say, many of those interviewed took their cues for social and political activities from intensely personal experience. As a result, even with a recognizable pattern of value orientation among the sixty activists interviewed, there is also a diversity of responses to questions of political and racial identity.

This diversity is based on socioeconomic, gender, religious, and other differences that separate one person from another, race notwithstanding. When coupled with the ill-defined notion of what constitutes the "black" phenotype, the respondents exposed a variety of positions on (*a*) self- and collective identification, (*b*) racial impediments to social mobility, and (*c*) multiple militancy.

Thirty-six of the forty-seven who gave more personal interviews raised the importance of black consciousness in their lives and within the movement. The thirty-six presented black consciousness in an inverse relationship with white dominance, thereby grounding their conscious identification with Afro-Brazilians in a power relationship.

This conscious identification among activists, many of whom attended college in the 1970s, came about during a period when blacks had more access to universities and more information about historical currents outside of Brazil. Greater access to information about other peoples of the African diaspora broadened the awareness of many Afro-Brazilians of this period. As excerpts from the following interviews will demonstrate, many activists of the movimento negro felt linked to a broader collectivity during this period, even though they were separated by language, culture, and geography.

Tier one: Internal Dimensions of Racial Consciousness

As Hasenbalg notes, one key element of heightened racial consciousness during the 1970s can be attributed to the inability of black professionals to obtain employment opportunities in their fields. When denied job opportunities that they were qualified for, many of the respondents developed a consciousness of racial discrimination that they did not have previously. Subsequently, many of the respondents began to criticize racial discrimination in their country and organize against it.

One example is Orlando Fernandes, one of the founders of the Institute for Study of the Black Cultures (IPCN). Fernandes said during his interview that one of his most painful motivations toward black activism came from the fact that he was refused a job with a Brazilian airline company because of his color:

> I was in a pilot training program in Rio in the 1960s, and at the time I had no real sense of myself as a black. I thought of myself as mulatto [*moreno*]. I had completed all the requirements for the program and received the highest examination marks of all the students. I was ranked the best student in the class. . . . All that separated me from an assignment with the company was a routine physical examination, which would have allowed me to fly. . . . Before assessing my heart rate, the doctor asked me to run up and down a flight of stairs several times. After doing so for about a half an hour, the doctor then checked my heart beat. . . . It was decided that I was physically unfit to be a pilot, on the basis of my heart beat. . . . It was only years later, after I met another doctor who worked for the same company, who told me that it was a tactic used to discriminate against black pilot trainees, did I realize what they had done to me, destroyed my career because of my color.[20]

Fernandes's experience lends a glimpse of possible tensions that result from whites and blacks competing for positions of social status, and the subtle but nonetheless consequential repercussions for black professionals seen as a threat to the racial order. The doctor's response to black excellence in the training program is paradigmatic of racial discrimination in private, institutional form. It also underscores the futility of analytic distinctions between interpersonal and institutional relations when racial discrimination is the most salient feature.

Thereza Santos, a cultural activist now living in São Paulo, recalled her precarious location as a black child in a white, lower-middle class community in Rio de Janeiro. Her experience also holds racial tensions, which became articulated in class terms:

> As a child I lived on a street which had two black families . . . a two-block street that ended where a *favela* [slum] began. The favela was all black. . . . So in my family we tried to give the impression that we lived on the asphalt— not on the hill; those on the hill were not our equals, we must be treated differently from the blacks on the hill. There always existed in our house a worry to appear as the "exception," the pretty little black girl, but the moment there was a fight with other white children on the street I was called "urubu," "macaco" [monkey]. . . . on the other hand when everything was

tranquil I was called "the black girl with the white soul." It was this way I began to discover the difference of being black. . . . At times I ask myself about the lack of black consciousness. . . . I say [to myself], but my experience was not different; all blacks are discriminated against from the moment they are born, and why did I have the opportunity to formulate a consciousness while other blacks did not? Perhaps because many blacks did not live on the street where I lived, in the predicament I lived in?[21]

Middle-class neighbors and the slum posed dilemmas of an existential and geographical kind for Santos, forcing her to identify a racial distance from the whites on her street, and identify *with* the black favelados. While her socioeconomic location created the distance from blacks nearby, her marginalization did not.

Racial slurs blurted out by whites during moments of childhood conflict accesses the subtext of Santos's and Fernandes's comments. Aggression, tensions, challenges that would be resolved through some form of competition when people of the same racial group are involved, become translated into racial conflict in disjunctures involving people from different ethnic or racial groups. In short, conflict may serve as a catalyst for racial violence, symbolic or physical, lying in wait during periods of social inactivity. Both its latent and manifest forms may be predicated upon the circumstances in which the individual or group initiating the violence finds itself.

For Fernandes and Santos, their locations in middle-class professions and middle-class communities did not shield them from discriminatory practices that, while new to them in form, were substantively familiar. Their move from one socioeconomic location to another brought about new, racially grounded contradictions.

Two forms of consciousness arise at the point of realization, in Fernandes's and in Thereza Santos's case. In the first form, discriminatory practices are encapsulated by the acknowledgment of their existence, which is cognitive. The subsequent form of consciousness, an offspring of the first, is forged through the resistance to discriminatory practices in subsequent encounters. In this regard it is similar to the oft-noted Marxian distinction between a social class of itself and the social class that operates for itself.

Yet as I have noted in Chapter 1 and have elaborated in the present chapter, the very notion of a singular, unitary consciousness that can mobilize an entire social group is problematic, given the array of cleaving variables (gender and class among them) that complicate forms of identification. An uncritical effort to highlight the relative autonomy of ethnicity and racial dominance vis-à-vis class relations shares with orthodox Marxian analysis the risk of reductionist determinism, if one is not careful. Moreover, these incidents display complexities of power relations between racial groups, of which market inequality is merely one facet. Neither class nor racial or other forms of social-cognitive unity is enough to reverse structured forms of oppression.

The Second Tier: The External Dimension of Afro-Brazilian Consciousness

Carlos Alberto Medeiros, participant and founder of several organizations during the 1970s, addressed the issue of external influences that came to Brazil through mass media: "At the end of 1969 . . . I started seeing and buying black American magazines, *Ebony*, principally, which in this period had a revolutionary rhetoric. This journal (*Ebony*) reflected what was occurring in civil rights and nationalist movements in the world, and it reflected this in a very strong way, especially the esthetics element, the Afro hairstyle and Afro clothing. It was love at first sight. . . . It was a new image of blacks that came from the United States."[22]

The "new image" to which Medeiros referred was novel for black Brazilians in two important respects. Prior to the 1970s, black Brazilians had little information about U.S. blacks due to the barrier of language, and received more information about African nationalist currents, particularly in the Lusophone countries. Second, what black Brazilians were witnessing, perhaps for the first time, were people they resembled constructing oppositional, positive images of themselves in contradistinction to the West. Medeiros and others talked about how they were introduced to these new images and in turn, introduced them to other black Brazilians. As discussed in Chapter 6, this Afrocentric[23] imagery was a symbolic catalyst for the Black Soul movements in Rio, São Paulo, and other parts of the country.

This emboldened many black Brazilians of this period. It provided them with a link to a larger community, which reminded many of the relative ideational impoverishment of Brazilian blacks. The irony that Brazil, the country with the largest population of blacks in the New World, had a black population with one of the lowest levels of racial consciousness in the Americas was not lost on black Brazilian activists of the epoch.

Like these other movements, black Brazilian activists clung to two common traits. The first, a belief in a common oppressor across three continents and at least three centuries that, conversely, united blacks across time and space. A related but distinct belief construct was the notion of Africa as a place of common origin, an ontological vortex for all people of "African" descent.

While the two beliefs were, and are, collapsed in numerous circumstances, they are categorized separately here to mark the two overarching political strains within the movimento negro. Some groups favored the first belief construct over the second, and vice versa, which resulted in differing political views, differing organizations and distinct courses of action.

Thirty-four out of forty-seven respondents interviewed stated that they perceived a common racial origin of oppression for blacks worldwide. Thus, reflections on their experiences were at once personal and collective. The following two examples from Rio de Janeiro attest to this: Joselina da Silva, member of the African bloc Agbara Dudu, community based organizer in Duque de Caxías and an activist for the Center of Articulation for Marginalized People (CEAP or Centro de Articulação de Populaçoes Marginalizados), commented on her social location as a black woman in Brazilian society: "The question of discrimination of the black woman exists . . . on three levels, because of the fact that we are women, black, and for historical reasons the great majority of the black population in this country is poor."[24]

Consider her observation alongside the following by Ivanir dos Santos, a PT militant, CEAP activist, and an ex-student of FUNABEM, a state-run orphanage created after the 1964 coup to cope with the increasing number of abandoned children in Brazil's urban centers: "My experience is not a very good one; the son of a prostitute who was first raised and educated in FUNABEM. It is an experience . . . of all black children and the poor who are in this country."[25]

Joselina da Silva and Ivanir dos Santos have made general points about the black Brazilian condition based on specific experiences. Da Silva speaks in terms of a "great majority" of black women being poor for historical reasons (i.e., racial discrimination). Dos Santos states categorically that his experience is symptomatic of the plight of black children writ large. What distinguishes da Silva from dos Santos is their self-conscious ordering of a constellation of experiences, each with their respective priorities and emphases.

The plural nature of individual identity is apparent in these examples. This plurality suggests a concurrent process of identifications as multiple selves, in addition to being "negro." In the strictest sense, when stripped of the metaphorical flesh of personality, each linked poverty and marginalization to being black in Brazilian society. The differences between the two emerge when poverty and marginalization become personalized, (i.e., Joselina—woman; Ivanir—man, son of a prostitute).

Faint and strong resemblances, then, are not fixed or "given" in any primordial way but are constructed, reconstructed, even deconstructed in the face of individual or collective concerns. They also co-exist with other forms of resemblance (black feminist, in da Silva's case; orphan in dos Santos's case). Neither individual operates solely within a "black" sphere, but in multiple arenas simultaneously.

All forty-seven respondents spoke of dual activism. Nineteen spoke explicitly of more than two forms of identification (black, woman, poor, etc.) as justification for participation in several movements or tendencies within a single movement. It appears in this context that multiple identification influences multiple activism.

A multiplicity of identification and activism may assist in the tracing of faint and strong resemblances among the activists, and the role of ideological differences in delimiting group tendencies. As mentioned earlier, none of the respondents considered racially specific black institutions (political or religious) as logical sources of mobilization. While many of the respondents are affiliated in supraparty organizations they are not all in the *same* organizations. In a discussion of the low probability of either a unified black movement or single political party, Afro-Brazilian congresswoman Benedita da Silva commented during her interview on the segmenting function of ideology in the movimento negro: "The concept of a party which I have expresses an ideology. It could be to the center or left or right. The black movement, as a social movement, contains blacks of all three political positions. The moment that you have a unified black movement using ideology as an organizational reference point, it is very difficult to organize all black activists on that basis. It needs to be well understood what is a social movement and what is a political party."[26]

Her analysis separating political party from social movement pinpoints the lack of ideological definition among many black activists (faint resemblance), which is actually helpful for the rudimentary agglutination of diverse advocates for issues like race-related violence and noted black Brazilians in history textbooks. Ways to actually effect these issues in civil society are much more difficult to coordinate, because they require the coalitions, disputes, and negotiations of politics.

Conclusion

This chapter seeks to highlight the nuances of racial identification among Afro-Brazilians in Brazil, through the responses and reflections of Afro-Brazilian activists interviewed for this study. Faint and strong versions of racial identification were conceptualized in this chapter to help distinguish attitudes and inclinations toward basic identification (faint resemblance) from behaviors that seek to politicize basic awarenesses of identification in the form of social mobilization (strong resemblance).

What has been made clear through the experience of these activists is an overemphasis on faint resemblances, and a lack of strong resemblances. This has been attributed, by activists themselves, to the absence of coherent, ideological positions and the preponderance of culturalist exercises within the movement.

At the same time, however, those seeking to mobilize Afro-Brazilians politically along racial lines are hindered by the low level of racial solidarity among them. This has been confirmed at various moments during the political history of the black movement. The FNB prior to 1945 and the 1982 municipal elections of São Paulo are just two examples.

Moreover, even when resemblances are articulated in political activities, racial identification has not sustained political organization and mobilization. Africanistas and Americanistas, two collectives with high degrees of ethnic identification and solidarity in Rio de Janeiro, had tactical disagreements over the scope and manner of Afro-Brazilian struggle, which hindered their coalition.

This underscores two elements of identification that obtain in most, if not all, situations involving the construction of identities and affiliation; first, that the conscious identification with a particular group or collectivity is an insufficient basis for political mobilization; second, even when groups-collectivities are mobilized on the basis of race or ethnicity, there are other factors (class, ideology, region) that complicate the coming together of groups, which may undermine the initial premise of group solidarity. In some instances, the premise of solidarity may eventually be transformed because of other factors.

In summation, while racial solidarity is an indispensable facet of what little Afro-Brazilian solidarity exists, it is also, as in other multiracial polities, an insufficient basis for constructing and maintaining a social and political movement. Even when the racial transformation of attitudes to behaviors does occur, it does not occur absolutely, independently of economic, historical, and cultural parameters. Its transformation is part of a broader social totality. The next chapter will explore the relationship between Afro-Brazilian political identities and this totality, through a reading of Afro-Brazilian social movements in the post–World War II period.

FIVE

MOVEMENTS AND MOMENTS

O movimento negro e, na verdade, um movimento dos negros.
[The black movement is, in truth, a movement of blacks.]

T HE COMMENTARY above was an often-heard phrase uttered by activists in cities in 1988 and 1989. In one sense, as articulated by Lelia Gonzalez (Gonzalez and Hasenbalg 1985), the black movement is actually a series of movements with distinct ideological commitments and political strategies. In another sense, though, it is also a movement of groups with little political coherence or relation to one another. As a movement or a series of movements, it is without direction.

Sectarianism, for one, has plagued the movimento. The innumerable factions and groups in Rio de Janeiro and São Paulo reflect the absence of concrete strategizing and coalition-building as much as it suggests individual initiative. As of 1988, Rio de Janeiro and São Paulo had 76 and 138 groups, respectively, that were affiliated with the movimento,[1] the largest number of groups of all the states in the federation. These numbers however, can be misleading. One has only to glance at subsequent catalogues of movimento organizations to discover that many that appear one year may be defunct the next. Other organizations are not organizations in any literal sense, but meetings of a few people with ill-defined objectives. Hence, the statement that the black movement is only a movement of blacks is unfortunately accurate. This chapter will show how culturalism, the preoccupation with genealogical inquiries and artifacts of Afro-Brazilian expressive culture, has led the movimento negro away from strategies of contemporary political change and more toward symbolic protest and a fetishization of Afro-Brazilian culture.

Afro-Brazilian political activity and expressive cultural practice have been inextricably linked since the third decade of the twentieth century, ever since Gilberto Freyre's anthropological inclusion of Afro-Brazilian cultural practices into the matrix of emergent national identity. One of the marked ironies of Brazilian racial politics has been that the paternalist, functionalist glorification of Afro-Brazilian culture, as well as more radical uses of it, emerge from the same source—the recognition that Brazil was as much an African nation as it was a country of the New World, and the attached genealogical excavations of the sources or "essences" of Africans in the New World.

Freyre, along with both white and nonwhite intellectuals created the first centers and institutes for the study of Afro-Braziliana in the 1940s. Diana Brown and Mario Bick (1987) have noted how *Candomble* and *Umbanda*, African and Afro-Brazilian derived religious practices, were frowned upon as forms of religious worship by whites until the 1940s. The academic and artistic production of these intellectuals became the basis for the study of African cultures and peoples in Brazil, as well as grounds for the critique and subsequent dismissal of these studies by later generations of scholars and activists.

Within this quasi-academic realm, scholarly and political debates about Afro-Brazilian cultural practices first emerged. Those debates subsequently led to the creation of institutes and community organizations by Afro-Brazilians themselves. It could be said that Afro-Brazilian social movements after the 1940s sprang from the academy, as opposed to the suburbio or the favela. These origins would become one of the recurrent problems intrinsic to Afro-Brazilian political development throughout the 1970s.

Until recently, most Afro-Brazilian leadership emerged from Samba schools, associational and religious groups, and athletics. Understandably, this leadership drew its strength from the arenas that spawned them. With virtually no representation in state apparatuses, political or educational institutions on a national level, Afro-Brazilian activists have had to utilize their constituencies and organizations in often indirect, veiled ways for political purposes. Thus, the politics and aesthetics of the movimento negro have always been intertwined out of necessity. Yet with this close interconnectedness, many Afro-Brazilian activists equate the micropolitics of cultural representation with the macropolitics of racial violence, market inequalities and lack of formal political representation.

The absence of linkages between various political and cultural activities has left the movimento negro episodic, fragmented, without self-sustaining organizations. The ever-present challenge for the movement is the unification of culture and politics and, more importantly, the differentiation between culture as folklore from culture as a valuative basis for ethico-political activity. The historical interpretation presented in this chapter suggests that there is no necessary correlation between cultural and political practice in any social movement, including the Afro-Brazilian movement. The various tendencies and internal conflicts within the movement over this issue have resulted in the movement's fragmentation and hence such mocking references such as "o movimento negro e um movimento dos negros" by some of its own militants.

Chapters 5 and 6 intend to provide both a selective historical overview and critical assessment of the movimento negro in Rio de Janeiro and São Paulo, Brazil, between 1945 and 1988. This overview highlights tensions within the movimento negro over issues of ideology, identity, and praxis; conflicts between civil elites and black activists over self-determination; and finally, the interaction between the Brazilian state apparatus and various tendencies of the *movimento negro*. These chapters focus on the efforts of Afro-Brazilians to chart what can be categorized as the "third path" of political mobilization. This "third path" is defined as a political position that attempts to transcend the narrow confines of the left-right continuum to create organizations that confront the specificities of racial oppression in conjunction with the general issues of state violence and economic exploitation. Such a position, as explicated by West (1988), is autonomist in relation to labor and other movements, but is not necessarily micropolitical. As will become clear shortly, the limitations of both patron-clientelist and leftist politics had, by the 1970s, made a "third path" necessary for Afro-Brazilian mobilization. These efforts are also similar to those of other communities of the African diaspora who have attempted a similar course of political praxis, steering away from both "bourgeois"- and "proletarian"-based movements.

There is a certain irony in the fact that while these movements in Brazil and elsewhere evolved out of the dynamics of racial inequality, they are generally ignored by a social movements literature at pains to discover forms of protest that are not directly linked to "old" loci of collective action—the trade union, syndicate, or political party. In my conclusion to this chapter, I will identify what I consider to be new avenues of research for the location of racial politics within the social movements literature.

Historical Coordinates

To comprehend the contemporary dilemmas of the black movement in Rio de Janeiro and São Paulo, it is necessary to first identify the limitations of the Brazilian left as well as the right in relation to the *movimento negro*. Regardless of regime type, Brazilian political parties have minimized the politics of racial difference in Brazil. Thus in terms of racial politics, there are no "givens" with respect to correlations between a politics of race and party or ideology in Brazil. Although stemming from distinct presuppositions about Brazilian society, both the Brazilian left and the Brazilian right have been exclusionary with respect to Afro-Brazilian concerns.

The Brazilian right, which has ruled Brazil through politico-military regimes for nearly two generations, has subverted Afro-Brazilian politics through corporatism and patron-clientelism (when it has not used coercive mechanisms) at least since the period of Estado Novo in 1937. Unlike labor-based politics, however, Afro-Brazilian politics has had its basis in associational groups, not unions or syndicates. Therefore, state and elite tactics to defuse Afro-Brazilian activists have been distinct from those employed against union organizers and other labor leaders. Culture and not class has been the operative political category for most interaction between black activists and white elites in civil, bureaucratic, and state functions.

According to Gramsci, the fusion of political and cultural categories is a principal characteristic of totalitarian societies, in which state and political party are one. Together they are sole representatives of civil society. In these societies, Gramsci posited that a political party's functions

> are no longer directly political, but merely technical ones of propaganda and public order, and moral and cultural influence. The political function is indirect. For, even if no other legal parties exist, other parties in fact always do exist and other tendencies which can not be legally coerced; and against these, polemics are unleashed and struggles are fought . . . . It is certain that in such parties cultural functions predominate . . . political questions are disguised as cultural ones, and as such become insoluble.[2]

While the Brazilian state has never been totalitarian in the strictest sense, the specific repression and denial of Afro-Brazilian protest movements has spanned both military and civilian regimes. For this reason, left-right or authoritarian versus liberal distinctions must be qualified when discussing matters of race. In this respect, Gramsci's discussion of the insolubility of politics and culture is applicable to racial politics in Brazil. From the prohibition of all political parties and racially specific political organizations after the installation of Estado Novo in 1937, to the climate of terror during the epoch of military rule after 1964, Afro-Brazilian activists have had to couch their language and praxis in indirect, ambiguous, and fragmented forms under the veil of cultural practice, and even then, according to state and elite definitions of what constituted Afro-Brazilian and Brazilian culture.

On the other hand, until very recently the Brazilian left was not particularly hospitable to discussions of race. The rather ossified brand of Brazilian Marxist-Leninism had consistently, up until the late 1970s, maintained that "the social problem" is of class and labor, not race or gender. As recently as 1990, Pedro Wilson Guimaraes, a PT militant talking to a U.S. audience in Philadelphia responded to a question about the party's stance toward racial and gender issues by stating that "these issues are important, but we have our priorities. We are primarily concerned with the social problem of working class exploitation in Brazil."[3]

Guimaraes's narrow understanding of "the social problem" begs a simple question: does racial or gender-based discrimination, indeed any form of discrimination, exist outside of a social context? If not, then don't they help constitute "the social problem" as well, inasmuch as blacks and women carry their "secondary" forms of discrimination with them into labor markets? Guimaraes's comments, taken representatively, point to two major problems the Brazilian left has historically had in dealing with and understanding racially based mechanisms of exploitation in civil society, and its subsequent reproduction in leftist intellectual circles.

Such reductionist understandings of the intersections of race and class can also be traced to the academy. The Marxist historian Octavio Ianni offers a more nuanced reading of the problematic that racial difference poses for historical materialism but ultimately pulls upon a determinist leash to pull racism away from its *merely relative* autonomy within capitalist social relations. Literally and figuratively, Ianni reminded an audience at the end of a roundtable discussion on historical materialism and the racial question that in the last instance "the base of the racial question is the fact that capitalist society functions as if it was a machine of human alienation. And prejudice is in a certain way an expression of alienation that marks the daily life of the society."[4]

While Ianni's position is an advance from Guimaraes, we can begin to measure the strategic and ontological problems that leftists, academic or otherwise, have posed for Afro-Brazilian activists. Ianni still maintains the equation between racism and capitalism. As Aronowitz (1981) and Robinson (1983) posit, analyses such as Ianni's neglect the simple fact that racism *predates* capitalism. As noted in Chapter 3, racist sentiments and practices in Iberian culture against people of African descent have been traced back to at least the fifteenth century, well before global mercantilism, the Industrial Revolution, or even the development of capital markets. It could not, therefore, be defined by a mode of production that postdates it. Moreover, based on this analysis of racial "alienation," one could not begin to make sense of ethnic and racial chauvinisms in contemporary societies that have supposedly transcended capitalism, namely China, Cuba, and the former Soviet Union.

Taken together, their observations partially confirm Abdias do Nascimento's assertion:

> For the dominant classes, exploitation, disdain towards the Afro-Brazilian and his aspirations remain unalterable. The Brazilian left, with its endorsement of "racial democracy" or with its systematic refusal to see social facts objectively, implicitly support the most retrograde positions regarding the possibility of a society truly multi-racial and truly multi-cultural. The attempt to mask racism, or better, the custom of substituting its identity by labelling racism as simple accident in the dialectics of class, in practice becomes a valuable service to the anti-national forces that threaten the legitimate interests of the Brazilian people, of whom African descendents are more than half.[5]

Nascimento's comments embody a striking parallel between Brazilian leftists and liberal-conservatives on the racial question. In denying the possibility of race as an organizing principle with material consequences all its own, many "orthodox" Brazilian leftists have employed Marxism as an ideology of domination much in the same way that paternalistic elites have used Freyrean tenets to construct a racial order of white superiority. In each instance, racial inequalities lurk outside the parameters of the "classless society" or "raceless society," which both hold as ideal-types. What distinguishes the "politically correct" Brazilian leftists from liberal and conservative elites is that the latter have held power while the former, until recently, has not.

In a somewhat muted critique, Andrews (1991) observes that white Brazilian elites have combined Freyre's and Fernandes's perspectives in an effort to explain—and neglect—contemporary racial prejudices and tensions, a type of convergence of the two positions. This point is reminiscent of a similar formulation by Joel Rufino dos Santos (1985), who has argued that white Brazilians, regardless of their political affiliations, share a "transideological" position when it comes to thinking about race relations. What this may indicate more poignantly, however, is how both the Brazilian left and right were spawned from the same racial-cultural matrix, thereby limiting their ability to envision and understand forms of oppression outside their immediate experience.

This is not unique to Brazilian racial politics. The Communist party USA (CPUSA) was chastised by none other than Lenin himself for not attracting more blacks to the party by addressing the specificities of racial oppression, due to their religious ascription to "classical" Marxism. In disillusionment, black intellectuals such as Richard Wright and Harold Cruse left the CPUSA. Similarly George Padmore, the Trinidadian, left the British Communist party in disgust in the 1930s and became one of the founders of Pan-Africanism (James 1984; Robinson 1983). These examples are chosen merely to pinpoint issues for comparative analysis of the common obstacles shared by Afro-Brazilian activists and black activists in other multiracial polities.

1945–1964: The Aftermaths of "New State" and "Revolution"

Nineteen forty-five signalled more than just the end of World War II. It also symbolized the demise of the Axis powers within a new global reconfiguration and a halt to the modern Jewish Holocaust. In Brazil, it symbolized the fall of the Estado Novo regime of Getulio Vargas. While Vargas did not openly promote anti-Semitism as Brazilian president, correspondence with government officials and discussion by subordinates of its potential merits in Brazil suggest a bigoted undercurrent to the administration not revealed in public depositions and propaganda (Tucci Carneiro 1988). Levine (1970) writes that the Vargas regime tolerated the rise of anti-Semitic activity "particularly by the fascist Integralists whose virulent anti-semitic campaign borrowed directly from Nazi propaganda materials."[6] While this is not a central theme of Estado Novo, it provides a clue to the public and private distinctions made concerning racial difference in Brazil up until 1945, distinctions that were also made with regard to Afro-Brazilians during this period.

While the ideology of racial democracy was being promulgated by Vargas and other elites, efforts were made to project an image of an Anglo-Saxon Brazil in mind and body to the rest of the world. Levine further notes that during the 1930s and 1940s, beauty contestants and invariably beauty queens were selected according to a criteria of beauty emphasizing aquiline features. "Middle class culture displayed an embarrassment at primitive survivals in its midst, such as spiritualistic *Umbanda* and *Macumba*."[7] These and other discriminatory practices occurred simultaneously, but privately, within the parameters of state discourse, as the ideology of racial democracy was articulated and worked upon in civil society. Many blacks considered Vargas a savior, however, because he "destroyed the Partido Republicano Paulista, which blacks regarded as the bulwark of the aristocratic class of former slaveholders"[8] and supported the October Third club, the most militant wing of Vargas's supportive base in 1930, just before he assumed power.

Seven years after his installation in presidential office, Vargas shut down the Frente Negra Brasileira's political organization in 1937, along with all other political parties. This was a major casualty for *a gente de cor*, as many activists of the period referred to themselves. Black Brazilians lost one of the few political outlets available to them.[9] Vargas's corporatist strategy engulfed political parties and organizations that willingly or reluctantly succumbed to his tactics of incorporation. More rebellious social movements, such as labor, were often dealt with in more coercive ways.

At least one activist from the FNB believed that the black movement in Brazil lost important ground during Estado Novo (Leite in Berriel 1988), not only because of its incorporation under Estado Novo, but its ideological distortion. As Berriel (1988) observes, the elitist and accommodationist tendencies of the Frente were only exacerbated by the Vargas regime. Most students of the black movement in Brazil have identified a normative shift on the part of the black movement from the 1930s, with a belief in Integralism and whitening (*branqueamento*), to anxious ruminations about white superiority and the proper trajectory of social (i.e., bourgeois) ascent by the 1940s. This is evidenced in Moura's (1988) and Berriel's (1988) analyses of the black press of this period, suggesting a correlation between a change in black activists concerns and those of the white middle classes in general.

This shift on the part of black activists and the middle classes stems largely from the emergence, in São Paulo and Rio de Janeiro, of an Afro-

Brazilian middle-status group that characterized an insurgent mode of capitalist development. Liberal professions flowered in these two cities in a manner and speed unprecedented in Brazilian society, due to the success of coffee production and other developing industries.

Afro-Brazilians who seized upon the rare opportunity of a professional education used this new climate to their advantage, obtaining training and skills in medicine, law and other white-collar professions. Caution should be used however, in describing these individuals as middle class, for they would not constitute the middle class in the terminology of an Adam Smith or Marx, but perhaps in a Weberian sense, since they did achieve a certain status from their social roles which distinguished them from their working-class counterparts.

While this was a necessary advancement for a small but influential segment of the black communities in these two cities, it only widened the distance between the minuscule black petit-bourgeoisie and the black working classes that the FNB, to a certain extent, tried to narrow. This distance was marked by the emergence of new organizations and publications after 1945 catering to black "elites" who believed in uplifting their race, one at a time. This understanding of community uplift was based upon the existing realities of social ascension in an increasingly competitive, market-oriented ethos that had already driven large segments of the black labor force to Brazil's economic periphery one generation earlier.

At the same time, it reproduced the tension between uplift and condescension found in the white middle classes in their own treatment of Afro-Brazilians as a whole. Thus the "whitening" ideal came to assume a signifying function in addition to its phenotypical and material function, in the sense that the black elites of this period came to apply the dominant cultural categories pertaining to race and social mobility upon their own people.

In Rio de Janeiro, a small group of black professionals, artists, and activists founded an organization devoted to Afro-Brazilian aesthetics and cultural advancement in 1944, just one year before the war's end. Named Teatro Experimental do Negro (TEN) it was led by Abdias do Nascimento, a multitalented performance and plastic artist. He was, and continues to be, one of the most dynamic, controversial figures within the black movement in Brazil.

TEN was founded with the primary intention of being a theatrical production company, but took on other cultural and political functions soon after its inception. In addition to conducting plays such as Eugene O'Neill's *Emperor Jones* (1945) and Albert Camus's *Caligula* (1949), TEN was also the driving force behind the journal *Quilombo* (1948–1950) and small-scale literacy campaigns and courses in "cultural initiation" between 1944 and 1946.[10]

In the third edition of *Quilombo*, Nascimento elaborated on TEN's multifaceted activities: "The Black Experimental Theater is not, in spite of its name, only an entity with artistic objectives. . . . it was inspired by the need of a social organization for people of color, with the elevation of their cultural level and individual values in mind."[11] TEN's written constitution also acknowledges the existence of a black intellectual elite and the use of theater as an instrument of struggle and redefinition of the black image.

As a consequence, TEN created the basis for contradictions between its vanguard and the masses, as well as between white and black elites. While ambitious, their cultural and ideological stances were conflicted. Maues (1988) notes that most of TEN's cultural activities involved more white intellectuals than blacks of any kind. She notes how the First Black Brazilian Conference of 1950 was a rather elitist gathering. There Nascimento declared that "The mentality of our population of color is still *pre-literate* and *pre-logical*" [emphasis mine], as justification for the need of a group such as TEN that would help the black masses rise to the cultural level of "the middle and upper classes of Brazilian society."[12]

Intellectuals—such as Guerreiro Ramos, a mulatto who was quite helpful and influential in TEN's pedagogical activities; Gilberto Freyre; Thales de Azevedo; and others who would later be severely criticized by the next generation of black intellectuals and activists in the 1960s—were involved with TEN during this period and participated in many of its events. White and black intellectuals converged in TEN because of a common belief in the African essence. "Primitivism, emotion, passion and exoticism appear as proper qualities of the 'black soul' and represented, in the opinion of its elites, the black contribution to the revitalizing process of the West."[13] This contribution, if recognized by Brazilian elites, would help counter white tendencies toward artistic and intellectual abstraction.

Here, rather starkly, we witness the inherent contradictions of Nascimento's earlier position, which internalized two reactionary features of the dominant ideological process. First, on an ethical-strategic level, it would be difficult to attract black masses, let alone literate and "logical" black critical intellectuals who were not part of this group, to such a position. Second, if one were to extend the essentialist logic of this group regarding the primordial elements of African culture, the "African oral tradition" would preclude the necessity of becoming literate at all, if being literate is defined by an ability to read and construct written text.

In an earlier analysis of the black intellectuals of TEN, Maues cogently stated that "the interpretations of the racial question produced by this group of black elites were incapable of effectively breaking with the parameters of dominant thought."[14] As noted at the outset of this chapter, the contradiction for black activists in the 1940s was the adherence to a notion of highly individuated social ascension coupled with advocacy of mass betterment, beliefs that were congruent with the paternalism of white elites. Yet at the same time, the activities of TEN and other groups in Rio de Janeiro and São Paulo after World War II provided the foundation for more confrontational groups in later periods that would valorize Afro-Brazilian and African culture. In this regard, as Maues notes, TEN was the segue between the ideologies of whitening and negritude.

Several black organizations and newspapers flourished briefly in the postwar period in Rio de Janeiro and São Paulo, with aspirations similar to those of TEN. In São Paulo, O Associação dos Negros Brasileiros, founded in 1945, also started the *Alvorada* as their official newspaper. The Associação Cultural do Negro, founded in 1954, published *O Mutirão*, which began in 1958. Other newspapers such as *O Novo Horizonte*, *Senzala*, and *Hifen* existed in the period between 1945 and 1960. Each publication had the normative strains of its time: social ascension, the necessity of a black elite, and a clamor for equal rights.

The first antidiscrimination law was enacted in 1951, known as the Afonso Arinos Law. Ironically, as Hasenbalg (1979) notes, the law was the result of an incident involving a black dancer from the United States, Katherine Dunham, who was barred lodging in a São Paulo hotel. Her subsequent protest led to a law that made racial discrimination a penalty subject to fine, but not imprisonment, amounting to a motor vehicle infraction. It would not be the last time that a U.S. African-American "import" would be a vehicle for exposing racial discrimination in Brazil.[15]

Also emerging in São Paulo in the 1950s and 1960s were small clubs and group associations catering to Afro-Brazilians. These clubs reflected the greater complexity of black petit-bourgeois and working class communities in São Paulo, as these Brazilians were entering the organized labor market for the first time, having been largely excluded through state policy and foreign immigration for forty years after abolition (Andrews 1988; 1991; Bastide 1965).

The founding of clubs such as Elite and Aristocrata were also responses to the exclusion of "new blacks" (Fernandes 1989) from groups and associations formed by whites—Italians, Portuguese, and other ethnic groups. As Raul dos Santos, founder of the Aristocrata Clube stated, "The Italians had a club, the Portuguese had a club, everyone else had a club—but not us (blacks)."[16]

Founded in 1961, the club sponsored debutante balls and student scholarships and provided financial and administrative assistance for several black political candidates for public office in the state of São Paulo. Clube Renascenca was formed in Rio de Janeiro with organizational intentions similar to those of Aristocrata Clube. Emergent black professionals who had been subtly and not-so-subtly barred from recreational facilities throughout the city formed a club of their own to accommodate a small but growing "elite negra" of white-collar professionals and clerical or service workers.

It should be noted that very little activity occurred during this period on the black left, which was a minority to begin with in the Frente Negra Brasiliera in São Paulo, and among the various groups in Rio de Janeiro. There were, in the 1940s, small socialist-oriented nuclei within existing black groups in Rio de Janeiro, São Paulo, and several other parts of the country, but they had few allies within these groups or in other, predominantly white organizations (Cunha 1988).

The "revolution" of 1964 brought most alternative political activities to a halt, with the exception of groups and individuals who engaged in armed conflict or public dispute with the military regime first headed by Castelo Branco (Skidmore 1988). The movimento negro was no exception and did not resurface in a public, organized manner until the early 1970s, as did other contestary groups. When it did resurface, however, the black movement assumed a character it never had prior to 1970.

1970–1990: Negritude, Afro-Marxism, and the Movimento Negro

The "new" character of the black movement in Brazil was in fact an old, latent trait that was developed and pronounced in the 1970s. That trait was leftist politics, which trudged along in fits and starts at the borders of several black organizations since the 1940s but, as implied above, was a "residual"[17] element in black political culture. What was unprecedented about the upsurge of groups and protest organizations during the 1970s was the confluence of race and class-based discourses within the black movement. Activists and followers alike abandoned the accommodationist and social mobility credos of the 1930 and 1940s respectively. By the end of the 1970s, those two forms of political discourse were discredited and marginalized within the black movement. Both came to be associated with statist, elitist values. Evidence of this ideological reversal can be found among numerous conferences and publications in this epoch.

The merging of internal and external tributaries, both historical and political, contributed to the reversal of longstanding political practices of acquiescent, clientelist exchanges with white political and cultural elites. The first, an internal factor, was the process of *distensão* (decompression) initiated by General Geisel during his tenure as presidential ruler of Brazil. With the offer of political amnesty to those in exile in 1979 and the increase in students entering colleges and universities as a result of distensão both new and old activists of the center-left had greater space for private debate about new tactics, as well as public criticism of the slowness of the decompression process. Former exiles who gained political insights in encounters with New Left groups in Western Europe, the United States, and other parts of Latin America shared these insights with the insurgent generation of activists and with the remaining militants of the pre-1964 era.

These so-called New Leftists attempted a more coalitional politics in Brazil, one which paid attention to issues such as race, ecology, and gender. Thus it is no accident that when political parties on the left were reconstituted in Brazil, most appeared with greater heterogeneity in terms of popular support and organizational agendas than those prior to 1964.

The second external tributary to influence the black movement in the 1970s was the proliferation of nonwhite or "Third World" insurrectionist movements in Asia, Africa, Latin America, and the Caribbean. As noted in Chapter 4, these events greatly influenced the tone and rhetoric of black activists in Brazil, although no one sought to replicate the full-scale revolt or openly confrontational tactics to be found in other "Third World" scenarios.

What had greater purchase among Afro-Brazilian activists in Brazil were the symbolic manifestations of nonwhite insurrection. A Negritude movement of sorts took place during this time, with supra-ideological manifestations among various segments of the movimento negro. So did a Black Soul movement in Rio de Janeiro, and in São Paulo with less resonance. As representations of the unification of national and international dimensions within Afro-Brazilian consciousness, these phenomena also signified a weariness with existing modes of cultural practice that had become commodified and in an existential sense, deracinated. Samba and Umbanda had become so nationalized that large segments of the white middle classes had pounced upon and claimed them as their own, in contrast to earlier points in the twentieth century when samba was considered the domain of the lower classes, black as well as white (Hasenbalg 1979; Schwarcz 1988).

In one of the few analyses of Umbanda within its socioeconomic and political context, Brown and Bick (1987) describe how Umbanda actually gained legal and social legitimacy during the period of military dictatorship after 1964: "This was facilitated by the new prominence of Umbandista military officers in leadership positions in Umbanda federations and churches. Their presence was a signal of the political conservatism represented in Umbanda's ideological emphasis on individual destiny and fate, and its ritual and cosmological focus on patronage relations, which did little to threaten the state."[18]

This is not to suggest that *escolas de samba* and *casas de Umbanda* were entirely white enclaves, or that Afro-Brazilian practitioners of samba or Umbanda wholly succumbed to the slow erosion of their spaces of cultural autonomy. Composers such as Nei Lopes and Paulinho da Viola, intrepid preservationists and innovators of Afro-Brazilian musical idioms, are two personifications of the role that Afro-Brazilian artists can play in political and cultural resistance. The dominant, almost gravitational pull of national politics and culture, however, made innovators such as Lopes and da Viola the rare agents of identity-based politics within samba schools.

The consequences of this pull were largely positive for the black movement. Masses of black Brazilians, who had never before gathered around issues of race, were attracted to the Brazilian versions of Negritude and Black Soul in the 1960s. Black militants created institutions, some ephemeral, that represented a path between extant left-right politics and the patron-client relationships normally utilized by Afro-Brazilian community leaders.

The last internal tributary to flow into these cultural and political reservoirs were black college-educated professionals. Many black professionals entered universities without racial consciousness, but through student activism and personal circumstance became militants for the black movement. As Hasenbalg (1979) acutely notes, this segment became politicized when it became clear to them that race, not training and education, was the principal key or impediment to socioeconomic advancement. All of these factors contributed to the rise of the *movimento negro* during this period. First we will turn to the cultural phenomena of the 1970s, Black Soul and Negritude.

Black Soul: A Threat to the National Project

Black Soul was one of several phenomena of the African Diaspora where people of African descent in one national-cultural context appropriated some of the symbolic and material forms from another. Anthropologist Peter Fry (1982) asserts: "The proliferation of Afro-Soul dances in São Paulo and Rio are instances where black Brazilians create new symbols of ethnicity, in accordance with their social experience. While some people believe that these phenomena are examples of 'cultural dependency' or of the capacity of the multinationals to sell whatever product, I have no doubt that, just the same, they represent a movement of major importance in the process of identity in Brazil."[19]

In contrast, Pierre-Michel Fontaine (1985) downplays the movement's significance because Black Soul had its genesis in the United States, and not Brazil. Fontaine's criticism of Black Soul, though brief, implies that the importance of a movement such as Black Soul is based upon its "authenticity," its originary gestation within an Afro-Brazilian matrix.

My interpretation of Black Soul parallels Fry's initial observation. Primary materials, events, and interviews with key figures of the Black Soul movement provide ample evidence to suggest that the Black Soul movement had as much to do with the "process of identity" creation among blacks in Brazil as with the alleged "importation" of cultural symbols. In fact, Black Soul, like Negritude, was a catalyst for an identity-based politics that continues today in the African Blocs and in several other organizations. Filo, one of the leading protagonists of the movement, stated during his interview, "Black Soul was not a fashion, it had an origin. A fashion does not last for fifteen years."[20] Filo was referring to the reconstitution and survival of many of the themes and rallying points of Black Soul in the phenomenon of "Funk" and "Charme," forms of dance and musical celebration that emerged in the 1980s with Black Soul's imprint, all of which have a basis in the development of a specifically "Afro-Brazilian" identity.

There is no official date for the start of the Black Soul movement, but its emergence was precipitated by the nascent popularity of U.S. "soul music" in Brazil. A white Brazilian disc jockey known as Big Boy is credited with first playing "soul" music on commercial public radio in 1967, on a show called *O Baile da Pesada*, which first attracted the attention of black Brazilians from Rio de Janeiro's Zona Norte.

Dance and party organizers in the north zone of the city began playing "soul." People such as Osseas "Mr. Funk" Santos, considered the originator of Black Soul and Filo developed reputations as able purveyors of this music, its attendant dances, styles of dress, and symbolic modes of protest. For many followers of Black Soul, James Brown was the principal interlocutor of this form of musical expression, with songs such as "Say it Loud (I'm Black and I'm Proud)," a major hit in the United States and among Black Soul participants in Brazil.

The music soon found its way into more traditional samba clubs and neighborhood associations, and ultimately into the Clube Renascenca—Rio's answer to the Aristocrata Clube—an exclusive club for upwardly mobile blacks. By 1970 the club's membership had changed greatly. It was no longer an enclave where working class and petit-bourgeois blacks with middle-class aspirations socialized among themselves. The external forces of the day, compounded by the new demands of civil society that were rooted in *abertura*, posed a challenge to clubs like Renascenca to adapt to new social realities.

There Filo and others began organizing and holding soul music dances, which attracted black Brazilians known as *Noites do Shaft* (Shaft's Night), named after the well-known 1974 U.S. film. This was two years before Black Rio was reported on as a social phenomenon by major daily newspapers like *Jornal do Brasil* and magazines such as *Veja*.[21] According to Filo, the influx of black Brazilians into Clube Renascenca with Afro hairstyles, high-heeled shoes, and other reified elements of the U.S. black experience during this period caused some dissonance among many of the club's leaders. This was due, in part, to the generational differences between participants in Black Soul and the black petit-bourgeois establishment of Renascenca. Yet the signifying forms of Black Rio were unprecedented, and may be a more important reason for the dissonance. Never before had black Brazilians collectively identified with cultural forms that were black but neither African nor Brazilian, the two categories through which sputterings of racial consciousness occurred in samba schools and houses of religious worship. In many instances, this process of identification had domestic repercussions in homes where black identity and consciousness was negated or repressed. The young women and men who participated in Black Soul often found themselves in conflict with parents, or as catalysts for family members who never before had confronted issues of racial oppression and identification. Thus hair and clothing styles became important not only in their symbolic representations but in their association with a collective identity that could not be defined solely within the boundaries of Brazil.

Dances organized by Mr. Funk or Filo in Zona Norte attracted three thousand to ten thousand people. Soon the popularity of these dances expanded beyond the confines of Clube Renascenca. The organizers of the dances at Renascenca left the club to form their own group, Soul Grand Prix, and held parties in various parts of Rio. Soul Grand Prix soon became a television show.

Soul Grand Prix also developed into a traveling multimedia event with slide presentations full of racially-specific imagery. Pictures of U.S. blacks in protest and self-adulation were abundant, which pleased many of the black participants but offended some whites. Grand Prix members thus altered the slides to suit the audience, deleting racial content from visual presentations in white clubs.

In situations where the constituency was overwhelmingly black, however, the slide presentations were a success. Newspaper reports and interviews with partygoers from the epoch confirm gestalt-like revelations by many individuals. Scenes of black people crying while viewing the slides and U.S. movies like *Wattstax*, and relating the imagery of blacks in the United States and elsewhere to their own experience, were not uncommon in clubs and dance halls where Soul Grand Prix produced events.

This facet of what came to be known as Black Soul brought consternation to both military and civilian elites. It must be remembered that Black Soul, as well as the proliferation of Afro-Brazilian groups in general, coincided with the most profoundly repressive phase of the dictatorship (1969–1975). At the level of propaganda and communication, a disseminated image of national unity was paramount, and any mention of racial discord, either within or outside of Brazil, was prohibited. Film censors were instructed to assess whether a film depicted racial problems in Brazil, dealt with the Black Power movement in the United States, or referred to racial problems in any way that could impact upon Brazil (Johnson and Stam 1982) as part of the criteria for censorship.[22] In an example of race-specific censorship in print journalism, one sentence of a reprinted article on chess from Britain's *Manchester Guardian* was censored: "The whites have great material advantage while the blacks have almost no legal opening."[23]

By the time Black Soul received media coverage in the late 1970s, it was criticized by the military government, which sought to invoke the increasingly bankrupt ideology of racial democracy, and by civilian elites who opposed the dictatorship but nonetheless believed that the exponents of Black Soul were fomenting racial hatred and conflict. Both cadres viewed Black Soul as a phenomenon that needed to be brought under control.

Because it was independent of white elite definitions of both national "Brazilianness" and Afro-Brazilian cultural practice, as well as resistant to appropriations by white elites. Black Soul was subject to criticism and, ultimately, repression. In a *Jornal do Brasil* article on Black Rio in 1977, the municipal secretary of tourism in Rio de Janeiro stated, "Black Rio is a commercial movement with a racist philosophy," with its development attributable to "a socio-cultural problem."[24] Pedro de Toledo Pizza, then municipal secretary, added that the movement was without any trace of authenticity.

Also on the issue of authenticity, a report was published in *Folha de São Paulo* regarding a teacher's denunciation of "external" musical influences of Black Rio which sullied Brazil's musical heritage of Afro-Brazilian music: "What is most tragic, above all, is that they are imposing a rhythm, a harmony, and a sound that has nothing to do with *our* [emphasis added] musicality. Worse still they are deceiving a band of innocents, who can not evaluate the importance of our musical treasure which has an African heritage."[25]

Criticism like the above was symptomatic of the emergent tensions between practitioners of Black Soul, and the many arbiters, white and black, of nationalized Afro-Brazilian culture. Several prominent sambistas and escolas de samba opposed Black Soul on the perceived basis of its invasion upon their turf and their own shrinking islands of cultural relevance. This was an ironic stance on the part of the more conservative samba schools, in light of the fact that it was commonplace for police to enter samba schools during this period and make indiscriminate arrests of up to two hundred young black males at one time, in the middle of the dance floor. As criticism intensified, it became clear that Black Soul could not coexist with the existing paradigm of national culture.

The reason it could not was based only in small part on the musical and symbolic innovations of Black Soul practitioners. These critiques were arguably only a pretext for the more significant anxiety of white elites, both civil and military, that Black Soul was the harbinger of a protest movement by Afro-Brazilians. For such a movement to occur, Afro-Brazilians would have to develop forms of critical consciousness and organization that were specific to them, and therefore not national, inasmuch as national signified the repression of racial identities and race-specific claims. To allow such a process to occur would be to admit, nationally, to both racial discrimination *and* racial identification.

None other than Gilberto Freyre sounded the alarm against Black Soul for precisely the two-part rationale offered above. In a 1977 article published in *Diario de Pernambuco* entitled "Attention Brazilians," Freyre warned his fellow nationals of the threat Black Soul posed to both national identity and security:

> Perhaps my eyes are deceiving me? Or did I really read that the United States will be arriving in Brazil. . . . Americans of color . . . why? . . . to convince, Brazilians, also of color, that their dances and their "Afro-Brazilian" songs would have to be of "melancholy" and "revolt"? And not, as it is today . . . sambas which are almost all happy and fraternal. If what I have read is true, it is once more an attempt to introduce into a Brazil that is growing fully, fraternally brown (moreno)—what appears to cause jealousy in nations that are also bi or tri-racial- the myth of negritude, not of Senghor's type, of the just valorization of black or African values, but that which brings at times that "class struggle" as an instrument of civil war, not of the lucid Marx the sociologist, but the other: the inspirator of a militant marxism with its provocation of hatred. . . . What must be made salient, in these difficult times which the world is living in, with a terrible crisis of leadership . . . Brazil needs to be ready for work being done against it, not only of Soviet imperialism . . . but of the United States as well.[26]

The justification for such an extensive quote here is the links that Freyre's critique of Black Soul makes with denunciations of Negritude, Marxism, and two imperialisms. For Freyre, Negritude is mythical when emphasis is placed on militancy, protest, and not on the valorization of African culture. When the former is highlighted and not the latter, Freyre sees class struggle and, ultimately, militant Marxism lurking behind it.

Freyre was not alone in this belief. The widespread repression in the mid-1970s of even liberal critiques of the dictatorship, well documented in the São Paulo archdiocese report (Brasil: *Nunca Mais* 1985) on torture in Brazil after 1964 confirms that the anticommunist hysteria of the time was such that any dissenting voice was perceived as part of the broader Marxist conspiracy. Consequently, any group or individual protesting against the military regime and environment of terror, communist or not, could have been, and often was, subject to censorship or physical repression. Thus members of Black Soul in Rio de Janeiro and São Paulo—whose activities included passing around copies of Stokely Carmichael's *Black Power* and Frantz Fanon's *Wretched of the Earth* for group discussion, among other items—were (mis)identified as part of the conspiracy theory held and propagated by civilian and military elites. There is no documentation available on the surveillance and perceptions of Black Soul and the black movement in general during this period, due to the nature of the regimes during the dictatorship. However, a high-ranking official of the National Information Service, the resourceful intelligence arm of the state, confirmed during a personal interview that several black activists were closely monitored in the 1970s because of the state's belief that they were mere cogs in the ever-turning wheel of communist conspiracy.[27]

As for Freyre's criticism of Negritude, two things should be noted. First, Negritude took hold in a very diffuse way among individuals and groups in Brazil, mostly as an attitude, rather than a movement with a clear politics. Negritude as a belief system was one facet of a wider, insurgent recognition of things African, or of the "diaspora."[28]

Lastly, as for the recurring construction of "authenticity" in Brazilian culture, the criticism of Freyre and others neglect the fact that the "authentic" samba, which most Brazilians had come to know and exercise was a samba that had been appropriated by the white middle classes and elites in the post–World War II period, when it was discovered by these social groups as an inexpensive means of leisure. As Fry (1982), Brown (1974) and others have shown, samba, like Capoeira and Candomble, was considered a lower-class form of recreation reserved for very poor whites, and of course, Brazilians of African descent. Therefore, the appropriation of the practices relating to Black Soul by Afro-Brazilians was no less "authentic" than the elite appropriation of samba, which can be vividly witnessed in the yearly competitions and spectacles of Carnaval. In this sense Black Soul can be seen as a counterbricolage to extant constructions of Afro-Brazilian and therefore national identity.

Moreover, many Black Soul dances were held in samba schools, largely due to the high cost of renting dance halls, and the reluctance on the part of many white owners to allow throngs of black Brazilians into their buildings. Once inside, samba and Black Soul enthusiasts mixed, in most cases, dance and music without conflict. Indeed, this intersection also led in some cases, to new, more experimental samba compositions.

While Black Soul did have its political moments, it never left the confines of the dance hall. The principal figures of Black Soul in Rio de Janeiro were considered Americanistas (see Chapter 4) and were disparaged as crass materialists by several factions of the movimento negro. According to their critics, this image was confirmed by the involvement of

Filo and others in the production of several commercial record albums and in organizing concerts featuring black U.S. soul performers.

Part of the difficulty in bridging the chasm between political and cultural practices was the incorporation of Black Soul by the Rio de Janeiro tourist and entertainment industry, which soon became more than able competitors for the handful of black production companies who were turning a small profit. Monsieur Lima, a white Carioca club owner who sponsored *bailes soul* in Zona Sul (Botafogo) by contracting groups like Black Power and Soul Grand Prix, went so far as to suggest that the dances were not only commercially viable, but were forms of social control as well: "If not for these dances, what would the mass of people do on Saturdays and Sundays? How would they enjoy themselves? If they didn't have this I guarantee there would be a great increase in assaults on the weekend by these people who have nothing to do . . . the government must encourage it (the dances)."[29]

Thus, the sixteen to twenty-year-olds who flocked to the weekend soul festivals were viewed as a criminal element, despite the well-documented fact, as Vianna[30] and others have noted, of the absence of drugs, alcohol, fighting, and other forms of social disturbance. This distanced black participants and activists from the north zone from events which, after 1976, became increasingly commercialized.

In São Paulo, several activists of the mid-1970s mentioned during interviews however, that unlike the Funk and Charme parties of the 1980s, Black Soul events were fertile occasions for pamphleteering and dissemination of information regarding marches, discussions, and other events pertaining to the movimento negro. The Chã bridge (*Viaducto de Chã*), a major thoroughfare in the center of São Paulo, was the meeting place for "blacks" (i.e., those of the movimento "Black") and blacks who directly participated across the full spectrum of sociopolitical positions of the center-left in the 1970s. While Black Soul promoters and disc jockeys were perhaps sympathetic to the covert political activity during this period, they were not agents for such activities themselves. Here, we can distinguish political *empathy* and political *praxis*, insofar as political empathy can be characterized as a feeling for certain practices, while, praxis is articulated in the *assumption* of responsibilities *and* feeling of political participation. This was quite unlike the use of soccer matches in public stadiums in South Africa, or for that matter funerals or other public forums where African National Congress members met to strategize during numerous cycles of repression in the 1970s. Despite their symbolic repercussions, the parties were ends in themselves. Hence the divide between political and cultural practices of Black Soul and other, more explicitly political Afro-Brazilian groups of the period.

This view is echoed in the work of Rodrigues da Silva (1983), in one of the few scholarly analyses of the Black Soul phenomenon. Focusing on the emergence of Black Soul in Campinas, São Paulo after 1978, Rodrigues da Silva describes how its appearance there represented a process of ethnic identification as well as the material production of leisure. The empresarios of Black Campinas were the offspring of the traditional, middle-class black families well represented in samba schools and social clubs for upwardly mobile Paulistanos negros. While their activities within the movimento soul were in some respects counter to the traditional assumptions about black elites forgetting their ethnic and African origins, their functions belied the empresario's middle-class origins. There was an implicit acceptance of white, bourgeois values, evidenced in the preoccupation of both organizers and partygoers with *comportamento* (behavior), being well-groomed (which was purported obverse of blacks, who were generally unkept), and a desire to occupy a social space that heretofore had been denied to them in high culture.[31]

In contrast, Mr. Funk, Filo, and many other figures of Black Soul–Black Rio were from poor backgrounds, and built a following in the predominantly black north section of the city before attracting the attention of the mass media. Filo and Carlos Alberto Medieros penned a newspaper column pertaining to Black Soul events under the pseudonym of J.B.

By 1978 though, the attacks and discrediting in the mass media, coupled with the rising popularity of disco music, had telling effects on Black Soul. The parties, newspaper columns, record contracts, and television specials petered out. Funk and Charme, dance hall phenomena in the 1980s with their basis in black U.S. music was reminiscent of Black Soul, but without glimpses of alternative forms of racial identification found in the slide presentations, films, and literature circulating in and around their predecessor.[32]

How then to assess Black Soul? I concur with Rodrigues da Silva's assertion that final judgment of its merits is not an either/or proposition, a matter of determining whether either the commodification of leisure or ethnic agglutination was predominant in the movement. Clearly both are evidenced in the discussion above, with each made prominent in particular moments. Perhaps the most important barometer of Black Soul as a critical attempt at strong resemblance in Brazil is the reaction it evoked in white elites. They recognized a dangerous undercurrent to the images projected, in Brazil, of black social protest elsewhere, and its impact upon black Brazilians. Here is where the significance and the incompleteness of the Black Soul movement lies, in its valorization of forms of self-expression and identification that were previously repressed or denied by both whites and nonwhites in Brazil. That these new ways of self-expression and identification did not materialize into something broader reflects the boundaries imposed by white elites upon Black Soul, as well as its own limitations. Raymond Williams (1977) persuasively characterizes this facet of alternative cultural emphases and the inadvertent challenges under-studied "fashions" like Black Soul often pose for the status quo:

> Alternative political and cultural emphases, and the many forms of opposi-tion and struggle, are important not only in themselves but as indicative features of what the hegemonic process has in practice had to work to con-trol . . . . Any hegemonic process must be especially alert and responsive to the alternatives and opposition which question and threaten its dominance. The reality of cultural process must then always include the efforts and con-tributions of those who are in one way or another outside or at the edge of the terms of the specific hegemony.[33]

The Movimento Negro: New Organizations, the Movimento Negro Unificado

Black Soul was not an isolated phenomenon. Other, new Afro-Brazilian organizations emerged during the period of Black Soul. Their prolifera-tion signaled the emergence of a new generation of black intellectuals in major cities like Rio de Janeiro and São Paulo, but also in Salvador, Brasilia, and Pernambuco. In the postdictatorship period the task for in-surgent activists across the country was to attempt a new politics. Afro-Brazilian activists in the new age of emerging democracy did not want to regress to the previous limitations of either leftist economic determinism or the patron-clientelism of the right.

In Rio de Janeiro, the two most prominent organizations to emerge in the 1970s were the Society for Brazil-Africa Exchange (SINBA) and the Institute for Study of the Black Cultures (IPCN or Instituto de Pesquisa das Culturas Negras). They were founded in 1976 and 1975, respectively. While both organizations grew out of the same group discussions at Can-dido Mendes University in Ipanema, their existence reflected the emer-gence of differences, and divisions within the movimento over tactical and ideological affinities. As detailed in Chapter 4, SINBA was considered the more Africanist group, while IPCN was portrayed (somewhat disparag-ingly in some circles within the movement) as more Americanist. The pos-itive aspects of this perceived Americanism was the advocacy of direct so-cial protest for civil rights and the development of black institutions that would parallel white ones. Negative aspects were—in the minds of some of its detractors—a preoccupation with individual mobility and uncritical acceptance of capitalism as a dynamic social force.

In São Paulo both individuals and groups appeared to be far more com-prehensive and ambitious in their attempts at projecting the movimento negro onto a national stage than activists in Rio de Janeiro. While the Unified Black Movement (MNU or Movimento Negro Unificado) was the most obvious manifestation of this difference, there were important precursors to MNU. Grupo Evolução, formed in 1971 in Campinas by Carioca Thereza Santos and the São Paulo intellectual Eduardo Oliveira de Oliveira, infused political and ideological issues into their cultural presentations—plays, poetry readings, dances and festivals. Their use of culture, especially performance arts, as pedagogical and political devices to educate Afro-Brazilians greatly influenced the future leaders of MNU, such as Hamilton Cardoso, the late Vanderei Jose Maria, and Rafael Pinto, they saw these practices as powerful distinctions between the culturalism that plagued the *movimento negro* up to that point and cultural practices linked to party or organizational politics.

The Centro de Cultura é Arte Negra (CECAN), in which Santos and Oliveira de Oliveira were also involved, served a similar purpose for militants with still undecided political affiliations emerging from the shadows of political repression. Other organizations and events attempting a cultural-political synthesis were the first meeting of black organizations at São Paulo (I Encontro de Entidades Negras de São Paulo) and the first week of Black Art and Culture at São Paulo (I Semana do Negro do Arte e na Cultura de São Paulo) in 1975; the House Association of Afro-Brazilian Art and Culture (Associação Casa de Arte é Cultura Afro-Brasileiro or ACACAB), founded in 1977, and the Black Communitarian Festival—Zumbi (Festival Comunitario Negro-Zumbi or FECONEZU), which was first held in Araraquara, São Paulo, in 1978 in commemoration of the death of Zumbi of Palmares. Newspapers such as *Jornegro* and journals such as *Avore de Palavras* and *Cadernos Negros* undertook similar campaigns.

The period of dictatorship after 1964 compounded the difficulty of open discussion of racial issues in Brazil, and as a consequence, further reliance upon expressive culture as a vehicle for political discourse. Political organizations and activities that did not fall on the ARENA-MDB continuum, the only two political parties during the period of military dictatorship, were treated as criminal entities.

Maria Ercilia do Nascimento (1989) highlighted the predominance of culturalist groups during this period and the contradictions that culturalist positions posed for the black movement. She suggests that "the cultural question was decisive in the definition of the paths of the black movement in general and the Movimento Negro Unificado in particular. Black, blackness, negritude, are expressions that came to dominate the language and practice of currents and organizations."[34]

This is, to a large extent, true. The overwhelming majority of groups in Rio and São Paulo, not to mention the rest of Brazil, had on some level focused on an originary return to African "roots" as the basis of *any* political or cultural practice. Here Negritude operated as a cornerstone for the edifice of *negro* definition, the celebration of "otherness" and differentiation from the West. Its symbolic manifestations were found in the emphasis on wearing west African garb, name changing, the aforementioned donning of Afro hairstyles during the Black Soul period. Its political manifestations were in the attempts, slowly but increasingly successful, to expand the teaching of African and Afro-Brazilian histories in the Brazilian educational system.

Yet many sought to link this political practice of cultural grounding to demands for more egalitarian benefits for Brazilians of African descent in general—better health care, educational, and labor opportunities. Several activist-intellectuals recognized the need for a transitional step from expressive culture to cultural politics, the employment of cultural practices as a means to collective advancement and not as ends in themselves. This is evidenced in several self-critical articles that appeared in various newspapers and journals of the black press. As late as 1980, SINBA published an article entitled "The Black Movement and Culturalism," an example of this worry. Although no mention is made of specific culprits, the warning of its dangers for the black movement is made clear: "Those who believe that the idolatry of culture is a cultural practice are deceiving themselves. . . . the reverence of cultural values stops being conservative attitudes when culture becomes something dynamic, and a truthful cultural practice is necessarily creative and transformative. PEOPLE DO NOT WORSHIP CULTURE, THEY PRODUCE IT."[35]

The article proceeded to discuss how cultural practices should be a starting point for a trajectory toward political and ideological thought, and not an end in themselves. Interesting to note as well is how this passage reflects an identification of the relationship between culturalism and conservativism. While SINBA's criticism was explicitly aimed at conservative samba schools in general, this criticism could have also been made of SINBA.

For while many of the new groups, SINBA included, had rejected the old order, they had not yet created new organizational vehicles that bridged the gap between vanguard and mass. The problem, it appears, for the entities in these two cities was the inability of episodic, mostly artistic events to sustain the political interest and support of black communities. IPCN, which was located in the predominantly white Zona Sul, had more resources than its rival in Zona Norte, SINBA, but those proceeds were invested more in cultural rather than political activities. Paul Roberto, former president of IPCN commented:

> IPCN . . . I thought, was a euphemism for the creation of an entity that would seek to work not only on the cultural level, but would be able to be an entity of black political mobilization. But it ended up having, since its begin-

ning, not political activity, but principally culturalist work. I think that a group of people with economic power within the organization . . . the majority who were on the board of directors. . . . Thus this group, by virtue of the simple fact of having money . . . imposed certain taxes of character which were extremely culturalist. And what were these taxes? . . . a little show here . . . a little theatre there; this type of thing was very negative for the entity. In this respect, the people (IPCN) had a political loss.[36]

Roberto concluded by stating that IPCN's culturalist proclivities implicitly set the ideological tone for other fledgling groups in Rio de Janeiro.

The absence of a party-like structure hurt the movimento negro during this phase. In spite of the Black Brazilian Front's brief success as an organization and political party in the 1930s, most black protest in the country had been limited to relatively isolated individuals and associational groupings of lower-middle-class origins, making even the front's undertakings, on a national level, highly uncoordinated, even contradictory. The numerous groups of the 1970s continued this trend. What was needed was an organization with the structure of a political party but with modes of outreach like that of a social movement.

The catalyst for the development of such an organization was, ironically, a clandestine organization with an ideological basis in the Trotskyist version of Marxism, the Socialist Convergence (Convergencia Socialista). The Socialist Convergence was one training ground for several important intellectuals of the Unified Black Movement who later, out of frustration with the strategies of the Convergence, left its membership. Not, however, without developing valuable writing and political skills that were later employed in the movimento.

The Convergence was the most ideologically radical and militant cell of the remaining leftist groups in São Paulo after the institutionalization of the dictatorship. Many of its members were still committed to armed struggle years after the 1964 coup, when the military state had long institutionalized, if not legitimated, its power. Within the Convergence was a nucleus of black Trotskyists, led by Jorge Pinheiro, now a journalist in São Paulo. According to several former members of the Convergence who were interviewed, black militants were first attracted to the Socialist Convergence in the years immediately following the coup because of Trotsky's strategic collaboration with C.L.R. James. James was an Afro-Trinidadian intellectual and activist in the Marxist tradition whose political imagination informed various Pan-Africanist, anticolonial, and Black Power movements in Africa, the Caribbean, and the United States until his death in 1989.[37]

Trotsky had discussions with James over the linkage of struggles for racial equality in the United States with the worker-oriented concerns of the Communist party while Trotsky was exiled in Mexico in the 1930s. Those discussions were published, otherwise disseminated, and found their way into the hands of Brazilian leftists exiled in the early 1970s in France, Great Britain, and other Western European countries.

Their conjuncture of race and class was eagerly received by black militants who had been historically alienated by the materialist positivism of the white Brazilian left. Flavio Carrança, Hamilton Cardoso, the late Vanderlei Jose Maria, Milton Barbosa, Rafael Pinto and others joined the Convergence cell in São Paulo. They would later emerge as pivotal figures in the creation of the Movimento Unificado Contra Discriminação Racial, which later became the MNU.

Versus became the periodical of the Convergence, and was published between 1977 and 1979. In keeping with the nucleus's ideological orientation, members of the black socialist nucleus formed their own section within *Versus*, entitled "Afro-Latino America." Hamilton Cardoso, Jamu Minka, and Nueza Pereira wrote the first articles for the section, although other black militants would later craft essays and commentary.

"Afro-Latino America" reflected the diversity within the emergent black movement with writings on African socialism, police violence, dialogues between blacks and indigenous Brazilians, the three-tiered oppression of black women, literature, and many other issues. While periodicals that were the direct output of the black movement existed such as *Avore de Palavras* and *Jornegro*,[38] none were as editorially sophisticated and wide-ranging as *Versus*; nor were they directly linked to an oppositional political formation, as "Afro-Latino America" and its producers were. This is not to suggest that "Afro-Latino America" was a mere organ of the Convergence. It was not. In fact, constant differences over the editorial direction of *Versus*, due to conflicts over the direction of the Convergence, resulted in the departure of many black militants from its pages, and their departure from the Convergence altogether.

While many of the articles in "Afro-Latino America" reflected the youth of their authors (most were in their early twenties), they signified a process of speculation over the degrees to which the subordination of black Brazilians was conditioned by racial exploitation with material subordination as one of its principal forms. While most articles did not downplay the social reality of class antagonisms in Brazil, there was an explicit refusal to subsume race under the category of class. Marx may have turned the Hegelian dialectic on its head, but the writers for "Afro-Latino America" turned Marx's own dialectic of historical materialism on its side, to construct, as others had done in nationalist movements in Africa and the Caribbean, a parallel analysis of race and class in national society and culture. While decidedly in favor of the creation of a socialist party with an emphasis on labor politics, they advocated a contingent

Afro-Brazilian stance *within* the party in relation to the party's treatment of issues of discrimination, police violence, and labor market segmentation. An example of this, taken from an "Afro-Latino America" article in support of the eventual creation of a labor party and not a social-democratic one, follows:

> Blacks, with all of their problems, will only have a solution, if instead of accepting this alternative and being towed into this party, create nuclei which depend upon culture, political discussion, ideological armament. Create black ideology and theories relating to their problems. If these nuclei do not form a unity, a front of thought to formulate a solution for the situation in Brazil separate from UDN, PSD, MDB, and ARENA, that will signify that the black has still not assumed a position of ideological independence, capable of restudying their problem within Brazilian society.[39]

This, in effect, contains the ideological embryo and "third path" position of the Unified Black Movement, actualized not only during MNU's founding and subsequent activities but in the creation of Afro-Brazilian nuclei within the Partido dos Trabalhadores (PT) and the Partido Democratico dos Trabalhadores (PDT) in the 1980s. Soon afterward several other political parties such as PCB would follow suit.

The confluence of race and class issues within a political formation of leftist activists from a subordinated group is not unique to Brazil. The rhetoric of Pan-African socialism in the Caribbean or Africa and the failed projects of racial egalitarianism undertaken in Guyana and Suriname are some examples of this. What is unusual about the Brazilian case is that activists linked to MNU seemed to permanently oscillate between the spheres of party politics and the *movimento* negro rather than opting for party politics at the expense of the black movement, or vice versa. This was helped, in large part, by the mutual accommodation of the labor movement and the black movement to their respective—often common—concerns, which had not occurred prior to the 1970s.

The increasingly untenable positions of the Convergence, such as its romantic adherence to Trotsky's notion of permanent revolution and the compartmentalization of the "Afro-Latino America" team within the journal caused disillusionment among section members.[40] Writers like Vanderlei Jose Maria and Hamilton Cardoso left *Versus* and the Convergence by the time of *Versus*'s final publication in 1979. Nevertheless, *Versus* was a site of gestation for black intellectuals. The staff of "Afro-Latino America" became important figures in the formation of one of the few explicitly political, nonculturalist attempts at a national black movement in Brazil.

To tie up an earlier point then, the tactical and ideological positions taken by "Afro-Latin America" was a precursor to MNU. These positions were decisive for both MNU and the movement in general, as were the ambiguous strains of culturalism. For the first time in Brazil, the advocacy of a race-class position was not marginalized by the Afro-Brazilian intelligentsia, and in fact had come to supplant accommodationist, assimilationist paradigms as the dominant position of the black movement. What was missing, by the latter part of the 1970s, were events to propel these intellectual and political positions into forms of praxis.

The event that galvanized black activists in São Paulo, and subsequently in other areas of Brazil, including Rio de Janeiro, was the torture and murder of Robson Luz, a black taxi driver, at the hands of São Paulo police in April 1978. This was neither the first nor the last act of racial violence perpetrated by the state against blacks, but it was seen by activists as one that warranted a response. The militants of São Paulo and Rio decided a public act would be the first real attempt to recapture the public space lost during the dictatorship, and a test of the state's purported commitment to democracy and racial harmony. In June, the Movimento Negro Unificado Contra Discriminação Racial (MNUCDR) was created by militants from Rio de Janeiro and São Paulo, where it was decided that their first public act would be a demonstration in front of the municipal theater in downtown São Paulo.[41]

On 7 July 1978, an open letter to the Brazilian population was read to approximately two thousand people on the steps of the Teatro Municipal in São Paulo:

> Today we are in the street in a campaign of denouncement! A campaign against racial discrimination, against police repression, underemployment and marginalization. We are in the street to denounce the very poor quality of life of the Black Community. . . . The Unified Black Movement Against Racial Discrimination was created as an instrument of struggle for the Black Community. This movement must have as its basic principle work to permanently denounce all acts of racial discrimination, the constant organization of the Community in order to confront whatever type of racism . . . For this reason we propose the creation of CENTERS OF STRUGGLE OF THE UNIFIED BLACK MOVEMENT AGAINST RACIAL DISCRIMINATION in the neighborhoods, towns, prisons, lands of candomble, our lands of umbanda, in the workplace, in the samba schools, the churches, everywhere black people live: CENTERS OF STRUGGLE that will promote debate, information, consciousness raising and organizing of the black community. . . . We invite the democratic sectors of society that support us, creating the necessary conditions for a truthful racial democracy.[42]

Soon afterward, CT's (*Centros de Luta*) were formed in Salvador, Bahia, Porto Alegre, and Espirito Santo. The ambitious, yet motivating principle of MNU was to be an overarching entity for all black militant

organizations in the country. MNU, like most other Afro-Brazilian political organizations of the epoch, was organizationally biased against
political conservatives, black or otherwise, who were less visible and self-
congratulatory after the failures of the economic miracle and quasi-totali-
tarian policies of the mid-seventies. The strategic positions of liberals and
conservatives on the one hand, and those of MNU on the other, were
mutually exclusive.[43]

One of MNU's first thrusts into national debate was over the question
of amnesty for political prisoners in November 1978 in São Paulo. MNU
wanted to expand the category of "political prisoners" to include blacks
imprisoned for materially based crimes (theft, robbery, etc.) on the
grounds that while these "crimes" appear to be individual acts, they are
nonetheless political responses to an elite that denied employment, housing, and education to a majority of its citizens. MNU went further in their
condemnation of the conditional amnesty by arguing that blacks, who are
more prone to be arrested than whites to begin with, are disproportionately subject to beatings and tortures, which, in effect, makes their predicament analogous to white political prisoners.

In their criticism of the restrictive amnesty program that was instituted
by the Brazilian government, MNU declared, "The hand that indiscriminately assassinates blacks is the same that arrests students, workers, with
the same result; to keep the population oppressed . . . and disorganized,
and in the end maintain the privileges of the minority that is seated in
power."[44]

In December 1979, the first national Congress of MNU was held in
Rio de Janeiro. Resolutions were enacted regarding national organization, structure, and support of various political candidates in electoral politics. Like church and labor leaders who were voices of dissent during the
1970s, MNU also called for more radical agrarian reform, protection of
squatter settlements, workers' rights to unionize, and a revamping of the
educational system as part of their sixteen-point plan of action.

Regarding the specific agenda for Afro-Brazilians, some of their points
included references and proposals for the discrimination against black
woman, homosexuals, and prostitutes. MNU, along with feminist and
other organizations, coordinated their second public demonstration at
the Teatro Municipal, followed by a march in protest against increased
harassment by the police against prostitutes, homosexuals, blacks, and the
poor in general on 13 June 1979.

These activities initiated by MNU and black groups that supported
them worried some white elites. Gilberto Freyre, in an oblique reference
to MNU, relayed his response to a United Press interview on Brazilian
racism in a *Folha de São Paulo* editorial in 1979: "I have news of a movement calling itself anti-racist in São Paulo. I believe that it is a considerable

imitation—voluntary or organized, of the revindications of the so-called "black american" of the United States. Now, in Brazil there is no "Black Brazilian," separate from the national brazilian community. There exists, yes, Brazilians of Black—African origin, some of which suffer discrimination, not of a racial character, but of class."[45]

Another example of elite anxiety regarding the upsurge in black activism, this time on an international scale, are the following comments by Antonio Neder, president of the federal supreme tribunal in 1979. What is remarkable about the comments below is that they were made during a speech in honor of the International Day against Racial Discrimination, March 21. With ambassadors from several African countries present, Mr. Neder stated that racism "must be eliminated, well before, the stupidity of racism, so that their grandchildren [read whites] do not come to be victimized, tomorrow, by the vengeance of a black Hitler, defender of the races defined as inferior by the erroneous doctrine . . . of Gobineau."[46]

With the absence of available documentation of state behavior pertaining to the surveillance of black militant groups and assumptions about their actions, responses like the ones above provide only glimpses of broader, more comprehensive belief systems that motored the defense of racial democracy. Nonetheless, MNU activities were considered to be examples of reverse racism, whereby black militants unnecessarily perpetrated acts of racism by claiming racism's existence in Brazil. Freyre categorically denies the existence of race prejudice in Brazil to begin with. Therefore, according to Freyre, the claims made by "Brazilians of African origin" were disingenuous.

Neder's "innovation upon racial democracy," as an editorial in *SINBA* characterized it, is surprising when one considers that he was invited to present a commemorative address at Itamarati about racial discrimination and struggles against it.[47] What unites Freyre and Neder is the presupposition that claims of, or even revenge against, racist practices are tantamount to claims of racial superiority and hence racism itself. These are just two more examples of the theoretical claim made earlier about racial democracy's hegemonic ability, in the actions of white elites, to reduce most debates about the substantive manifestations and consequences of racial discrimination in Brazil to disagreements about whether racial prejudice exists at all. Indeed, although no charges against MNU were filed by the state, several government officials suggested after MNU held its second national assembly in 1979 that the organization was violating the Afonso Arinos Law!

MNU's view of supporting political parties was that of an independent. Although many of its members were part of the PT by the time of the party's founding in 1980, MNU operated separately from it and other parties. MNU aided only those parties and individual candidates whose stance on race and other issues were congruent with its own. Its support of individual candidates, however, appear to have had little bearing on the outcome of elections, given the overall weak presence of blacks in electoral politics. With the exception of the 1988 election of Luiza Erundina as mayor of São Paulo, few candidates having the backing of MNU have been voted into public office.

After the initial fervor of the late 1970s and early 1980s, MNU appears to have lost some of its momentum. By the late 1980s, however, a new generation of MNU activists emerged in various parts of the country. Ambitious to begin with, the centers of struggle vary widely in activity and influence in communities nationwide (Gonzalez and Hasenbalg 1985). While they are active in areas where the black movement in general is visibly operative, the MNU has become just one organization among many, rather than the overarching entity that it was intended to be. There were too many groups, often with competing programs, for any single organization to function in an umbrella-like fashion. This problematic is similar to Campello de Souza's 1989 analysis of the Party of the Brazilian Democratic Movement (PMDB) during the abertura, when multiple ideological tendencies could no longer be contained within a single party, and the party's base of support began to wane with the proliferation of political parties and organizations. It remains to be seen whether MNU, like PMDB, will lose its importance within the movement as a consequence of political mobilization, or if it will become restructured in pursuit of new strategies in the 1990s.

Sparse material resources have been a major obstacle to the implementation of projects and the creation of policies that reach into predominantly black and mulatto-based favelas in Rio de Janeiro and São Paulo. Several key members of MNU leadership have been also involved in labor disputes and strikes, thereby depleting the already paltry finances of MNU. Milton Barbosa, a member of transit worker's union and a labor activist as well, has been involved in protracted labor strikes through the 1980s. Neither MNU, nor many of the other organizations are financially self-reproducing and rely on grants, community and personal contributions for their existence.

This material deficit points to a major structural difference between "middle class" activists within the movimento and their white Brazilian counterparts, exposing the precarious socioeconomic location of the black middle status group members who are engaged in political activity. Many are one generation removed from illiteracy and poverty. A general strike, severe medical ailment or other potential form of material deprivation can—and often did—place several activists of the 1970s and 1980s nearer to the material circumstances of their parents than those of Paulista or Carioca liberal professionals. In this respect, their ambiguous location within relationships of production is more reminiscent of E. Franklin Frazier's "black bourgeoisie" than the institutionally based, emergent, powerful class a host of German sociologists have written about as the motive force of the Industrial Revolution. Again, the socioeconomic impact of race fundamentally alters the neat axis of class analysis.

The "resource mobilization" approach of Aldon Morris (1984) concerning the cultural-structural basis of the U.S. civil rights movement is relevant for an analysis of the limited resources available to the movimento negro in Brazil. Morris posits that collective action grows out of pre-existing structures and political processes, suggesting further that a dominated group's ability to organize, mobilize, and manage valuable resources determines the extent of its social protest.[48] The dependence of many Afro-Brazilian organizations on noncommunity funding sources, particularly those of grant institutions outside of Brazil, coupled with minimal infrastructure within their own communities to raise funds independently, keep records of expenditures and profits relating to cultural events designed to generate revenue, has greatly hindered the development and mobilization of material resources for cultural and political purposes.[49]

Race, Gender, and Religious-Based Mobilization

São Paulo activist Sueli Carneiro has described the black women's movement as "an intersection between the black movement and the women's movement," which is an accurate description of both the theoretical and practical complexities of the role of Afro-Brazilian women within the movimento negro, and their own autonomist position in relation to white feminists. While there is a rich literature on women's movements in Brazil and Latin America more generally, there is very little scholarly work on Afro-Brazilian women.[50] Like the subject of race in Brazil, the dearth of scholarly literature on Afro-Brazilian women's movements will only be remedied by the production of scholarly work by Afro-Brazilian feminist activists and by Afro-Brazilian women who are sensitive to the issues therein.

The location of Afro-Brazilian women in Brazilian society, like the predicament of women of African descent elsewhere, is largely informed by the three-dimensional relationship between race, class, and gender. As highlighted in Chapter 2, Afro-Brazilian women have had both market opportunities and limitations determined by their gender. Work by Peggy Lovell, Charles Wood, and George Reid Andrews have noted how Afro-Brazilian women have had greater employment opportunities than Afro-Brazilian men in less skilled areas but less employment opportunities in highly skilled professions. This predicament is not unlike the relationships and disparities between U.S. African-American women and men in relation to labor markets.

In political terms, Afro-Brazilian women and men are also at similar disjunctures with regard to racial and class oppression. While several groups such as MNU developed feminist perspectives and agendas by the late 1970s, there was also the reproduction of patriarchical activities within the movement that fostered discord between male and female activists. A well-worn phrase, "The personal is political," aptly characterizes the frustrations experienced by women within the movement in the mid-1970s. Many Afro-Brazilian male activists preached equality between the sexes as part of their political rhetoric but expected Afro-Brazilian women to perform the tasks of the conventional housewife while they participated fully within in the movement and sometimes in relationships with other women.

For Afro-Brazilian women involved in the movimento, this disjuncture served to underscore the need for political strategies and theoretical positions that were independent of the masculinist version of the movimento. The masculinism within the movimento not only led to tensions between Afro-Brazilian men and women, but also led to a hierarchy and prioritizing of issues along gender lines as well.

On the other hand, the white Brazilian left often reproduced the elitism of their professional socialization and personal experience, neglecting the manifestations of racial and gendered inequality in their own homes. One incident best characterizes this paradox. By 1980, discussions concerning the formation of a new Labor party (PT) were taking place in São Paulo in the homes of many key intellectuals of the left. Black activists were taking part in these discussions and articulating the need for PT recognition of importance of race in structuring social inequalities. Rafael Pinto and Francisco Marcos Dias, Afro-Brazilians who were then active in MNU, attended a meeting at the home of Eduardo Suplicy, a well-respected intellectual and one of the founders of PT. Before the start of the meeting, both men claimed that two black maidservants appeared and were instructed to lead several children from the room because "the adults were talking." Pinto and Marcos stated that they then suggested to Suplicy that the women should be included in the meeting. "I suggested to Suplicy" recalled Marcos, "these two women should be present at a discussion of the formation of a worker's party, since after all, they are the *real* workers in the room."[51] Suplicy quietly but angrily conceded, and according to Marcos and Pinto, then refused to talk to either Pinto or Marcos for the remainder of the meeting, or for years afterward.

Afro-Brazilian women encountered similar difficulties with white women feminists. Much like the tenuous alliances between black and white women feminists in Britain and the United States in the 1970s and 1980s, Afro-Brazilian women activists often found their *camaradas brancas* to be neglectful of the fact that they too oppressed Afro-Brazilian women. Black women, as several Afro-Brazilian women interviewed pointed out, have been the caretakers of white families. This structural advantage in the relationship between black and white women enabled the latter to pursue educational and career opportunities that they would not have been able to do otherwise in a conventional heterosexual relationship in which women are expected tend home and hearth. This was brought home on several occasions during the 1980s at meetings where white and black female feminists confronted each other and their respective issues.[52]

Despite these difficulties, the Afro-Brazilian women's movement has successfully pursued several courses of action to alleviate the conditions of Afro-Brazilian women who are mostly poor, with little skills or education. In fact, one of the distinct advances of their movement has been the ability of certain organizations to address issues that disproportionately, but not solely, affect Afro-Brazilian women, such as child care, abortion, and reproductive rights. Agbara Dudu, the womanist African bloc founded in Rio de Janeiro in 1982, has made some inroads in the impoverished community of Baixada Fluminense by attracting black women of the Baixada through their involvement in everyday activities, from nutritional education to protecting families against police violence by advising them of their constitutional rights.

GELEDES, a black women's institute founded in 1990 by São Paulo activists, is one of the few organizations of its kind to aggressively confront racial discrimination within the framework of the Brazilian legal system. GELEDES, like other proactive women's organizations, has the advantage of issue-specificity. With an emphasis on reproductive rights, labor market discrimination, and other concerns directly related to Afro-Brazilian women's health, they have the potential to achieve short-term aims for ameliorating living conditions for some women while having the long term effect of bringing attention to the specific problems Afro-Brazilian women face in civil society.

Similarly, religious groups like Black Pastoral Agents (Agentes de Pastoral Negros) and the Commission of Fathers, Seminarists and Black Religious Practitioners of the State of Rio de Janeiro (Comissaõ de Padres, Seminaristas e Religiosos Negros do Estado do Rio de Janeiro), founded in 1987, confronted racism within the Brazilian Catholic church and its hierarchy. Their members have worked in communities like the Baixada Fluminense in Rio de Janeiro and in the slums of São Paulo. Their outreach has included open protest against the killing of children (many of them black) by vigilante squads in places like São João de Meriti and

Duque de Caxias in Rio de Janeiro; dissemination of educational materials on liberation theology and the history of blacks in Brazil; and increasing dialogue with leaders of Afro-Brazilian religious denominations. It seems as if issue-oriented groups that are already integrated into predominantly black communities have had more success as social catalysts than associational groups who are defined primarily by their affiliation with the movimento. The black women's movement and black liberation theologians are just two examples of this. Groups already situated in certain communities have a greater organizational base and experiential knowledge of those communities than "black" research and activist organizations formed outside of the community. This seems to concur with Rex's suggestion that the key issue to an ethnic-based movement may *not* be ethnicity but class, power or some other indicator of inequality that becomes an organizing principle.[53]

In contrast, the movimento, as distinct from either church or gender-*and* race-based organizations, has displayed a penchant for extended, rather academic debates over ideology and "proper" politics in lieu of organizational discussions of broad strategy within civil society. Gonzalez and Hasenbalg (1985) note how discussions centered around the flaws of Quilombismo, Abdias do Nascimento's purportedly scientific explication of communalist practices of quilombo slave societies, as well as other issues of ideology, not practice. This tendency has also been detrimental to its outreach toward people for whom running water, housing, and food are more pressing issues than the epistemological merits of Quilombismo. This is not to suggest that these issues remain muffled, but placed in their proper perspective.

Given the greater instability of racial categories in Brazil than in other politics, the utilization of religious and gender identification as vehicles toward racial consciousness may have more short-term advantages in Afro-Brazilian mobilization for other reasons as well. Since *being* "negro" is a relatively new phenomenon, identifying oneself as woman, poor, or Christian may be an easier, less conflictual self-reference than referring to oneself as black. There is evidence of internal debates between pretos and pardos within the movement itself over what constitutes black, often with exclusionary consequences. In 1988, at the first national conference for black women in Rio de Janeiro, there was a *putsch* to dislodge the Rio de Janeiro representative from the national organizing committee because she was considered too fair-skinned to be representative of black women.[54] During a debate between black candidates for municipal offices in Rio de Janeiro in 1988, the commentary of one person was discounted by a black PT candidate for assemblyman because he was mulatto and therefore, could not provide a relevant analysis.[55]

Such seemingly petty yet significant conflicts are rooted in the complexity of racial identification in Brazil, but they are persistent in other multiracial polities as well. Phenotypical differences between lighter and darker skinned blacks produce social tensions within black communities as well as between black communities and white society. Yet while they are *factors* or variables in racial identification and politics, they are not automatic *barriers* to political participation for blacks of any skin complexion (though, admittedly, they were at one time).

Race, State, and the Movimento Negro

In the 1980s, a new generation of activists demanded organizational positions and spaces within government administrations at the municipal level. Demands by activists in São Paulo for state councils and accessories specifically for the black community of São Paulo led to the creation, by Governor Franco Montoro, of the Council of Participation and Development of the Black Community in 1984. The stated objectives of the council were to develop relevant studies of the condition of the black community, propose ways in which the community can defend its civil rights, and to eliminate the discriminatory practices that affect the socioeconomic, political, and cultural life of blacks on a daily basis.[56]

The council, which was dominated by PMDB members (Montoro's own party), received funding from the state of São Paulo since its inception. Shifts in governmental funding priorities, generally precipitated by changes in gubernatorial administrations, have hampered the council's efforts toward conducting research and aggressively pursuing other stated objectives.

Personal feuds within the council have also been detrimental to the active mediation between interests of the government and those of São Paulo blacks. Adultery, personal ambitions, and other puerile but crippling episodes involving council members have lent the aura of a *telenovela* (soap opera) to the council's activities. As of 1989, many activists and cofounders of the council expressed dismay at its increasingly personalized character and have distanced themselves from the organization.

In 1988 a municipal council of the black community was formed by black activists of PT in São Paulo, with the intention of agitating for the needs of blacks in a manner consistent with the earlier practices of MNU. By 1989, the council was dissolved after Luiza Erundina's victory, with the assumption that new, popular councils would be devised under her tenure that would be commandeered by various segments of society (women, blacks, etc.) rather than the government. These councils, however, were not actualized as of 1990. Moreover, the likelihood of their creation, during Erundina's period in mayoral office, is slim, given the limited resources available to state government.

The 1982 state elections of Rio de Janeiro made PDT leader Leonel Brizola governor of the state of Rio de Janeiro. Once in office, Brizola fulfilled an earlier promise made to black activists of his party by appointing blacks to important positions within his cabinet. Carlos Alberto Cão was made secretary of labor; Edialeda Salçado Nagcimento was made minister of social promotion, and Carlos Magno Nazareth was appointed head of military police in Rio de Janeiro. Although their appointments shocked some sectors of the political establishment, severe financial crises at the national and state level between 1982 and 1986 greatly impeded prospects for transformative municipal policies either in race or class-specific terms.

The unifying problematic for both Rio de Janeiro and São Paulo electoral politics, as they affect the lives of black Brazilians and their political practices, is the ephemeral nature of gains made through specific political administrations. As evidenced by the dissolution of the municipal council for the black community in São Paulo once Erundina assumed office, the inroads into the state apparatus of city government made by black activists within one administrative epoch can immediately be eroded during another.[57] Thus it would appear that a social movement—if it successfully brings enough pressure to bear upon governments, politicians, and technocrats—has the potential for political effects of longer duration. Several activists and groups have expressed distrust of electoral politics and distaste for those individuals and groups who have advocated the need for the black community to "occupy space" within government. The dangers of coaptation, corporatism, and the old Brazilian "jeitinho" style of politics are usually cited as reasons for avoiding the pitfalls of both electoral politics and electable politicians.

This leads to the fundamental lacuna of the movimento negro, the dearth of significant *national* institutions whose foremost, explicit purpose is the politicizing of racial inequalities. Without an institution, or complex of organizations with institutional bases to make Afro-Brazilian subordination a focus of national political concern, the responses by white elites in civil and political society will be piecemeal, idiosyncratic, and state-based (as opposed to federally based).

The incorporation of black activists into positions of state authority is not automatically a bad omen. The special councils and intermediary organizations created in the two cities during the mid 1980s are direct descendants of social formations that emerged in the 1970s and that clamored for greater sensitivity, at the state level, toward Afro-Brazilians. In this regard, state and societal activities are intertwined, and are not a priori, separate or contradictory encroachments upon racially discriminatory practices occurring in civil society or within the state itself. It is true that approaches toward the alleviation of racially discriminatory practices do reflect ideological and strategic orientations of say, blacks from MNU as opposed to racially conscious blacks who are members of PMDB. In the case of the former, there is a general aversion of "ghettos" within bureaucratic structures of municipal or federal governments, while blacks of PMDB, in keeping with the more statist politics of its party, have been more eager to occupy spaces within city and state councils in São Paulo.

One positive aspect of incrementalism is its ability to operate as an alter ego in the public sphere, forcing state actors to function in the benefit of a certain community in general even while operating to the detriment of a particular activist group. This is a point echoed in Andrews's positive assessment (1991) of Afro-Brazilian advances into the state apparatus in the 1980s. Rarely do demands or concessions made by agents in a state apparatus or in civil society operate in zero-sum terms. That is to say, most decisions—on whether to make demands, and whether to accede to certain demands and not others—are not made in isolation, but after relative consideration of available options. Those options, at the state level, are to ignore demands at the risk of higher social unrest and the rise of more radical agents-demands or to address them in order to affect greater civil stability and neutralize conflict. Under each option there is usually an identifiable array of agents whose demands and activities are considered more or less desirable than others.

These general demands and activities are as much a part of political calculations by state and civil actors in specific instances as are the immediate factors attributable to the instances themselves. While this assertion is rather commonsensical, it is made here to emphasize both the context and the composition of the relations between black Brazilian politicians-activists and the various governments in Brazilian society, and to suggest that the dilemmas that governmental-electoral activity poses for all racially conscious black activists are part of the broader paradoxical relation between state and civil society. It reflects the problems inherent in the attempt to wear two hats; as an activist figure representative of a particular constituency in civil society who ultimately becomes reconstituted in the state apparatus as a mediating agent between that constituency and state interests.

Once an activist assumes this responsibility, the activist's political movement is bounded by the limitations and dynamic tensions of the relationship between state and constituency. Thus, such mediators are not merely state representatives or civil activists in and of themselves, but the dialectical result of the relationship that created their position within the state in the first place.

This, by most accounts, leads to a still unanswered question for the movimento negro in Rio de Janeiro and São Paulo: can activists, once inside a state-formed organization created to negotiate the claims of a particular constituency in civil society, remain faithful to the articulations and demands of that constituency while in a state position? The early returns from São Paulo, in the form of the previously mentioned state council of the black community, shows at least one instance of failure.

Newly formed organizations such as the accessory to the black community in São Paulo, an adjunct office created under the Erundina administration in 1989, and the Palmares Foundation, created by presidential decree in 1988 and administered by black activists in Rio de Janeiro, are just two of several offices created by municipal or federal law to address specific concerns of black activists. The administrators of these offices have no immediate answers to the above question, stating that a positive or negative response is contingent upon the degree of relative autonomy for activist–state agents and the offices that they occupy, and the receptiveness of bureaucratic-administrative superiors to the political stances they assume. This will subsequently determine the ability of activist-agents to secure policies through governmental, bureaucratic processes that reflect the articulated interests of the communities that they serve.[58]

Perhaps the best and most recent example of this process lies at the macropolitical level, in Section II, Article 5, paragraph 42 of the 1988 Brazilian Constitution. This written passage makes an act of racial discrimination a crime subject to imprisonment without bail. Despite its vague wording, which makes it difficult to actually prosecute cases of racial discrimination (although there are several documented cases with jail sentences administered) it represents a significant advance over the Afonso Arinos Law, which, as previously mentioned, amounts to a traffic ticket for "infractions."

While there was overwhelming support for this article among assembly members, principally among those of the center-left (PSDB, PCB, Partido Verde), PT congresswoman Benedita da Silva was the primary advocate for its inclusion. Like any other politician operating within the framework of a representative political system, Congresswoman da Silva was responsible to multiple constituencies—PT, the Nucleo Negro do PT, the movimento negro, those who were directly involved in the drafting of the article and finally, the constituent assembly itself. The last constituency may be the least obvious one insofar as its objective interest was the drafting and ultimate institution of a new constitution. That objective, however, was the constituent group's raison d'etre, and produced interest groups, negotiating and haggling of its own. Various politicians and representatives, operating en bloc or individually, tried to effect a certain slant to the final document, which most reflected their positions. Thus certain measures which were raised were voted down, others modified. Many articles and sections of the constitution were the final result of melding complementary positions and discarding the most conflicting ones.[59]

Similarly, such a view is generally held of Carlos Alberto Cão, the former PDT congressman who first drafted the congressional amendment making racial discrimination a criminal act in 1988. Although the amendment was defeated when first voted on in congress (with "leftist" PT politicians among those who voted against it), it was subsequently passed by majority vote. It is an example, in both instances, of two black politicians operating within the conventional political matrix and pushing for laws that benefit black Brazilians in particular and society writ large, regardless of their political-ideological affiliations. In theory, any individual or group can employ this legal code as a basis for jurisprudential action in response to a racially discriminatory practice.

The distinguishing characteristic of these two examples, in relation to the more microlevel operations noted earlier, is that both Cão and Benedita da Silva hold national positions, rather than federated state positions within a specific council or accessory for black communities. Their stances then, are defined more by party, constituency, and personal issues than by the more ephemeral preoccupations of council funding and administrative inclination. While national politicians are not immune to these issues, these variables are less of a factor in their calculus for policy creation, implementation, and advocacy.

Conclusion

This chapter is an overview and analytical synthesis of the major events and issues pertaining to the movimento negro in Rio de Janeiro and São Paulo after 1945. While considerable empirical detail is provided, this chapter should not be read as a comprehensive historical account of the period in question. There were other incidents and formations, too numerous to mention here, that would round out this abridged version of Brazilian racial politics and history after 1945. What has been provided, however, is more than sufficient evidence to identify the most critical issues and impediments (externally and internally imposed) of the movimento negro.

Externally, the most visible impediments to activists have been a combination of resource deprivation (material and institutional), racial hegemony, and culturalism. Without the financial resources to maintain Afro-Brazilian newspapers and organizations, there have been many short political lives within the movement. We have also seen throughout the intermittent but consistent denial and deferral of racial conflict. This has been evidenced in the behavior of white elites at the ideological level, *regardless* of ideological position, and at the level of state discourse and practice, where the myth of racial democracy has been energetically sustained, even when its very sustenance required intimidation or coercion.

What has not been addressed are the problems that the movement has created for itself, the spoiled fruits of its relation to dominant institutions and values. Material constraints and outside hostilities do not explain the overall lack of integration within the movement itself. Neither the elitist Teatro Experimental do Negro nor the more recent, more popularly based Movimento Negro Unificado was successful in orchestrating a mass-based movement with coordinated, simultaneous linkages between various sectors in civil society.

The lack of definition of many groups is reflected in the movimento negro as a whole, if the present ensemble of "cultural" religious, political, and social organizations can be referred to in any single, comprehensive way. Two major problems, it appears, lie in the absence of a definition of what constitutes a social movement, Afro-Brazilian or otherwise.

Black Soul and the MNU were two distinct instances of cultural and political activity in the 1970s. Though each had its epochal moment in terms of culturalist or political mobilization, only MNU made an organizational effort at broader coalitional politics. This effort was hindered by limited resources, but also by strategies that often emphasized academicist debates at the expense of community outreach. Black Soul, while a more popular manifestation of identity-politics and cultural articulation, never really left the confines of the dance hall. As such, it was both an expression of resistance and a form of commodified leisure that was ultimately appropriated for mass production, circulation, and consumption.

Yet it would be an error to regard these instances as absolute failures. As examples of politico-cultural imagination, they helped spawn the Blocos Afros (African Blocs), the "race-first" entities that came to dominate culturo-political activities in the Northeast in the 1980s. The modes of racialized consciousness that emerged from black pastors, Black Soul, Afro-Brazilian feminisms, and MNU revitalized various spheres of Afro-Brazilian cultural production with a racially cognitive dimension that had been previously erased.

Thus while these movements had their shortcomings, each represented significant advances from previous generations of Afro-Brazilian activism which relied heavily on the patron-clientelist matrix of traditional Brazilian politics for individual favors and advancements. At the same time, however, the fetishization of cultural artifacts and expressions, which characterized previous generations of "Afro-Brazilianists" of varying points on both racial and ideological continuums, was reproduced in both the *national* and *international* tiers of Afro-Brazilian racial consciousness in the 1970s.

This is most evident in Black Soul, where Afro-Brazilians internalized the symbolic aspects of Afro-diaspora that were most easily translatable—the artistic and ideological expression by blacks of the New World and Africa. The practical dimensions of this expression, that of community outreach, grass-roots politics, were largely ignored. More importantly, there were no Afro-Brazilian versions of boycotting, sit-ins, civil disobedience, and armed struggle in its stead.

It is the absence of these last forms of struggle in the Brazilian context that highlights the culturalist tendencies of the movimento negro of the 1970s and, indeed, the 1980s as well. The extraction of artifacts and expressions from external social and cultural forces is certainly not unique to Brazilian racial politics or Afro-Brazilians. Almost any interaction between individuals or social groups from distinct collectivities will entail such activity, in one form or another, on a continuous basis. Yet cultural practices that aim at political mobilization do not mobilize people by themselves. They must be part of *whole social processes*—at once ideological, cultural, and material—in order to have coherence.

Perhaps this can partially explain the contradiction between the "nationalization" of the transnational rhetoric and symbolism of the Afro-Diaspora, and the inability to nationalize organized resistance based on Afro-Brazilian mobilization and concerns in Rio de Janeiro, São Paulo, or Salvador—Bahia, for that matter. While the movement had the ideational space to incorporate discourses of Negritude, Pan-Africanism, or Black Power, it did not have the *practical* space to accommodate forms of "peopled resistance," the historical moments of rebellion and revolution from which such artifacts and expressions came. It could be said, then, that these appropriated discourses were bled of their historical content and functioned as myth, rather than history, at a general level of Afro-Brazilian political thought and activism.

Once these myths were bled of their historical content, the prospect of grounding them into praxis vanished. A gap existed between the circulating products of cultural and political production, whether indigenous to Brazil or not, and the processes of cultural and political activity peculiar to the movement itself. Several São Paulo activists interviewed in the 1980s perversely lamented that although numerous Afro-Brazilians have died from malnutrition, violence, and police brutality, not one Afro-Brazilian has died in the name of the movimento negro.

This leads directly into what I consider to be the most significant tension for Afro-Brazilian movements from the 1970s to the present, which is, the tension between content, form, and meanings of struggle, and the need for activists to distinguish one from the other. This is not, as some readers may conclude, an excessively formalist exercise, but one that is inextricably bound to the conceptualization of practical activity within the movimento. Admittedly, social movements are replete with narrative and signification, those generated by movements as well as those attributed to them. In this sense, the relationship is indivisible. Yet on another level, which I will relate shortly, they can be distinguished.

The residual effects of the U.S. civil rights movement can be found not only in contemporary U.S. racial politics, but in the feminist and gay rights movements as well. Civil disobedience, songs such as "We Shall Overcome" are just two of numerous echoes from a previous epoch of black activism that resonate within other, more recent paradigms of political contestation involving politically subordinate groups. Music from the 1960s has reappeared in everything from angry "rap" songs conveying recalcitrance to televisual advertisements hawking leisure, teenage sexuality, and the awakening of the U.S. libido.

South African apartheid has often appeared in dramatic form for foreign consumption. The film *Cry Freedom*, plays like *Sarafina!* and *Master Harold and the Boys* represent very palatable depictions of a situation that remains, for many South Africans, unpalatable.

What all of these permutations suggest, and share in common with the culturalist tendencies of Afro-Brazilian activists, is that *all* forms of expression, along with the meanings first attributed to them, can be *appropriated* and *rearticulated* by either dominant or subordinate groups. Thus it was no accident that Black Soul was both a moment of racial identification *and* a conversion of Afro-diasporic expression into commodified leisure. There appears to be, in each national context, a correlation between the degree of popularity and socialization of a creative practice peculiar to a subordinate racial group and the likelihood that practice will be repressed or rearticulated by the dominant racial group. In multiethnic, multiracial polities where the most powerful members of a dominant racial group seek to *lead* as well as *rule*, the process of rearticulation is crucial to the maintenance of racial hegemony, whether to present alternative or insurgent practices as things to be accommodated or conversely, as figures to be worn down. In both scenarios such practices must be managed, dealt with.

What resists rearticulation is social struggle encapsulated in movement, in the sense that movements can be interpreted in innumerable ways, but cannot be reproduced in the *same* way in which they first appeared. Attempts at either reviving preexisting political practices or retrieving them via historiography entail reliving those practices, which, for both historiographers and common folk, is an impossibility.

Objects, gestures, and antics from one era can be glorified or caricatured in another, and re-presented in subsequent epochs as a history writ large. Such activities, however, are based upon norms and intentions steeped in the present. They can never alter what occurred in the past, only the meanings attributed to it. Meanings of the past become politically viable only when they intervene in debates and practices rooted in the continuous present. This type of intervention, so crucial for subaltern historiographers desirous of affecting the politics of their own epoch, has been undertaken by Afro-Brazilian activists with only limited success.

In Brazil, South Africa, and the United States, intellectuals of subaltern groups have utilized history, in one form or another, to contest the fragmented rearticulations of the dominant group that are presented as whole. In South Africa, for example, Steven Biko had to die before a movie such as *Cry Freedom* could be made about Donald Woods, yet the film does not alter his death. With few clear linkages between culture and politics since 1945, there has been a tendency within the movimento negro to appreciate culture for its own sake.

Here the movimento negro appears to be at an impasse. It remains to be seen whether further inroads will be made via electoral politics. Moreover, explicitly racial politics without issue orientation in a country where race identity is up for grabs has been, and will be, a dead end.

Like the labor unions, Christian base communities, and other formations that emerged in the epoch of *abertura*, the movimento negro will have to undergo a process of reconstruction within a political culture that is new to Brazil, that of a representative democracy with participatory social movements debating in public spheres. The movimento negro, with its history of culturalism, will have to reformulate its presence within this new political culture if it is to remain a political locus for black Brazilians in the 1990s and beyond. The politics of the centennial commemoration of abolition, analyzed in the following chapter, are emblematic of the movement's struggles toward reformulation.

SIX

RACIAL POLITICS AND NATIONAL
COMMEMORATIONS: THE STRUGGLE
FOR HEGEMONY

THE 1988 COMMEMORATION of abolition in Brazil was the single most important event for the movimento negro in the post–World War II era, for two reasons. It was the first time that the manifold forms of racial inequality against Afro-Brazilians became a principal theme in national debate. For Afro-Brazilians, the events of the abolition represented one of the few times in the postwar period when Afro-Brazilians undertook collective action against state practices, both discursive and nondiscursive, and commonsensical attitudes in civil society about the history and ongoing legacy of Afro-Brazilian oppression.

Commemorative celebrations in multiracial societies are often contestations over national identity; dominant groups stretch the mythical canvas of "national unity" to include representations of subordinate groups; subordinate groups contest myths of national unity that the state presides over. The 1988 centennial celebration of abolition in Brazil contained these dynamics in the relations between representatives of the Brazilian government and those of Afro-Brazilian communities.

The events of 1988 brought forth several contradictions of Brazilian racial politics. In micropolitical terms it exposed the Afro-Brazilian movement's struggles to define itself in relation to Brazilian society, and ultimately, in relation to its own history as a movement.

At the macrolevel, tensions existed between white elite strategies to "manage" the tone and force of the commemorations and tactics employed by leaders of the movimento negro to disrupt the continuity of "national" memory in the events of *o centenario*. What became obvious after the yearlong events of 1988 is that national, collective memory is plural, full of internal contradictions, and often revealing what members of dominant and subordinate groups choose to forget as well as remember. What they remembered—and what they chose to publically forget— was invariably bound up with their perceived relation to Brazil's past, whether as descendants of Italian immigrants or the great-grandchildren of former slaves.

This resulted in a third, discursive tension within Brazilian racial politics, between an eroding myth of racial democracy and the emergence of competing political discourses about race, inequality, and power in contemporary Brazil. While the myth of racial democracy and the ideology of racial exceptionalism has been greatly eroded, it has not been yet supplanted by a new "common sense," as the recounting of the following events in Rio de Janeiro and São Paulo make clear.

The Centennial and The Harnessed March: A Commemoration of Subordination

> The heart of Brazil would not be the same without the contribution of African culture, arts, and dances. Our ability to overcome adversity and our happiness undoubtedly comes from Africa.[1]

Former President Jose Sarney's comments mark the paradoxes inherent in common and official constructions of the African contribution to Brazilian culture. Afro-Brazilians have always fit neatly within Brazilian social mythology as the "heart" of Brazil, filled with passion, emotion and sensuality. The work of the mind was someone else's responsibility.

The excerpt from Sarney's opening speech touched upon the most important facets of the paternalistic, patron-client relations between whites and Afro-Brazilians. The adversity that Sarney refers to suggests black resistance to slavery and the now quasi-national hero Zumbi of the Palmares *quilombo*. Happiness translates the archetypical "happy negro" or negress, known for their exuberance in most colonial and slaveholding societies in North and South America. Even in celebration, Sarney's commentary is a synopsis of the hierarchical, cultural functionalism of Brazilian racial hegemony.

Ironically, the centennial commemoration signified a radical shift in the manner in which Brazilians discussed the topic of race. In the years preceding the centennial, the ideology of racial democracy, with its presumption of harmony between racial groups, discouraged the very type of racial discourse promoted in 1988.

The tenor and complexity of political discourse in Brazil amplified with the return to civilian rule in 1986, and race was just one of several topics that were part of the process of political amplification. Racial prejudice and oppression were components of a more comprehensive national dialogue regarding *cidadania* or citizenship. "How can Brazilians begin to talk to each other as citizens if there is no civil society?" was the question underlying debates about racial inequality in Brazil.

This emergent discourse was precipitated largely by a new generation of

Brazilian as well as non-Brazilian historians and social scientists in the 1960s, who questioned the premises of racial democracy and previous assumptions about the moral and cultural economies of Brazilian slave systems. Brazilian activists, mostly black, also helped in the creation of this new perspective. Representative figures from both the activist and scholarly communities in Brazil were participants in the events of *o centenario*, as were private business organizations and institutions. From state and civilian-sponsored events alike, the centennial projected the image of the "great refusal"[2] of traditional historiography on Brazilian racial politics.

As I have noted in a cross-national assessment of the role of national commemorations in multiracial societies, celebrations of national life, which often seek to suspend racial antagonisms and inequalities for the sake of national harmony, often highlight extant relations of inequality between dominant and subordinate racial groups.[3] What distinguishes Brazil from other racially heterogeneous societies is the relative infrequency of public debate regarding the nexus of racial-national identity.

Its occurrence in 1988 exemplified the multivalent conflicts over the meaning of racial discrimination in Brazil, as well as proof that however small, Afro-Brazilian resistance to prevailing interpretations of their history and identity in Brazil does exist. In general, the movimento negro's response to *o centenario* was a politics of confrontation, exposure, making explicit what was once implicit.

Also exposed, in an unprecedented manner, were three tensions in the movimento negro, present since the 1970s. The first is the relation between black elites and the cultural apparatuses of municipal and national governance. Afro-Brazilian protest in the late 1970s and early 1980s led to the creation of accessories and committees in Rio de Janeiro and São Paulo to mediate relations between the state and black activists. During *o centenario*, black activists who assumed positions in these adjunct organizations were confronted with the choice of either maintaining political space within the state on behalf of the black community or rejecting those spaces altogether. The latter choice risked continued exclusion of demands made by Afro-Brazilians on policy agendas at a municipal, state, or federal level.

This quandary reappeared in various debates, panel discussions, marches, and countermarches during the commemoration of *o centenario*. Blacks who had recently assumed roles as state-appointed or elected representatives were criticized by activists outside the state gambit for their attempts to mediate events. The ebb and flow of state "mediators" and "authentic" black activists was the second major tension highlighted by the remembrance of abolition.

The third tension concerns the "authentic" activists, those who contested the motivations behind the national appropriation of Abolição. Many of these activists chose not to partake in the official presentation of events, or did so only to subvert them. As a reading of several crucial events will show, the state was quite hostile to all forms of commemorative subversion. Attempts to reverse the order of the dominant-subordinate equation were met with verbal condemnation, and in some instances, physical reprisal.

The three tensions help outline the course through which macrofocused activities of the state in the realm of "culture" were received and worked upon by diverse segments of the Afro-Brazilian community. The tensions are also trace elements for origins of confrontation between state apparatuses and Afro-Brazilian activists, and between activist tendencies within civil society.

The centennial celebration of Abolição and Zumbi were major cultural events in both Rio de Janeiro and São Paulo, as well as in other parts of Brazil. Both were public testaments to the significant contributions of Afro-Brazilians to national culture and economic development and served purposes that extended far beyond the objects of commemoration. Samba schools, nationally renowned politicians and celebrities, sports figures, as well as local activists and community groups took part in the activities related to the event.

The abolishment of slavery in Brazil on 13 May 1888 was considered a far more significant date in Afro-Brazilian history than 20 November, which commemorates the death of Zumbi, the principal symbol of resistance in Afro-Brazilian culture.[4] "In 1987 the black movement decided to concentrate their forces on a critique of the official day [of abolition] and program marches for 13 May in all capitals in Brazil."[5]

While 20 November signified national black consciousness day to most activists, 13 May represented the national day to combat racism. For most white and government officials, Schwarcz (1989) noted an ambience of guilt that pervaded their participation in many events. White participation in *o commemoração* suggests a common memory shared between white and nonwhite Brazilians. Yet common memory, like Gramsci's notion of common sense, is invariably plural. When infused with the dynamics of power and inequality, the memories that constitute common (i.e., national) memory are related but distinct. Thus the central issue for an understanding of shared memory in the case of the centennial celebration is not the commonality between socially distinct groups, but the ways in which their distinctive memories function in response to social inequalities past and present.

"Shared" memory in multiracial or multiethnic politics is clearly a power-laden process. Simply put, one may share a loaf of bread with another and only relinquish one or two slices rather than half the loaf; sharing does not automatically mean equality of opportunity or access to distributed resources. Providing or "sharing" resources is a power-laden facility. It places those who initiate a dialogue of sharing with the responsibility of distribution and allocation, of providing one interpretation of a historical moment and not another, and presumes a need or desire on the part of the recipient for this act of incorporation.

The reasons for participation in the events of 13 May differed as widely as the participants themselves. Some took part in the events out of a sense of national duty. Others claimed that the commemorations were proof that Brazilians, regardless of racial differences, were coming together. Still others formed discussions and events to question the need for celebration, given the continuing plight of Brazilian blacks.

The overarching sentiment was a recognition of the past and present marginality of black Brazilian existence, best expressed in *Veja*, the Brazilian equivalent of *Time* magazine in the United States:

> The Centennial of Abolition is, above all, an invitation to observe the spectacle of the unresolved issue of labor in Brazil, its economic exploitation and its political consequences. The centennial spectacle, embalmed within a history in which a very good princess saved the blacks from senorial hell, will be feted this week in mummified ceremonies which run the risk of not knowing what occurred until 1888, in order to avoid the knowledge of what is occurring today.[6]

Supported by a panoply of statistics, the *Veja* article was one of countless articles and presentations by commercial mass mediums that took up the banner held by social activists and radical historians twenty years previously. The purpose of this, it seemed, was to denude conventional interpretations of Abolition and slavery, which presented Abolition as the usher of a new era of racial and socioeconomic relations and portrayed Brazilian slavery as the least harsh in the New World.

In another example of the use of the centennial as a vehicle for this new, official critique, an editorial in a Paulista Catholic church magazine presents Aboliçao as a juncture from which to view the past as well as the present:

> Upon completing the century with the symbolic gesture of Princess Isabel, nearly everyone prefers to wash their hands of the previous crimes. Few confess to their complicity with the sins of the past, sins which exist today. Whoever does not understand the links with the past will also not understand the slavery of today, shackling 60 million blacks, and not only blacks but the majority of Brazilian people, condemned to live at the margin of social life due to the arrogance of today's powerful, direct descendants and continuers of the crimes of the men of yesterday.[7]

The above quotes reflect the decisive shift of positions and sensibilities regarding "the social problem" in Brazil. Unlike any previous celebration of Abolição, the centennial had a national character, with an expressed concern for the "social" inequalities in Brazil. Yet absent from the above quotes, and from most events tied to the centennial, was a discussion of racial prejudice as an ongoing process in the structuring of social inequalities.

The quotes also expose the cultural logic of the yearlong "celebration." The centennial provided a forum for white recognition of glaring social inequalities past and present, but with an overwhelming emphasis on the past. In keeping with the political culture of racial dynamics in Brazil, much of the commentary and discussion during the commemoration focused on Afro-Brazilian culture, resistance and oppression in the past tense. Afro-Brazilian activists had few forums to engage in debates about contemporary discrimination. Thus a duality emerged that held a congruence between official and activist versions of abolition in one sphere, and a relative silence on more recent asymmetries in another.

In one of the most comprehensive analyses of the yearlong commemoration, *Catalogo: Centenario da Abolição*, a tabulation of events and issues points to similarities between state and civil-oriented emphases of the centennial. According to the data within the catalog, the largest event category was "black culture." Brazilian social anthropologist Yvonne Maggie (1989) posits that this encompassed all events that pondered "the difference between 'blacks' and others"[8] in terms of dance, music, clothing, diet, and other consumptive or commodified rituals.

Out of 1,702 tabulated events in capital cities throughout the country in 1988, 500 were promoted and presented under this heading, the single largest segment of events. Of the 500, 224 were under federal, state and municipal auspice. Sixty-four were backed by the black movement. The second most popular rubric was "blacks today" (295), colloquially understood to be "the marginalization of blacks," which was "the fruit of slavery." The third most operative category was "abolition," with 236 events in capital cities nationwide.[9]

In contrast, the category of race relations had the lowest total for any single category (38). Only the category of "other" had less (36). Of the 38 under the race relations title, 5 were sponsored by the black movement, 13 by federal, state, and municipal authorities. Similarly, the politics category had only 72 events, the second lowest issue-category and the third lowest category overall, exceeding only the "race relations" and "others" categories.[10] Ironically, as Maggie notes, the race relations category "denotes the production of inequalities caused by the contemporary social system."[11]

Two interesting patterns can be culled from this data. First, the three most employed categories (black culture, blacks today, and abolition) address social inequalities for blacks that were putatively related to their prior conditions in slavery, and not present circumstances and mechanisms that aided in the reproduction of inequalities. The categories that dealt with contemporary issues were least cited, and are not among the top three categorizations. Slavery is seen not only as the source of racial inequality but as a timeless explanation for contemporary racial dynamics.

Secondly, among the first three issue-categories, there is a positive correlation between events sponsored by the movimento negro with those sponsored by federal, state, and municipal governments in capital cities. The three categories most used by governmental entities, those noted above, are also the three most used by the black movement. The only significant differences between governmental and black movement sponsorship occur at the fourth and fifth positions. For the black movement, politics and discrimination occupy positions four and five, respectively, with no marked decrease in the number of events sponsored. The fourth most used category under governmental auspice is slavery; the fifth, discrimination.[12] The relatively large numerical drop off between three and four, and four and five among governmental categories, indicates much less state interest in promoting events outside the first four categories.

Thus the duality, mentioned earlier, was sustained through sponsorship of events that addressed the presence of blacks in Brazil in various arenas, but rarely within the context of the twentieth century. It is even more ironic to note, as Maggie does, similarities between the state's emphasis on past events in Brazilian race relations and the revisionist positions of Florestan Fernandes and the São Paulo school of sociologists. Both looked toward the past, rather than the continuous present, for explanations of Brazilian racial inequalities—although, perhaps, with different motivations.[13]

The movimento negro appears to have followed this path as well. In São Paulo, 13 May was a day for internal disputes between segments of the movimento negro, in addition to being a day of protest against racism. The march against the "farce" of abolition was "marked by a clear political dispute for internal hegemony. More than a historical act, what was in question was the monopoly of words, political words, in the hands of the participants."[14] Schwarcz is here referring to tensions between leaders of Afro-Brazilian religious practices, the black movement, and party politicians who vied for the most visible and commanding presence in the events of the day, including the march.

The Unified Black Movement treated the march as a "great protest" against racism in the country and state-sponsored events. The paradox of their "nonevent" was their de facto participation in the march, which left their ritualized mark upon the commemorative events. The state government, which approved of the 13 May march, had done so with the assumption that it was done in homage to the signing of *Lei Aurea* by Princess Isabel in 1888.

The state secretary of social relations, Oswaldo Ribeiro, who considers himself black, intended to lead the march from Largo do Paissandu, a major thoroughfare in the center of São Paulo. Members of MNU wanted to lead the march with a banner of protest. After much discussion between state representatives and members of MNU, it was finally decided that the latter would head the march. MNU members also succeeded in altering the course of the march, as well as making a public declaration against the state's position at the march's end.[15]

Circumstances were quite different in Rio de Janeiro, where differences over the interpretation of the day's march almost led to violence. Government troops would accept no divergence from the original course and intent of the 11 May march to commemorate the "farse" of abolition, two days before the actual date.

It began in a manner similar to what occurred in São Paulo, tensions among and between various segments of the movimento negro. Damasceno and Giacomini (n.d.), in an ethnographic essay on the march, noted tensions between black nuclei from competing political parties; PT, PDT, PSB, PC do B, and others, and conflicts between several organizations of the nonpartidarian kind within the movement. There were also "institutional divergences and conflicts; some with the state, others against the state, depending upon the moment and the conflict in question."[16]

The original plan for the march was for its participants to walk down President Vargas Avenue, a major street in downtown Rio, past the monument and tomb of the Duke of Caxias, past the former building of the army ministry, and terminating at Eleventh Square (Praca Onze) which has a statue of Zumbi of Palmares. Caxias, from the slave and plantation-owning class of the previous century, was a patron of the army who fought in the War of Paraguay. Historians have noted that the majority of Brazilian soldiers conscripted for the Paraguayan war were black, as were the overwhelming majority of Brazilian casualties. The historical irony of the 1988 march in front of deceased general's statue was lost upon neither the activists nor the Brazilian government.

The army commander of the western part of the city stated he received information shortly before the march suggesting that the marchers would make hostile gestures in front of the monument and the former army ministry. Consequently, the march was altered immediately before its procession, despite vociferous protest from the movimento negro. Helio Saboya, the state secretary of the civil police who had originally approved of the march, was the one who ordered its alteration. In a four-part justification for the change, the western section military commander stated that he had "confirmed information of the intent . . . of activists to utilize the commemorations of the centennial to upset the tranquility of the city of Rio de Janeiro" and present to its citizens "unpatriotic proposals to create antagonisms, even hate, among brothers of whatever race and color."[17]

Furthermore, he added in another justification reported in *Veja*, the activists had the "improper intent of some citizens to make Caxias out to be a man who condoned slavery." Under those conditions, the army could not permit "offenses of whatever nature to historical landmarks,"[18] namely the duke's tomb and the old army ministry. Two days later, before the march in São Paulo, military police surrounded a statue of the duke to avoid its possible desecration.

Approximately six hundred soldiers and military police blocked the entrance of three thousand participants to President Vargas Avenue. During the abbreviated march that started late and took less than one hour to complete, "political discussions were not permitted . . . party flags had to remain behind the representative flags and banners of black culture."[19] Nevertheless, marchers chanted various slogans of the black movement. They made references to Zumbi, criticized Brazilian racism, and even taunted the black shock troops with chants: "Who represents the majority of the military police? Blacks!"[20] This repressive act highlights the residue of authoritarian political culture in Brazil two years after the return to civilian rule. More specifically, it underscores the limits of expressive freedom for Afro-Brazilian activists even in the "democratic" or democratizing era.

Clearly, the military and civil police in Rio de Janeiro and São Paulo were intent on keeping the respective marches "cultural," without racialized, political content. Most importantly, their actions were informed by the old logic of racial exceptionalism and democracy, not new logics of the commemoration or *abertura*. This is evidenced in Colonel Saboya's assertions that the activists had "unpatriotic proposals" as justification for the intervention into the march by the state's coercive apparatus. His assertions represent the transposition of logic that is rooted in racial hegemony—claims of racial mistreatment become calls for racial division or conflict. This too is made obvious by the colonel's assertion that the activists were seeking to foment antagonism and "even hate . . . among brothers of whatever race and color."

Lessons of Memory, State, and Culture

In cultural terms, the harnessed march exposes the peculiarities of Brazilian racial hegemony and the repercussions for Afro-Brazilians who contest the prevailing norms of racialized discourse in public forums. Unlike *Carnaval* and its attendant *carnavalesque*, there were no symbolic inversions within the *content* of the march that were preordained, sanctioned by the state. The *Commemoração*, however, like these two national rituals, was a staged event. The actions of the coercive apparatus served to remind the civilian participants who was doing the staging.

Indeed, the march exposed the limitations of symbolic inversion as a form of political expression. While important as *critical* interventions into prevailing discourses, symbolic inversions rarely offer alternative formulations of how things could or should be, emphasizing instead the reversal of dominant-subordinate relations. In this sense, the march was a more radical form of political articulation than *Carnaval*, for its constituents eschewed the conventional symbols and rituals of Brazilian racial politics. Instead, they devised and utilized new rituals of their own.

In his essay "Injustice and Collective Memory," Sheldon Wolin distinguishes between collective and private, individual memory. The former is a memory of manipulation, convenience (remembering and forgetting) and is defined as the formation, interpretation, and retention of a public past . . . preserved in public art and architecture, public rites, ceremonies and rituals, the rhetoric of public authorities, the educational curricula, and the ideological themes that pervade these.[21]

Moreover, the events of 1988 in Brazil suggest that collective (national) memory is in fact an *ensemble* of discordant, multiple memories out of which one dominant memory prevails. This dominant memory however, does not successfully repress *en toto* the collective, articulated memories that differ from it. Other memories often work to problematize the recollections that the dominant, ostensibly "national" memory has of itself and by extension, the nation.

At the same time, "other" memories must compete with a "public past" that is itself the result of the ability of a dominant social group to preserve certain recollections, *deemphasize* or otherwise *exclude* others in "public art and architecture, public rites, ceremonies or rituals, the rhetoric of public authorities, the educational curricula, and the ideological themes that pervade these." In this sense, the activist march, as collective memory, had to contend with the dominant memory of the Duke of Caxias, Princess Isabel, slavery, and ultimately the mythology of Brazilian national development. Thus, the harnessing of the Rio de Janeiro march suggests that as of 1988, Afro-Brazilian collective memory could critique—but not quite override—the prevailing constructions of *national* memory in the public sphere as articulated by public, statist authorities. The universality of the meaning of national memory was questioned, but not yet overruled.

At the level of the state, there are theoretical and practical lessons to be drawn from this incident. The decisive actions of the military and civilian police to curtail the final marches of *Abolição* may appear to run counter to the Brazilian government's overarching policy of historical atonement and encouragement of national discourse about slavery and the centennial. Yet the harnessed march exemplifies the multivalent, ambiguous, and often contradictory activities of state apparatuses, activities that often occur *simultaneously* and seemingly in conflict with each other. Invariably, the state's role in overseeing civil society is to manage contradictions, not resolve them, as characterized by the actions taken in Rio de Janeiro.

Another lesson of the harnessed march is that state practices are also racialized, as most social and political practices in multiracial societies are, in response to the struggles and contestations over meanings of race and racial discrimination in civil society. Omi and Winant write, "State institutions acquire their racial orientations from the processes of conflict with and accommodation to racially based movements. Thus, 'reform', 'reaction', 'radical change' or backlash . . . is constructed through a process of clash and compromise between racial movements and the state."[22]

The struggles of racial politics in civil society creep into the supposedly objective realm of state decision-making, as highlighted in Chapter 2. The coercion and repression of criticism of racism in Brazil in defense of the commonsense of racial democracy is another example of how racial politics informs state practices.

In the vast literature on the state apparatus there has been an increasing tendency to close the analytical gap between state and civil society, as state apparatuses no longer resemble the nineteenth century liberal ideal-type, the institutional complex with "checks and balances" that presides over civil society but is also constrained by it. Poggi (1978) has argued that tensions between state and civil society have dialectically resulted in the development, by state apparatuses, of bureaucratic armors to shield itself from societal pressure. The outcome has been the disproportionate accumulation of power in certain arenas of the state, the diminution of other state sectors in relation to those sectors that have increased their autonomy, and ultimately, the systemic collapse of state self-regulation.

The military dominance of both the state and civil society in Brazil is an example of state distortion in the absence of the procedural elements of liberal democracy. This is linked to the exclusionary character of civil society in Brazil noted by O'Donnell (1986). Without a long-standing tradition of civil liberties, there is even greater propensity for the state's unchecked growth. As a consequence, the state-society distinction has eroded as well, as those state components with increased autonomy and power not only operate more aggressively within the state but also in civil society. With reference to Brazil, Alfred Stepan posits that the state is a "continuous administrative, legal, bureaucratic and coercive system that attempts not only to manage the state apparatus but to structure relations *between* civil and pubic power and to structure many crucial relationships *within* civil and political society."[23]

Yet the state, in addition to the characteristics that Stepan cites, is also a *normative* system. Both its officials and subjects are in some way or another bearers, transmitters of a normative system, a *mobilization* of bias, to use Bachrach and Baratz's terminology for understanding organizational behavior. In the case of the harnessed march, race appears to have triggered a normative alarm. This alarm, however, with its synaptic relationship to the coercive dimension of the state, may sound in response to numerous other articulations in civil society. Once unleashed, the coercive forces of the state aim to thwart perceived hostilities toward the ideological constructions of racial democracy, which in turn was perceived as a threat to the state. This further collapses the analytic distinction between state, civil actors, and their respective functions, because after all, state institutions are occupied by human beings.

The end result is that Afro-Brazilians stand accused of agitation during the centennial. Their grievances are reduced to a matter of interpretation, namely the interpretation of white Brazilians. This is best expressed by Pedro Gastão de Orleans é Bragança, whose grandmother, Princess Isabel, freed Brazilian slaves. After characterizing those who criticized his grandmother as "misinformed," Dom Pedro asserted that Afro-Brazilian activists were "negating the gesture of abdegnation and altruism of my grandmother," who "risked everything, her throne, the Brazilian crown and still ended up in exile."[24] Tellingly, there is no mention of the plight of the former slaves, who as of 13 May 1888 were written into freedom, but not full citizenship.

In the aftermath of the centennial commemoration, there was mention of the more contemporary predicament of at least one Afro-Brazilian just one day after 13 May 1988. Geraldo Máximo de Oliveira, a black male carioca, reported to the *O Dia* newspaper that he was beaten by Rio police on Saturday, 14 May. In a newspaper photo, he is shown with one front tooth missing; a consequence, he stated, of the beating. Oliveira stated that he was asked to produce his identification papers and when he protested he was beaten. One of the police officers was reported to have said to Oliveira as he was beating him "Your head is full of May 13. . . . the day for blacks has already passed."[25]

Conclusion

In this chapter we have seen the power relations between white Brazilian elites and Afro-Brazilian activists manifested in the interface of the state and civil society, constructions of race and the state, and in internal struggles within the movimento negro itself over the meaning of the centennial commemoration of abolition. At stake in these dynamics was the degree of democratization in postauthoritarian Brazil, the role of the state in managing public contestations of racial politics, and attempts by the movimento negro to affect cohesion and collective action among a variety of groups. The relations between whites and Afro-Brazilians, between white elites and Afro-Brazilian activists, and between the activist community and the state apparatus speak to currents and crosscurrents of national identity in Brazil.

The centennial commemoration leads us to one of the precepts of racial hegemony outlined in Chapter 2: when confronted with accusations of racial discrimination, white Brazilians, both elite and nonelite, tend to identify those who critique Brazilian race relations as the source of discrimination. The consequence, as noted in Chapter 2, is the nondeliberation over the actual practices of discrimination in contemporary Brazilian society.

Lastly, this chapter represented the response of Afro-Brazilian activists to the hegemony of white elites during the centennial commemoration as one of the few instances where the movimento operated as a movement, a collective social force headed toward particular forms of protest, contestation, and demands for change. The next and final chapter will attempt to synthesize historical and contemporary features of Brazilian racial hegemony as it relates to the movimento negro, and evaluate avenues and prospects for change in Brazil's racial politics.

SEVEN

CONCLUSION

It ain't where you're from, it's where you're at.
—*I Know You Got Soul*, by Eric B. and Rakim.
Island Records, © *1987.*

Recapitulation

T HE LYRIC above encapsulates the two principal themes of this
investigation of the movimento negro in Rio de Janeiro and São
Paulo, Brazil, between 1945 and 1988. First, the movimento
negro has attempted to bring attention to the legacies and ongoing practices of racial discrimination in Brazil, amidst a process of racial hegemony
that denies the existence of racial inequalities while simultaneously producing them. Second, the movimento negro has attempted to accentuate
the positive aspects of Afro-Brazilian and African history in order to ele-
vate the racial awareness of Afro-Brazilians without losing sight of the
everyday realities of racial oppression in Brazil.

Chapter 1 presented the terms, methodology, and concepts of the racial
politics perspective utilized in this study. As a consequence of being left
out of most comparative assessments of contemporary racial politics, recent innovations in racial theory have not been incorporated into the literature on Brazilian race relations. This chapter served to orient the reader
toward several new approaches to the study of race, and to justify their
application to the dynamics of race in Brazil.

Chapter 2 contained a brief review of the literature on Brazilian race
relations, namely a consideration of the two major schools of thought on
the subject, the determinist and structuralist schools. This chapter detailed their contributions to the dismantling of the scholarly apparatus
that upheld the ideology of racial democracy, but also pointed out the
need for an approach that synthesizes the *ensemble* of social, political, cultural, and economic forces that constitute racial hegemony in Brazil.

Chapter 3 provided an explication of racial hegemony in Brazil, the
simultaneous production and denial of racial inequality. It outlined its
historical antecedents in the ideologies of racial exceptionalism and racial
democracy, as well as its present-day consequences in the racialization of
daily life in which Afro-Brazilians are subordinated in nearly every socializing institution in civil society.

This chapter also showed how the state, from the inception of the Brazilian republic, was never racially neutral, but consistently denied Afro-Brazilians access to job and educational opportunities. In cultural terms, the presence of blackness in Brazil was scorned, while the folkloric presence of African-derived expressive culture was glorified. At the same time, expressive culture was one of the few activities in civil society that afforded racially conscious Afro-Brazilians the opportunity for political association and collective action.

Chapter 4 outlined the contours of Afro-Brazilian racial consciousness through analysis of selected interviews with Afro-Brazilian activists in Rio de Janeiro and São Paulo. Contrary to claims of the absence of racial solidarity among Afro-Brazilians, many activists interviewed for this study displayed clear recognition of the racial basis of their social oppression. Their existence exemplifies the limits of racial hegemony in Brazil, forms of alternative political, and racial identification.

Chapter 5 provided an overview of the movimento negro in the two cities between 1945 and 1988, a sense of the modes of racial consciousness that emerged in and informed struggles with the Brazilian state, elites, and the Brazilian left. The most significant groups within the movement attempted to chart what was characterized as the "third path," a politics that was autonomist in terms of its racially based analysis while mindful of social and political forces in civil society writ large. As noted in Chapter 4, the absence of a critical and ideological perspective signaled the demise of Africanista groups such as SINBA, as well as many other groups of the 1970s that operated without political visions extending beyond racially charged symbols and forms of expressive culture. In this respect, the movimento was vulnerable to culturalism in a manner similar to the vulnerability of earlier, more elitist political and cultural movements aimed at ameliorating living conditions for Afro-Brazilian people. Resource deprivation, the precarious state of the Afro-Brazilian middle status group, and the indirectness of cultural politics were presented as limitations to the deepening of Afro-Brazilian social mobilization. Though these were crucial limitations to the broadening of the movimento negro's social base, its impact can be felt in more recent cultural organizations such as the Blocos Afros and the nationalization of political discourse about race and racism.

Chapter 6 focused on the intersection of race, nation, and an authoritarian political culture in the 1988 centennial commemoration of abolition. The "event" of the centennial was one of the few instances where racial discrimination and prejudice became a topic of national conversation. Yet it was also submerged beneath an emphasis on the legacy of slavery and the contributions of Afro-Brazilians to the Brazilian nation. Afro-Brazilian activists in Rio de Janeiro and São Paulo attempted to publically confront racially discriminatory practices of state and civil society.

Directions Toward Comparative Analysis

As mentioned in Chapter 1, the aim of this analysis of Afro-Brazilian social movements was not to make sustained cross-national comparisons. Instead, I have utilized literatures on racial theory, discrimination, and inequality of other polities as comparative referents, to emphasize that there are more similarities than dissimilarities between racial politics in Brazil and in other polities where people of African descent reside.

While comparative studies of slavery systems are abundant, there is little investigation of the contrasts and parallels between racially based social movements among people of African descent. If racial inequality and Afro-Brazilian social movements are to be reincorporated into comparative racial politics studies, I suspect it will be done by students of the African diaspora in the New World, not social movements scholars. My reason for this assertion is also justification for not providing extensive consideration of the movimento negro as it relates to the social movements literature; in general, the contemporary social movements literature rarely considers race.

Other than work on the civil rights and other racially based movements by McAdam (1981), Morris (1984), Piven and Cloward (1977), recent theorizations of "new" social movements, particularly by West European scholars have ignored racially based politics altogether, focusing exclusively on gender and sexuality based, ecological, and other "new" sociopolitical phenomena.[1] This is an unfortunate omission, since not only does it continue the legacy of theoretical impoverishment within the literature on racially based movements but ahistoricizes the actual formations of these other movements as well. Recent volumes of "new" social movements in Western Europe make no mention of S.O.S. Racisme in France, a specifically antiracist movement begun in the 1980s in response to the rise in race-related violence there, nor the evolution of similar groups in the Netherlands, Germany, and Italy (Dalton and Kuechler 1990).[2]

Why such glaring neglect? On one hand, it could be that many social movements scholars find racially based movements difficult to compartmentalize within their "new" social movements schemes. Afro-Brazilian social movements, for example, could not be rightly characterized as "post-materialist," a common refrain utilized by social movements scholars attempting to describe formations that can not be situated along the party-union-sindicalist axis. The forms of prejudice, discrimination, and inequality movements that MNU or Agbara Dudu have responded to certainly have a material dimension. Nor are they single issue, for as evidenced throughout this book, politics of race overlap with manifold forms of social oppression and identification.

On the other hand, there are less charitable explanations for why present speculation on new forms of collective action excludes racial issues. To my mind, lurking within the writings of some of the most prominent social theorists is the desire to hierarchically order social movements based upon "materialist" criteria, which is at best reductionist and economistic, and at worst ethnocentric. An example of this is Jurgen Habermas's brief comparative assessment of feminist and African-American movements in the U.S.:

> After the American civil rights movement—which has since issued in a particularistic self-affirmation of black subcultures—only the feminist movement stands in the tradition of bourgeois-socialist liberation movements. The struggle against patriarchal oppression and for the redemption of a promise that has long been law gives feminism the impetus of an offensive movement, whereas the other movements have a more defensive character. The resistance and withdrawal movements aim at stemming formally organized domains of action for the sake of communicatively structured domains, and not at conquering new territory.[3]

While directed toward U.S. African-American movements, the implications for a critique of racially based movements more generally are clear. Aside from displaying a certain amount of ignorance concerning the impact of the abolitionist and civil rights movements upon the feminist movement in the United States, Habermas's comments are also replete with wrong-headed assumptions I noted just above concerning the so-called particularist basis of racially based movements for social change.

The biggest consequences for students of social movements—whether indigenous or environmental, gendered or racially based—is the lack of attention paid to the dynamic interaction *between* social movements. As recounted in Chapter 5, the movimento's encounters with the Brazilian left, white and black feminist movements, and political exiles led to tensions and conflicts. It also led to the recognition, at least in some circles, of the overlapping forms of oppression that people of different races, genders, and sexual orientations often share. As in most societies where there are multiple social movements, these encounters led to the transmission, exchange, and expansion of political strategies and imaginations. In this respect, both the movimento negro and students of comparative racial politics could benefit from investigations into the actual political development of racially based movements. Issues to be found within a study of the movimento negro are the process of moving from fragmented associational groups to broad-based coalitions, the timing and duration of movements, the tensions between legitimation and co-optation, the importance of timing in social protest, and an array of other concerns that are peculiar to social movements that do not fit within party or union paradigms.

Prospects for Counter-Hegemony

How can the various organizations, elements, and tendencies that constitute the movimento negro transform themselves into a more unified, di-
rectional, mass-based movement? As described in Chapter 5, the two basic
impediments to further seepage of the movimento negro into the institutions, discourses, and political practices of civil society have been culturalism, and resource and institutional deprivation. The paradox of these limitations is that activists have often had to rely upon the very culturalist
resources and institutions in order to further engage in alternative, sometimes directly confrontational, political practices. For the movimento
negro in Brazil, this is their Gramscian problematic.

The most immediate consequence of this problematic is that the
movimento, with the exception of a few isolated incidents and organizations, has engaged in what could be characterized as meta-politics, that is,
a politics once removed from direct action and engagement with forces of
white dominance. One of the positive consequences of the process of democratization in Brazil is that various political groups now have greater
ability to make their articulation of dissent more explicit, less veiled. If the
movimento negro is to be more successful in the 1990s, then it will have
to undergo a similar transition, all the more important given institutionalization of previously marginalized political issues and actors. At this juncture, the movimento would have to transform its fragmented and episodic
subaltern politics to an emergent politics of contestation.

One possibility would be the creation of a supraparty organization
whose purpose it is to create a threshold civil rights–nationalist agenda,
based upon a consensus among various groups regarding the basic needs
of black Brazilians. Those "basic needs," however defined, should emerge
from a critical presentation of data such as that presented in Chapter 3,
which details the socioeconomic, political, and cultural forms of Afro-
Brazilian subordination found in Brazilian society. This is the way in
which the movement can document the daily operation of discrimination,
violence, and miseducation that Afro-Brazilians are exposed to. If activists
are to "enlighten" hordes of white and nonwhite Brazilians about practices of racial prejudice that affect the whole of society, it will come via
consistent presentation of data and political language about Brazilian racial politics that contradicts official and unofficial, public as well as private
transcripts about racial democracy. This process of political documentation, "historicizing the present," could counteract the predilection for
reverting to discussions of inequalities related to a static conceptualization
of the past, as found in discussions of slavery and culture.

The process of historicizing the present could start at the community
level, through the development and coordination of national and local

groups to monitor cases of race-related violence and other forms of discrimination. Local, regional, and national meetings could then be assembled to discuss strategies for addressing these problems. This would give the movement a much more grounded base than it currently has, as evidenced by the ideologically dominated, academicist discussions at several regional and national meetings commented on in Chapter 5. It would serve another purpose as well, lessening the chances of ideological discord between various factions within the movimento.

Consciousness-raising, the clarion call of the 1970s and 1980s, will come about only after activists, along with academics and informed citizens of the polity, link it with practical political activity. An assumption often made in Afro-Diasporic politics is that consciousness-raising will automatically lead to recognition of repression and subsequently, resistance. Much like class consciousness, as noted in Chapter 4, racial consciousness does not automatically lead to collective action or thinking. Simply by presenting one form of consciousness as superior to another, without prospects for dialogue between them, amounts to a recipe-like formula of political activity, the substitution of some ingredients for others,[4] leaving a movement of blacks rather than a movement of specific, collective goals.

Potentialities for an Historical Bloc

Coalitional politics, the historicization of recurring inequalities, and consciousness-raising within masses all lead to what Gramsci referred to as tasks of an emergent social group whose duty it is to commander not only the economy, but the ethico-political contours of the entire society. This emergent social group is what Gramsci called a "historical bloc" (*blocco historico*), a unity of "structures and superstructures" that is rooted in "a reciprocity which is nothing other than the real dialectical process."[5] While Gramsci's cryptic reference alluded to an idealized agenda of critical intellectuals in the Communist party, his insights, made more explicit, can apply to the movimento as well.

The task of a historical bloc is to lead as well as to rule, to consolidate economic, cultural and political elements within a hegemonic alliance. Rule then, is an insufficient basis for hegemony. For Gramsci, "The realization of a hegemonic apparatus, in so far as it creates a new ideological terrain, determines a reform of consciousness and of methods of knowledge: it is in fact of knowledge, a philosophical fact."[6]

There is an architectonic aspect of a historical bloc that relates to a potentially reformed Afro-Brazilian social movement. Murphy (1990) observes that when translated from the Italian, *blocco* has two connotations.

The first, noted above, is alliance. The second relates a geometric resonance within the term *bloc(k)*, which Murphy explicates:

> A historical bloc(k) is a social order that must be looked at in different ways,
> whose different faces must be examined the way we might examine a block
> of marble, a child's building block, or a Rubik's cube. Only when we have
> looked at all of the faces of an historical bloc(k)—its economic face, its polit-
> ical face, its cultural and economic face . . . and have begun to understand
> the ways that they are internally connected to one another can we begin
> to understand what makes the characteristic form of its social development
> possible.[7]

In the case of the Afro-Brazilian movement this would mean, in addition to a coalition of Afro-Brazilian groups, an integration of techno-
cratic, entrepreneurial, educative, and community-based initiatives within
a single organization, or a cluster of organizations that share overarching
purposes. For Gramsci, this signifies "the attainment of a 'cultural-social'
unity through which a multiplicity of dispersed will, with heterogenous
aims, are welded together with a single aim, on the basis of an equal and
common conception of the world, both general and particular."[8] At present, splits within the movement have occurred between groups of similar organizational proclivities (struggles between cultural groups, for
example), with little effort to forge alliances between culturally and economically oriented organizations, to cite but one absent linkage. Consciousness-raising in the form of lectures and public debates should not be
substituted for the development of political organizations for the purpose
of organizing people. Thus, even as the movimento sets out to change the
hearts and minds of Brazilians, it must set out to reform its own hearts and
minds as well.[9]

Even in the chasm between groups with similar organizational biases lie
presumptions that any preoccupation with social mobility and capital formation infers a "bourgeois" agenda, or obversely, that cultural practices
are automatically folkloric. Such perceptions could have crippling implications for a broader, more integrated social movement. Taking Joel Rufino
dos Santos's previously noted cue regarding the movement's lack of relevance to world events, the movement faces a great paradox within the
context of recent world events that few emergent social movements have
come to transcend in the post–World War II period. Since 1945, as noted
in Chapter 5, the movement has shifted ideologically leftward in its appropriation of Marxist, poststructuralist and other political discourses associated with radical visions of social change. Ironically, postcolonial, anticolonial, and anti-imperialist discourses have foundered in the collapse of
socialist and social-democratic projects in Africa, Latin America, and in
the Caribbean in the same epoch.

With the complete exhaustion of its command economies in the 1980s, the entire communist bloc stumbled onto a similar path and now attempts (as *individual states*) an accelerated integration into a global, market-oriented political economy. Politically, this has translated into the need for new political and social thought to not only make sense of change, but to also intervene in national debates about the future of Eastern European nations, from qualified reappraisal of old doctrines and paradigms to total denunciation of once-dominant philosophies and policies, namely historical materialism and bureaucratic centralism (the two *are* distinct). Looming above this continuum is the recognition that the old dismissals of capitalism and liberal ideologies must be revised. As the twentieth century nears its end, it is capitalism, with all its intrinsic shocks and vulnerabilities, that has prevailed as the dominant mode of material and cultural production.

Similarly, if the movimento negro is to expand its base of popular support, it must find ways to situate itself in national, public debate and bring further pressure to bear upon formal politicians and their institutions. In this respect, it must become less diasporic and more national. With this in mind, the movimento negro can no longer afford sectarian divides between "bourgeois" and "culturalist," "Africanista" or "Americanista" to constitute itself. Crosscutting alliances within the movement among contradictory organizations is not, in a political sense, contradictory. That is to say, the affecting of compromises and subsequent alliances between distinct tendencies within Afro-Brazilian communities is precisely what is political and dialectical about the formation of an historical bloc. Brazil, perhaps more than any other nation-state in the region, is caught somewhere between the collapse of the cold war, modernization theory and its implementation, and postmodernism's absent prescriptions for the so-called Third World. Afro-Brazilian political actors, along with all other political actors in the country, must figure a way out of this triad and its constrictions.

A Modern Prince?

Gramsci believed that the only Italian Communist party, *the* representative of an alliance between peasants and workers, could lead the masses into class struggle from which they would emerge victorious. Based on the research and theoretical material presented here, though, we must reject the theoretical and practical implications of this position within the context of Brazilian racial politics.

First, Afro-Brazilians, as members of the Brazilian working-classes and the petit-bourgeoisie, possess heterogenous modes of consciousness, as

Chapters 5 and 6 demonstrated. As noted in the latter, consciousness is something that is contextualized, to be sustained in collective action only when an issue threatens the entire group. Even then, clustered and individual members may view a threat differently. Homogeneity, then, if it ever exists at the level of consciousness, could only be an epochal phenomenon. Moreover, it would be mere fantasy to expect Brazilians—from indigenous groups in Amazonas, to Italo-Brazilian metal workers in the state of São Paulo, to blacks in Salvador, Bahia—to unite as a single working class with a unilaterally consistent consciousness. Not only has each group been formed differently, but each group has also entered into relations of production in fundamentally distinct ways.

Secondly, due to the history of Brazilian racial politics, there are no "givens" at the level of class politics. We have seen from Chapters 3 and 5 that white Brazilians, regardless of their ideological stripes, have been spawned from *the same cultural matrix*. That matrix has been a barrier to greater dialogue between the white and Afro-Brazilian left, although there have been advances in this relationship since the 1970s. In this respect Januario Garcia's comment in Chapter 5, "I'm neither right nor left, I'm Black" is, in political terms, a limited but viable form of strategic essentialism (faint resemblance). Brazilian racial politics are such that being Afro-Brazilian radically problematizes facile left-right distinctions. Neither the left nor the right have positive histories with regard to Afro-Brazilian struggles. Consequently, Afro-Brazilian activists have had to chart a third path between left and right ideological positions.

The dissolution of a leftist coalition (PT, PDT, PC do B, PSDB) after the defeat of PT presidential candidate Luis Ignacio Lula da Silva in 1989, coupled with the overwhelming victory of center-right candidates in the 1990 municipal elections, suggest another reason why the existing party structures may have valuable, but limited utility for the concerns and needs of Afro-Brazilians unless the parties themselves become more expansive and pay greater attention to Afro-Brazilian concerns.

Nonetheless, the need for institutional development within Afro-Brazilian communities is paramount, whether in the form of political party or not. Degler (1971) recognized the relative absence of independent Afro-Brazilian institutions when compared to the evolution and proliferation of U.S. African-American institutions. For Gramsci, the Communist party was the most likely organizing institution for peasants and workers because the Catholic church, trade unions, sindicalists, and other loci of working-class coalescence had already been infiltrated and predominated by social practices and values aimed at social control, not societal transformation. For the movimento negro Brasileiro, there is no easy solution to this problem, but only they can decide what their "modern prince" will be.

Orpheus and Power

In the film *Orfeu Negro*, the French adaptation of the Greek tale of Orpheus that was set in Brazil, Orpheus is a gifted dancer from the slums of Rio. Euridice is a beautiful mulatta, entranced with Orpheus, god of music and dance. Death, however, dressed as himself during the festivities of *Carnaval*, intervenes. He covets, pursues, and ultimately captures Euridice and leads her, forlorn, into the underworld. She becomes, like so many others, a casualty of *Carnaval*. Orpheus's mournful search ends at a Candomble ceremony, where he hears Euridice's voice emanating from an old *mae santa*.

Euridice's voice comes to him from a distance, at his back. Orpheus yearns to visually behold Euridice but, like his Greek counterpart, is instructed to keep looking forward or risk a Euridice grown silent. Death grants Orpheus only so much. Yet Orpheus grows frustrated by this incongruity, and like his Greek counterpart, makes a sudden, passionate about-face. As in the original tale, Euridice retreats to the realm of the dead in the instant their eyes meet. With that backward glance, Orpheus loses Euridice forever.

Ironically, this tale is a fitting parable of Afro-Brazilian politics, for it captures the problematic of culturalism, with its emphasis on genealogical excavation and "we too" history within the movimento negro Brasileiro. As we have seen in Chapter 2 and especially in Chapter 5, the tensions between narrow culturalism and a broader cultural politics have been a recurrent impasse within the movement. Based upon the evidence presented and my analysis of Afro-Brazilian social movements in Rio de Janeiro and São Paulo after 1945, it appears as if the fundamental issue–problem for the movimento has been the backward glance, the gaze toward a monolithic, unitary Africa as a basis for collective identity, ideology, and action.

The efforts undertaken by both scholars and activists in the period to reconstruct "the whole" of Afro-Brazilian and African history have had positive results and implications for Brazilian historiography and the way in which Brazilians come to view themselves. These efforts have been a combative parallel to racist versions of Afro-Brazilians in Western histories, and to the distortions of African and African-influenced histories in Western histories more broadly.

Yet these efforts pose certain problems as well. The first is narrow forms of scholasticism and activism, which seek merely to rebut equally narrow interpretations of Afro-Brazilian dilemmas in Brazilian society by presenting either *quilombos* in Brazil, Bantu, or Yoruba communities in western Africa as inherently superior forms of social organization than either Brazilian slavery or capitalism. In formulating what I characterize as a "we too" approach to Brazilian politics and intellectual life, many scholars and activists of the movimento have constructed political histories of African and Afro-Brazilian communities that bear only idealized resemblance to actual, multidimensional social formations.

As we have seen in Chapter 6 in the consideration of *o centenario*, discussions of resistance within the movimento have often obscured the realities of social struggle—battles lost, civilizations obliterated, and internal conflicts sustained by human needs and quests for power. Moles and warts are expunged from "we too" murals of history.

There are immediate as well as long-term implications of this approach. One could just as easily criticize the patrifocal economy of quilombos or Yoruba communities as part of the inequalities and power disjunctures that exist in virtually all societies. An uncritical acceptance of all good things being African or, more broadly, non-Brazilian or non-Western can result in the defense of injustices and inequalities of a past, glorified history that contradicts present struggles.

In embracing the Quilombo or some variation of Quilombismo, does it mean women are to accept largely child-rearing, labor oriented roles within the contemporary Afro-Brazilian community? In embracing some form of Negritude, should we accept the essentialist notion that there exists a transcendental, transhistorical "African personality" found in some Negritude writings? Aside from personal reservations regarding both of these positions, suffice it to say that these elements are also parts of Brazilian and Pan-Africanist histories, as much as slave revolts and anticolonial movements.

Clearly, there are short-term gains to the glorification of African and Afro-Brazilian pasts in "we too" history; its powerful symbolism, the explosion of the pejorative correlation between blackness and civilization that is encompassed in the collective recognition by a people who now proudly state that yes, we have heroines and heroes all our own. Yet history is not a thing to have or possess, as Orpheus discovered the hard way. Orpheus's Euridice was timeless, unchanging, unwavering in her beauty and devotion. Euridice was a thing to be retrieved, in her entirety, despite the fact that she, as well as her relationship with Orpheus, had been transformed by Demeter, the god of death.

Histories are processes through which groups and individuals develop dialogical relationships. They are slippery, eel-like, with ever-shifting positions and interpretations. There can be no retreat to "the way things were," for even if we possessed full knowledge of how things "used to be," such moments no longer exist. With this recognition, it is the "used," rather than the "to be," which deserves emphasis. So far the black movement, like Orpheus, has neglected the former in pursuit of the latter.

Thus the second, long-term problem of the "we too" approach is an epistemic one of attempting to capture, hold and ultimately *know* the past, which is, as most scholars recognize, an impossibility. That does not, and should not, discourage activists or intellectuals from attempting to recapture the past for the purposes of articulating displeasure with an onerous present. However it should be recognized that the past can never be captured wholly, *en toto*.[10] It can only be reconstructed, and not without a high degree of manipulation.[11]

Both the Greek and Brazilian Orpheus, in their attempt to recapture the past through one last gaze, trespassed upon the ground of historical occurrence. Their disregard for the realities of Euridice's departure cost them the loss of dialogue between themselves and their beloveds, between the living and the dead, and ultimately, between contemporaneity and history. In their desire to recapture Euridice wholly, they lost her—entirely—through their confusion of memory and meaning with history.

Efforts to *know* the past, recapture and recast it in original form greatly reduce prospects for critical perspective. When combined with the "we too" approach, the consequences can be devastating for politically marginalized groups such as the movimento. Historical interpretation, a dialogue with history, is shunned in favor of cataloging events and personalities to project an appealing but superficial self-portrait. Solipsism creeps in as caricatures, both evil and good, are preferred over complicated figures. Caricatures are more comforting; they can be easily manipulated to project an image that counters all the negativities that a dominant group, in their own caricatured versions of history, may attribute to the less powerful.

The final result is a preoccupation not with history, but with parts of history that can serve as cosmetic accoutrements to enhance self-image—heroes, battles won, human rabbits that occasionally outwit foxes, and so on. Rebelliousness and indefatigable wills are presented not as elements of social struggle, but as expressions of cantankerous individualism and adventurist thinking, in a word, voluntarism. This form of self-absorption has as its consequence the limitations of political symbolism and semiotics.[12] Orpheus too suffered from the consequences of self-absorption. As we know from the original tale, Orpheus plucked his lyre endlessly after losing Euridice a second time, even in the presence of Maenads, followers of Dionysus who could be driven to violence by the sound of music and the taste of wine. The sounds from the lyre that had once spellbound Hades and Cerberus drove the Maeneds to a murderous frenzy. They tore Orpheus apart, limb from limb.

Part of a new political vision would have to entail not only internal organization and coordination, but a broader recognition of *global* forces occurring in contemporary politics. As Joel Rufino dos Santos (1985) has rightly posited, the movimento negro must become more cognizant of the national and international crises confronting not only Brazilian society but also those societies with black populations that Afro-Brazilians use as cultural and political referents.

As forms of political resistance in Africa bear greater resemblance to the polarities of the African National Congress and the Inkatha in South Africa, or those of FRELIMO and UNITA in Mozambique and Angola, respectively, intelligent, relevant answers to questions of strategy and mobilization for Afro-Brazilians in the 1990s will not be found either in the *Quilombo* of Palmares or the Mau Mau of Kenya, but elsewhere. Hasenbalg, in his explication of the limited utility of slavery as an explanatory variable for contemporary inequalities, posited (correctly, I believe) that slavery's explanatory power for contemporary racial inequalities decreases as Brazilian society is further removed, historically and structurally, from slave labor (1985). Conversely, neither slavery, resistance to enslavement, or African sociopolitical and religious organization preceding and during the first wave of Western imperialism three centuries ago will provide easily grafted solutions to Brazil's societal ills in the 1990s.

The continuous present, rather than a folkloric past, must be historicized if black and white critical intellectuals are to reveal ongoing, racialized disjunctures in Brazilian society. If the movimento is to avoid Orpheus' fate, there needs to be greater critical activity *within* the movimento, not only for exploding both self-laudatory and demeaning accounts of an Afro-Brazilian past, but most importantly, to historicize and thereby de-folklorize an Afro-Brazilian present. This is the only way for the movimento to rid itself of its own culturalism. A real attempt at dialogue with the Afro-Brazilian past will help produce more comprehensive—and more ambiguous—dialogues about its past history and politics, yet ones that will have greater integrity and invariably, greater strategic utility.

Orpheus believed he could simply exchange the limitations of dialogue for the selective expansiveness of meaning and memory, and in doing so retain the Euridice of his past. But Death, knowing fully that dialogue, however fragmented, was worth far more than memory, refused to be shortchanged. Hopefully the movimento negro will not succumb to the same frustrations, and will *choose* dialogue over the backward glance.

NOTES

INTRODUCTION

1. The figure of 44 percent represents the official IBGE 1980 census figure for the nonwhite population, consisting of *pardos* (browns) at 38 percent and *pretos* (blacks) at 6 percent, based on the 1980 census. Given the indeterminacy of racial categories in Brazil, the 1980 census was the subject of many disputes, especially over objective and subjective criteria for determining who precisely pretos and pardos are.

2. Thomas Skidmore, "Race and Class in Brazil: Historical Perspectives," in *Race, Class and Power in Brazil*, Pierre-Michel Fontaine, ed. (Los Angeles: Center for Afro-American Studies, UCLA, 1985), 13.

3. Verena Martinez-Alier's work on race, marriage, and social mobility in Cuba is a poignant example of how racial differentiation not only affects life and marriage choices, but informs social structures. See *Marriage, Class and Colour in Nineteenth Century Cuba: A Study of Racial Attitudes and Sexual Values in a Slave Society* (London: Cambridge University Press, 1974).

4. I personally attended all the conferences, debates and meetings referred to in this project, with one exception. The First National Conference of Black Women in Brazil, held in Rio de Janeiro in 1988, prohibited male participants. A research assistant attended on my behalf.

CHAPTER ONE
RACIAL POLITICS: TERMS, THEORY, METHODOLOGY

1. Emilia Viotti da Costa, *The Braziliam Empire: Myths and Histories* (Chicago: University of Chicago Press, 1985), 238.

2. Michael Hanchard, "Racial Consciousness and Afro-Diasporic Experiences: Antonio Gramsci Reconsidered," *Socialism and Democracy* 7, no. 14 (Fall 1991): 83–106.

3. Ira Katznelson, *Black Men, White Cities* (London: Oxford University Press, 1973), 14.

4. This term, as a descriptive category for the politics of people of African descent and as an occupational position within departments of political science, is dangerously misleading. It (*a*) erroneously implies that blacks—as opposed to whites—engage in a racial politics, while "whites" themselves do not and (*b*) that ethnic, regional, class, or other distinctions that threaten the monolithic characterization of "Black Politics" are secondary. Finally, the term on its own is an expression of power, insofar as it suggests that the politics that blacks engage in are, ipso facto, "black" while those of their white counterparts are national, regional, fiscal, federal, state, or a host of other spatially or institutionally identifiable categories.

5. Paul Gilroy, *There Ain't No Black in the Union Jack* (London: Hutchinson, 1987), 39.

6. Harold Hoetink, *Caribbean Race Relations* (London: Oxford University Press, 1967), 31.

7. The distinction that Hoetink and others refer to is the one first noted by Brazilian race relations scholar Oracy Noguiera, who has argued that a color problem exists in Brazil, while a race problem exists in the United States. For Noguiera, this is evidenced in the "prejudice of origin" in the United States versus the "prejudice of color" in Brazil, where "whitening" or "passing" is possible for people of mixed racial heritage. In the United States, the emphasis is on genealogy in determining a person's racial composition, with much less emphasis on physical features. See Oracy Noguiera, "Preconceito de marca e preconceito racial de origem," *Anais do XXXI Congresso Internacional de Americanistas* (São Paulo: Editora Anhembi, 1955), 409–34.

8. This term is used to refer to people of African descent in the Americas, North, Central and South, not just those who reside in the United States.

9. Gilroy, *There Ain't No Black* . . . , 38.

10. See Katznelson, *Black Men, White Cities,* especially chap. 2, "A Framework for Research: Priorities and Guidelines," 17–28.

11. See Phillipe Schmitter, "Still the Century of Corporatism?" in Frederick B. Pike and Thomas Stritch, eds., *The New Corporatism: Social Political Structure in the Iberian World* (Notre Dame, Ind.: University of Notre Dame Press, 1974), 85–129.

12. This is not to imply that immigration laws that did segregate incoming populations were not a form of de jure segregation, but to emphasize the apartheid quality of national legislation around race in a polity such as the United States, which divided all public interaction along racial lines.

13. Perry Anderson, "The Antinomies of Antonio Gramsci," *New Left Review* (special hundredth issue) no. 100 (November 1976–January 1977): 5–80.

14. For Gramsci's discussion of leadership and passive revolution as it relates to Piedmont, see "Notes on Italian History," in *Selections from the Prison Notebooks of Antonio Gramsci*, translated and edited by Quintin Hoare and Geoffrey Nowell Smith (New York: International Publishers, 1971), 104–14.

15. Hanchard, "Racial Consciousness," 83–106.

16. Stuart Hall, "Gramsci's Relevance for the Study of Race and Ethnicity," in *Journal of Communication Inquiry* 10, no. 2 (Summer 1986): 5–27.

17. In his eagerness to dismiss Gramsci's conceptualization of hegemony through a reductionist interpretation of false consciousness that equates false consciousness with the entire concept of hegemony, James Scott omits the more dynamic interpretation of hegemony as, a priori, a *relational* concept in which conditions of hegemonic power are temporal and incomplete. In doing so, the broader implications of the hegemonic-counterhegemonic relationship, and Gramsci's own ethical and practical concerns about this relationship, are missed in his critique of hegemony. Scott's "weapons of the weak" are also weapons of the strong. (See his *Weapons of the Weak*, [New Haven: Yale University Press, 1985], or "False Consciousness or Laying it on Thick?" in his *Domination and the Arts of Resistance*, [New Haven: Yale University Press, 1990]). Even more broadly, Scott ignores the implicit critiques of dominant ideology theses within Gramsci's oeuvre and in Marxist traditions, which would have complicated his own reading

of the relation between "dominant ideology," "false" consciousness, and hegemony. Raymond Williams, for one, rejects the facile equation of ideology with
true or false consciousness (or unconsciousness): "Hegemony is . . . not only the
articulate upper level of 'ideology,' nor are its forms of control only those ordinar-
ily seen as 'manipulation' or 'indoctrination.' It is a whole body of practices and
expectations, over the whole of living: our senses and assignments of energy, our
shaping perceptions of ourselves and our world. It is a lived system of meanings
and values—constitutive and constituting—which as they are experienced as practices appear as *reciprocally confirming* [my emphasis]. It thus constitutes a sense of
reality for most people in the society, a sense of absolute because experienced
reality beyond which it is very difficult for *most* [my emphasis] members of the
society to move, in most areas of their lives. It is . . . in the strongest sense a
'culture,' but a culture which has also to be seen as the lived dominance and
subordination of particular classes" (Williams, *Marxism and Literature* [New
York: Oxford, 1977], 110). These concerns are also present in aesthetic theory.
Pauline Johnson notes in *Marxist Aesthetics* [London: Routledge & Kegan Paul,
1984], 2), that the distinctive contribution of the Frankfurt School to aesthetic
theory was to attack so-called Marxist theories that maintain that "everyday thinking in capitalist society is simply a conceptually false representation of social life
designed specifically to further ruling class interests." This is not to suggest that
the conceptual problems of false or contradictory consciousness in Marx-inspired
cultural theory have been resolved or superseded (a *theoretical* impossibility), but
that some of the preexistent, more sophisticated readings of Gramsci and the role
of consciousness, in both revolt and everyday life, must be situated in any *comprehensive* exegesis of hegemony. Otherwise we are left with, despite Scott's claims
to the contrary, a strawperson in the form of hegemony, and an already disfigured
one at that.

18. This definition of *activist* is taken from Kristin Luker's *Abortion and the
Politics of Motherhood* (Berkeley and Los Angeles: University of California Press,
1984). One of its methodological attributes is its definition of activism in terms of
political participation—not visible leadership—which includes political participants who are among the "rank and file."

19. See Gramsci, *Prison Notebooks*, 24–43

20. Without a more ethnographic approach in interviewing strategies, many
facets of a racial politics are not revealed. For example, concealed racial motivations have undermined many highly quantitative research surveys on election results in major cities in the United States, where whites regardless of party or ideological commitments have voted for white candidates based on racial preference
(and prejudice), while maintaining in survey interviews that race was not a factor
in their choice of candidate. This is evidenced in surges of "racial voting" in the
final stages of the 1989 mayoral race in New York City and in the Virginia gubernatorial election of that same year. It remains unclear, in short, what "representative samples" are in fact representative of, particularly with regard to racial politics.

21. Raquel Rolnik, "Territorios negros nas cidades brasileiras (Etnicidade e
cidade em São Paulo e no Rio de Janeiro)," *Estudos Afro-Asiáticos* (Rio de Janeiro:
Centro de Estudos Afro-Asiáticos), no. 17 (1989), 30.

22. Many of the immigrants are considered *moreno*, a term used to characterize

nonwhite who are not, at least visibly, of African or Asian descent. The term *moreno* itself has undergone a transformation over the course of this century, as it was initially used to identify mulattoes. It increasingly has come to be identified with dark-skinned whites, and in the case of women, brunettes.

23. The phenomena of anti-nordestino sentiment in São Paulo has appeared prominently in regional and national media since 1988, as a result of Luiza Erundina's mayoral victory in the city of São Paulo. Eurundina, the Workers Party (PT) candidate who originally hails from Paraiba, receives tens of letters weekly from São Paulo residents who blame worsening economic conditions, the dirtiness of the city, and other urban maladies on the "invasão dos nordestinos," which includes the mayor of the city. See "O aparthied moreno" by Andreá Barros in *Veja* (Bahia), August 1992.

CHAPTER TWO
BRAZILIAN RACIAL POLITICS: AN OVERVIEW
AND RECONCEPTUALIZATION

1. Florestan Fernandes. *The Negro in Brazilian Society*. (New York: Columbia University Press, 1969), xv.

2. Ibid., 36.

3. George Reid Andrews, *Blacks and Whites in São Paulo, Brazil, 1888–1988*. (Madison: University of Wisconsin Press, 1991), 59.

4. Florestan Fernandes, *The Negro in Brazilian Society* (New York: Columbia University Press, 1969), 15.

5. Fernandes, *Negro in Brazilian Society*, 4.

6. Raymond Williams, *Marxism and Literature* (London: Oxford University Press, 1977), 80.

7. Williams, *Marxism and Literature*, 81.

8. Fernandes, *Negro in Brazilian Society*, 189.

9. Howard Winant, "The Other Side of the Process: Racial Formation in Contemporary Brazil," 13. The arguments in Winant's unpublished paper will be developed along much the same lines in his forthcoming book, *Racial Conditions: Theories, Politics and Comparisons* (Minneapolis: University of Minnesota Press, 1994). Winant provides an excellent review of Brazilian race relations literature produced by Brazilian and non-Brazilian scholars, offering an alternative explanation through a racial formation approach, as outlined in his *Racial Formation in the United States* (New York: Routledge & Kegan Paul, 1986). There are several variations on the reductionist theme. Carl Degler, *Neither Black nor White* (New York: Macmillan, 1971); Marvin Harris, *Patterns of Race in the Americas* (New York: Walker, 1964); Thales de Azevedo, *Cultura e situação racial no Brasil* (Rio de Janeiro: Editora Civilização Brasileira, 1966); and others have, in one form or another, posited the existent or increasing importance of class difference as a social construction that envelops all other points of social difference, including race. Given the focus of this project, there is insufficient time and space to devote to the complexities and nuances of each particular argument, especially since the authors mentioned above have overwhelmingly been preoccupied with periods in Brazilian history that precede 1945.

10. See for example W. E. B. DuBois, *Black Reconstruction in America, 1860–1880* (Cleveland: World Publishers, 1969); John Hope Franklin, *Reconstruction After the Civil War* (Chicago: University of Chicago Press, 1961); Kenneth Stampp, *The Era of Reconstruction 1865–1877* (New York: Vintage, 1965); C. Vann Woodward, *The Strange Career of Jim Crow* (New York: Oxford University Press, 1955).

11. Nelson do Valle Silva, "The High Cost of Not Being White in Brazil," in *Race, Class and Power in Brazil*, ed. Pierre-Michel Fontaine (Los Angeles: Center for Afro-American Studies, UCLA, 1985), 54–55.

12. Thomas Skidmore, "Race and Class in Brazil: Historical Perspectives," in *Race, Class and Power in Brazil*, edited by Pierre-Michel Fontaine (Los Angeles: UCLA Center for Afro-American Studies, 1985), 20.

13. See, for example, Donald Bogle, *Brown Sugar: Eighty Years of America's Black Female Superstars* (New York: Harmony Books, 1980); *Toms, Coons, Mulattoes, Mammies and Bucks: An Interpretive History of Blacks in American Films* (New York: Viking, 1973). For a broader consideration of miscegenation in the United States, see Paul R. Spickard, *Mixed Blood: Intermarriage and Ethnic Identity in Twentieth Century America* (Madison: University of Wisconsin Press, 1989).

14. Anani Dzidzienyo, *The Position of Blacks in Brazilian Society* (London: Minority Rights Group, 1971), 5.

15. Fontaine's argument signifies a shift from his earlier thinking on the subject of power in Brazilian race relations. Where he once argued that Brazilian blacks were powerless (1975), he states in the later article that Brazilian blacks have "interstitial power" (Fontaine, 1985). The more recent, more nuanced interpretation represents one of the few attempts to move from an endogenous base of black political and social activity to an exogenous realm of interaction between the two groups as each gropes for political space within the boundaries of their pre-established relationships.

16. Winant, "Other Side of Process," 16.

17. Much of the dual/segmented market literature strains to locate racial discrimination within the confines of Marx's reserve army of labor. While granting racial discrimination relative autonomy within the relations of production, those relations, which are material, invariably condition and determine the forms that racial discrimination assumes. This determinist conclusion thereby neglects racism's proliferation in spheres that are not defined by material production, spheres that in themselves can determine the forms that production and capital accumulation assume. Stanley Aronowitz, *The Crisis in Historical Materialism* (New York: Praeger, 1981), underscores the problems race and other social constructions pose for classical Marxism.

18. Fernandes and other members of the São Paulo school (Octavio Ianni and Fernando Henrique Cardoso, among others) had a profound impact on race relations scholarship in Brazil, so much that Fernandes, along with his contemporaries, were forcibly "retired" from the University of São Paulo after the military coup of 1964.

19. Pierre-Michel Fontaine, "Research in the Political Economy of Afro-Latin America," *Latin American Research Review* 15, no. 2 (1980): 130.

CHAPTER THREE
RACIAL DEMOCRACY: HEGEMONY, BRAZILIAN STYLE

1. Jay Cantor, *The Death of Che Guevara* (New York: Vintage Press, 1984), 10.

2. Gilberto Freyre, *The Masters and the Slaves* (New York: Alfred A. Knopf, 1946), xx.

3. Structurally, the logic of this mythology about Brazilian "racial democracy" is analogous to the mythology of American exceptionalism posited by Louis Hartz in *The Liberal Tradition in America* (New York: Harcourt, Brace and World, 1955); Werner Sombart's *Why Is There No Socialism in the United States?* (London: Macmillan, 1976), and in the "American and Fordism" section of *Selections from the Prison Notebooks of Antonio Gramsci,* ed. Quintin Hoare and Geoffrey Nowell Smith (New York: International Publishers, 1971), since the dynamics of social conflict—class struggles in industrialized Europe, the racial conflict of the United States—have not been replicated in *exact* form in the New World, racial and class conflict in Brazil and the United States, respectively, do not exist, or a best, are too minimal to warrant comparison. As part of a racial politics perspective, however, one can expect the dynamics of racial politics to be distinct from one multiracial polity to the next, while still finding overarching similarities to warrant a comparative method. Peculiarities of nation, state, and region constitute the differences in racial politics between nonwhites in the case of Brazil, and "whites" and "blacks" in the United States, without necessarily denying the similarities of enslavement, forced exile and hyphenated identities of "blacks" in both New World nation-states. This mode of racial politics analysis parallels the logic of Sean Wilentz's argument against the notion of American (U.S.) exceptionalism (see Sean Wilentz, "Against Exceptionalism: Class Conflict in the American Labor Movement, 1790–1920," *International Labor and Working Class History* 26 (1984): 1–24, specifically, that the absence of the precise, literal form of Western European class conflict in the United States does not mean that class structuration and antagonisms do not exist in the country, but that instead they have assumed distinct cultural and material forms.

4. Historiographic research has uncovered that the so-called race war of 1912 in Oriente province was in fact a massacre of Afro-Cubans by whites in various parts of the island. See Aline Helg, "Afro-Cuban Protest: The Partido Independiente de Color, 1908–1912," *Cuban Studies* 21 (1991): 101–21.

5. Robert Edgar Conrad, *Children of God's Fire* (Princeton: Princeton University Press, 1983), xx.

6. William D. Christie, *Notes on Brazilian Questions* (London, 1865); reprinted in Conrad, *Children of God's Fire,* xxi. All italics in citations are Conrad's.

7. Emilia Viotti da Costa. *The Brazilian Empire: Myths and Histories* (Chicago: University of Chicago Press, 1985), 165.

8. Maria Luiza Tucci Carneiro, *Preconceito Racial No Brasil-Colônia* (São Paulo: Editora Brasilense, 1983), 55.

9. Tucci Carneiro, *Preconcieto racial no Brasil-colônia,* 56.

10. Perry Anderson, "Portugal and the End of Ultra-Colonialism," *New Left Review,* no. 15 (May–June 1962): 83–102, especially 102.

11. Mary Wilhelmine Williams, "The Treatment of Negro Slaves in the Brazilian Empire: A Comparison with the United States of America," *Journal of Negro History* 15 (1930): 315–36, especialy p. 336.

12. David J. Hellwig, "Racial Paradise or Run-Around? Afro-North American Views of Race Relations in Brazil," *American Studies* (Fall 1990): 43–60. For more on this, see David Hellwig, *African-American Reflections on Brazil's Racial Paradise* (Philadelphia: Temple University Press, 1992).

13. David Helwig, "Racial Paradise or Run-Around? Afro-North-American Views of Race Relations in Brazil," *American Studies* 31 (Fall 1990), 46.

14. Freyre, *Masters and the Slaves*, xxix.

15. The term *brutal intimacy* is taken from Michael Jimenez's discussion of the relations between Colombian peasant women and landowners, in which peasant women were often central figures in a triangular relationship of labor, capital, and land. It was not uncommon for men to offer their daughters to landowners in exchange for property and other forms of security, or for women to willingly enter into relationships with administrators for long-term material favors (property, title, tax leniency). Jimenez sees peasant women in this dimension of brutal intimacy as wielders of sexual capital. This form of capital represents a transcript that distinguishes them from male peasants. Possible hidden transcripts of "passive slave girls" is unexplored by Freyre for he is concerned with intimacy (and a very limited notion of intimacy at that) not struggle or brutality. See Michael F. Jimenez, "Class, Gender, and Peasant Resistance in Central Colombia, 1900–1930," in *Everyday Forms of Peasant Resistance*, ed. Forrest Colburn (New York: M. E. Sharpe, 1989) 122–50.

16. Thomas Skidmore, *Black Into White* (New York: Oxford University Press, 1974), 17.

17. Ibid.

18. See, for example, A. J. R. Russell-Wood, *The Black Man in Slavery and Freedom in Colonial Brazil* (New York: St. Martin's Press, 1982); Conrad, *Children of God's Fire*.

19. Da Costa, *Brazilian Empire*, 239.

20. Eugene Genovese, *Roll, Jordan, Roll: The World the Slaveholders Made* (New York: Pantheon Books, 1969), 106–8.

21. Gramsci, *The Prison Notebooks*, 326.

22. Pierre Van den Berghe and Roger Bastide, "Stereotypes, Norms and Inter-racial Behavior in Sao Paulo, Brazil," in *Race and Ethnicity* by Van den Bergh (New York: Basic Books, 1970), 99.

23. Ibid., 104.

24. Ibid.

25. Yvonne Maggie, "O ilusão do concreto: Uma introducão a discussão sobre sistema de classificaçao racial no Brasil" (paper presented at the fifteenth annual meeting of ANPOCS, Caxambu, Minas Gerais, Brasil, 15–18 Oct. 1991.

26. An incident relayed to me by João Batista de Jesus Felix (known as Batista) a member of MNU and PT during an interview confirms Yvonne Maggie's explication of the complexities of color reference in Brazil. Batista stated that as part of the black movement's campaign to rid the term *negro* of its pejorative connotation, he and other movement members often wore *t*-shirts that read "eu sou negão" (I

am a big black). After entering a restaurant wearing this T-shirt and waiting to be seated, he overheard a waiter saying to an incoming customer that they would be seated "after that black man over there" (Batista). Upon hearing this, Batista stated that he walked over to the waiter and asked him to repeat what he had just said. According to Batista, the waiter stammered a bit, whereupon Batista pointed to his shirt and said, "It's okay to call me black—I am black," after which the waiter replied softly, "Well, I know that sir. I just did not want to offend you."

27. Among the many studies of racial stereotypes in Brazilian literature are Roger Bastide, "Estereotipos de negroes atraves da literatura brasiliera," in *Estudos Afro-Brasileiros* (São Paulo: Perspectiva, 1973), 113–28; Fluvia Rosemberg, "Discriminaçoes etnico-raciais na literatura infanto-juvenil brasileira," Rev. Bras., Bibliotecon. Doc., São Paulo, 12, no. 3–4 (July–December 1979): 155–66; David Brookshaw, *Raça e cor na literatura brasileira*. (Porto Alegre: Mercado Aberto, 1983).

28. R. P. Pinto, "O Livro didatico e a democratização da escola" (master's thesis, University of São Paulo, 1981).

29. R. P. Pinto, "A representação do negro em livros didaticos de leitura," *Cadernos de Pesquisa* 63 São Paulo: (November 1987): 88–92.

30. Ibid., 92, table 2.

31. Henrique Cunha, Jr., "A indecisão dos pais façe a percepção da discriminação racial na escola pela criança," *Cadernos de Pesquisa* 63(November 1987): 51–53.

32. Vera Figueira, "Preconceito racial: Diffusão e manutenção na escola," *Intercambio* 1, no. 1 (January–April 1988): 37–46.

33. Vera Figueira, "O preconceito racial na escola," *Estudos Afro-Asiaticos* 18 (May 1990): 63–72.

34. Ibid., 68.

35. Salvador Sandoval, "The Mechanisms of Race Discrimination in the Labor Market: The Case of Urban Brazil" (paper presented at the Fifteenth International Meeting of the Latin American Studies Association, San Juan, Puerto Rico, 21–23 Sept. 1989.

36. Taken from *Censo Demografico 1980 IBGE*, 1980.

37. *IBGE*, 1987.

38. Ibid.

39. Pesquisa Nacional Por Amostra de Domicilios, 1987, *IBGE*. This statistical data excludes the rural population from the north region of the country.

40. IBASE/Comissão de Religiosos(as) Seminaristas e Agentes de Pastoral Negroes do Rio de Janeiro, 1987.

41. Author's interview with Antonio Leite, 1989.

42. Alain Rouquie, "Demilitarization and the Institutionalization of Military Dominated Polities in Latin America," in *Transitions from Authoritarian Rule*, ed. Guillermo O'Donnell, Phillipe Schmitter, and Laurence Whitehead (Baltimore: Johns Hopkins University Press, 1988), 108–36.

43. Author's interview with Antonio Carlos Arruda, São Paulo, 1988 and 1989.

44. Ibid.

45. A wealth of ethnographic material exists that highlights the intricacies of

racial dominance and subordination in encounters between members of the same subordinate racial group, in which one represents a coercive dimension of the state apparatus and another does not. James Baldwin's account of the 1981 black child-murder case in Atlanta, Georgia, contains the following passage that underscores the paradoxical relationship between black policeman and black communities in the United States, the traces of self-hatred and denial that manifest themselves: "We used to say, 'If you *must* [*sic*]'—for we hardly ever did—'for God's sake, try to make sure it's a White [*sic*] one.' A Black policeman could completely demolish you. He knew far more about you than a White policeman could and you were without defenses before this Black brother in uniform whose entire reason for breathing seemed to be his hope to offer proof that, though he was Black, he was not Black like you." See *The Evidence of Things Not Seen* (New York: Holt, Rhinehart and Winston, 1985), 66.

46. See John Gaventa, *Power and Powerlessness* (New Haven: Yale University Press, 1980), 19; Stephen Lukes, *Power: A Radical View* (London: Oxford University Press, 1974), 22.

47. Gramsci, *Prison Notebooks*, 54–55.

48. By *symbolic dimension*, I mean the communicative aspects of real life; how people create symbols, markers, and signifiers from the materials of everyday life to express themselves individually and collectively. With race, gender, and other forms of social demarcation, elements of communication are often designed to speak to microcollectives (e.g., women, blacks, businessmen), with the assumption that those elements transfer and transmit information that its receivers easily identify with.

49. The advertisement first appeared in a supplementary feature of the *Jornal do Brasil* daily newspaper, Sunday, 2 Oct. 1988.

50. IPCN letter to the publicity board and civil police, 4 Oct. 1988.

51. "Propaganda de butique causa irritação no movimento negro, *O Dia*, 5 Oct. 1988."

52. New Brazilian Constitution, 1988.

53. "Empresária e babá-modelo se defendem." *O Dia*, 5 Oct. 1988.

54. Ibid.

55. Pierre Bourdieu, *Outline of a Theory of Practice* (London: Cambridge University Press, 1977), 165. The need to explain such symbolic constructs automatically renders them inarticulate, because explanations, in instances such as these, are attempts to "clean up" symbols whose meanings are no longer clear. Interestingly, one of the advertisers used a language of parallel suffering to absolve himself from any racist intent. He claimed that as a Jew, he had known discrimination, and he could not possibly have helped create a biased advertisement.

56. Roland Barthes, *Mythologies* (New York: Hill and Wang, 1972), 110.

57. Ibid., 143.

58. *O Dia*, "Empresária e babá-modelo se defendem," 5 Oct. 1988.

59. For a critique of the conceptual underpinnings of James Scott's *Weapons of the Weak* see Timothy Mitchell, "Everyday Metaphors of Power," *Politics and Society*, no. 19 (Newbury Park, Calif.: Sage, 1990): 545–77.

60. The key point that many of hegemony's detractors seem to miss is that the idea of a contradictory consciousness, of dialectical contradictions found in single

or collective ways of seeing ("world views") is as much an ethical observation as it is a coldly "analytic" or "objective" one. As I have stated earlier, I part company with Gramsci's narrow formulation of contradictory consciousness as something peculiar to working classes. Yet, it should be constantly kept in mind that Gramsci was concerned with a politico-cultural transformation of the Italian working classes, and used "contradictory," "false," and "true" not only as categories of analysis but as part of his ethico-political position. For better or worse, political leaders invariably have to make claims concerning good or bad, right or wrong politics, in the name of collective action.

61. This expresses it all, doesn't it? See "As aparéncias enganam . . .," *A Tarde* (espaço do leitor), 31 Dec. 1987.

62. See *Diario Popular* (São Paulo), 14 June 1990; *O Estado de Minas* (Belo Horizonte), 10 June 1990.

63. "Benetton's Magazine to Push Vision, Not Clothing," *New York Times*, 15 Apr. 1991.

64. Ibid.

65. *O Estado de Minas*, 10 June 1990.

66. As reported in the Brazilian press; see "Anuncio foi vetado nos EUA," *Folha de São Paulo*, 8 June 1990.

67. *Folha de São Paulo*, "O que voçe acha da campanha da Benetton," 8 June 1990.

68. "Outdoor da Benetton é pichado pelos negros," *Diario Popular*, 14 June 1990.

69. For an excellent theoretical consideration of controlling images of African-American women, see Patricia Hill Collins, *Black Feminist Thought* (London: Routledge, 1991).

CHAPTER FOUR
FORMATIONS OF RACIAL CONSCIOUSNESS

1. Author's interview with Joel Rufino dos Santos, Rio de Janeiro, December 1989.

2. Michael M. J. Fischer, "Ethnicity and the Post-Modern Arts of Memory," in *Writing Culture*, ed. James Clifford (Berkeley: University of California Press, 1986), 230.

3. Author's interview with Luis Carlos de Souza, Rio de Janeiro, 1989.

4. Ivanir dos Santos of the Workers party openly criticized Garcia's position during a 1989 interview. Garcia has articulated this position on at least two occasions; once, during a 1989 interview with the author, and at a conference on Brazilian social movements at the Catholic University in Rio de Janeiro that same year.

5. The best two studies of this phenomena in the U.S. civil rights movement are David J. Garrow, *Bearing the Cross, Martin Luther King Jr. and the Southern Christian Leadership Conference* (New York: H. Morrow, 1986), and Taylor Branch, *Parting the Waters: America During the King Years, 1954–1963* (New York: Simon and Schuster, 1988).

6. This notion of a strategic essentialism is taken from Gayatri Spivak's discus-

sion of essentialism in *In Other Worlds* (London: Routledge & Kegan Paul, 1988). Spivak has gone against several contemporary readings of ethnicity that have automatically equated ethnicity with essentialism, with obviously negative connotations. For Spivak, essentialism can be employed for the strategic, political purposes of mobilizing particular collectivities and is, in fact, one of the few ways in which individuals without a common rhetorical denominator can coalesce.

7. Author's interview with Padre Luis Fernando, São Paulo, 1988.

8. Author's interview with Padre Batista Laurindo, São Paulo, 1988.

9. Eugene Genovese, *Roll, Jordan, Roll: The World the Slaves Made* (New York, Vintage Books, 1976), 238. Genovese's assessment of the autonomous role of African-based religious practices in Brazil, both within the Catholic church and outside of it, however, is outdated and incorrect, in light of the diminishment of ethnic content to the religious practices in question. His broader assertions about Brazilian race relations are even more problematic. Genovese suggests that individuals who are visibly of African descent found in positions of authority in Brazil are proof of a more racially meritocratic social order. Individuated social mobility however, speaks nothing of the oppression and lack of opportunities for a social group *as a whole*. Moreover, Genovese's determination of people who are "visibly" black is based on the normative racial logic of the United States and other more dichotomous race relations paradigms, where darker-skinned people (even those not necessarily "black") are considered black or negro, and consider themselves as such out of practical or political necessity. In Brazil, those who may seem visibly black to a U.S. citizen may not seem black to a Brazilian. Nor do darker-skinned people in Brazil, as a given, consider themselves *negro*.

10. Baptista, "Aspectos do comportamento politico do negro em São Paulo," *Ciencia e Cultura* (São Paulo: FFLCH/USP) 34, no. 10 (October 1982): 1286–1294.

11. Author's interview with Ivanir dos Santos, Rio de Janeiro, 1989.

12. Ironically, Camargo stated during his interview that the black entrepreneur in the U.S. he most admires is John Johnson, black publishing magnate of Chicago, founder of *Ebony* and *Jet* magazines.

13. Author's interview with Adalberto Camargo, São Paulo, 1988.

14. After reading Patterson's version of the role of ethnicity in structuring "rational" choices, one could be led to develop a "pointed gun" concept of ethnic identity, where individuals are "forced" to choose ethnic affiliation at the expense of class, regional, and *all* other possible bases of social group formation (see "Context and Choice in Ethnic Allegiance: A Theoretical Framework and Caribbean Case Study," in *Ethnicity: Theory and Experience*, ed. Nathan Glazer and Daniel P. Moynihan (Cambridge: Harvard University Press, 1975), 305–50. Countless fluid approaches to the study of ethnicity demonstrate the contrary, beginning perhaps with Edmund Leach's 1966 study of ethnicity and politics in highland Burma. Perhaps the only instance when the pointed gun conceptualization applies is during war or other dramas of physical conflict where individual or groups must exclusively choose one form of affiliation over another. For an anecdotal example, see Crawford Young's personal, tragicomic dilemma noted at the outset of Chapter 1 in *The Politics of Cultural Pluralism* (Madison: University of Wisconsin Press, 1976). In southwest Zaire, 1962, he was asked by an angry police officer to

identify himself as Mumbala or Mupende, when he was, in fact, neither. Young interprets the exchange as the policeman's means of codifying Young within the parameters of existing local ethnic categories.

15. For an account of the early days of SINBA, IPCN, and other happenings of the black movement in the early 1970s, see Lelia Gonzalez and Carlos Hasenbalg's *Lugar do negro*, (Rio de Janeiro: Editora Marco Zero, 1985).

16. Author's interview with Yedo Ferreira, Rio de Janeiro, 1989.

17. Both Carlos Alberto Medeiros (Americanist) and Togo Ioruba (Africanist) stated during their interviews that the ethnocentricism of SINBA diminished their interest in the group.

18. Author's interview with Yedo Ferreira, 1989.

19. Author's interview with Aristedes Barbosa, São Paulo, 1988.

20. Author's interview with Orlando Fernandes, Rio de Janeiro, 1989.

21. Author's interview with Thereza Santos, São Paulo, 1988.

22. Author's interview with Carlos Alberto Medeiros, Rio de Janeiro, 1989.

23. The use of the term *Afrocentric* in the study is not meant as a reference to the Afrocentrism debate in the United States (though there are similarities). The term, as it is used here, refers to imagery and symbolism linking Brazilian blacks to Africa and its diaspora.

24. Author's interview with Joselina Da Silva, Rio de Janeiro, 1988.

25. Author's interview with Ivanir dos Santos, Rio de Janeiro, 1989.

26. Author's interview with Benedita da Silva, Rio de Janeiro, 1989.

CHAPTER FIVE
MOVEMENTS AND MOMENTS

1. *Catálogo de entiadades de moviemento negro no brasil,* (Communicaçoes do ISER [Instituto de Estudos da Religiâo]) no. 29 (Rio de Janeiro: ISER, 1988, 7.

2. Antonio Gramsci, *Selections from the Prison Notebooks of Antonio Gramsci,* ed. Quintin Hoare and Geoffrey Nowell Smith (New York: International Publishers, 1971), 149.

3. Guimarães, a PT intellectual and *militante,* stated this during a question and answer session of the *Brazil Network* organizational meeting of 13 Jan. 1990. He was questioned on this point by the author and by a black woman activist, Joselina da Silva from Rio de Janeiro, and repeated, in Portuguese, his position, thereby refuting the claim made by one organization member that the meaning of Guimarães's comments were lost in the subtleties of translation. Since both the author and da Silva speak Portuguese, this answer as well as Guimarães's interpretation were unsatisfactory.

4. Octavio Ianni, in "Mesa redonda: Materialismo historico e questão racial," *Estudos Afro-Asiaticos,* no. 12 (August 1986): 36.

5. Abdias do Nascimento, *Mixture or Massacre: Essays in the Genocide of a Black People* (Buffalo: Afrodiaspora, 1979), 181–82.

6. Robert Levine, *The Vargas Regime: The Critical Years, 1934–1938* (New York: Columbia University Press, 1970), 20.

7. Ibid., 21.

8. Michael Mitchell, "Racial Consciousness and the Political Attitudes and Behavior of Blacks in São Paulo Brazil" (Ph.D. diss., University of Michigan, 1977), 130.

9. There were significant tensions within the FNB by this time, however, that were internally produced. The party was driven by class conflicts between working-class, liberal, and petit-bourgeois members with distinct ideological and personal commitments, so it would be a bit romantic to suggest that Vargas's Estado Novo was the only threat to a unified, racially based Afro-Brazilian political party. José Correia Leite, one of the founders of the FNB, remarked on the tensions between democratic socialist and Integralist factions within the FNB, as well as the tendency toward petit-bourgeois leadership. For a detailed personal account of the FNB from the perspective of one of its founders see, Leite and Cuti . . . *E disse o velho militante José Correia* (São Paulo: Seçtrearia Municipal de Cultura, 1992).

10. For this and other information about TEN, see *Dionysos, Teatro Experimental do Negro,* no. 28 (Rio de Janeiro: minC FUNDACEN, 1988), which includes various articles and testimony.

11. *Quilombo* 3 (June 1949) 11, quoted in Maria Angelica de Motta Maues, "Entre o branqueamento e a negritude: O TEN e o debate da questao racial," in *Dionysos,* 92. Translation from the original. Abdias do Nascimento's personal odyssey, his oscillation between political and cultural spheres, is reminiscent of W. E. B. DuBois. While he adamantly opposes being described as an intellectual in the traditional, academic sense, his trajectory is similar to Dubois's. Nascimento's positions during the period of TEN are similar to Dubois's notions of a "Talented Tenth" in the early part of his career. Dubois would later discard this position as he developed into a Pan-Africanist, a member of the Communist party, and a self-described socialist. Similarly Nascimento, while maintaining some of the cultural activity of his earlier years, has become much more of a politician for the Democratic Workers party, a great departure from the Integralist position of his earlier years.

12. Maues, "Entre," 93.

13. Ibid., 100.

14. Maria Angelica de Motta Maues, "Negro sobre negro: A questão racial no pensamento das elites negras brasileiras" (paper presented at the ANPOCS conference, Brazil, 1987).

15. There is, however, an alternative explanation for the motive causes leading to the Afonso Arinos Law. In a discussion in the Brazilian congress, Afonso Arinos explained that he decided to create an anti-discriminatory law after discovering that a family chauffeur who was black, Jose Augusto, was barred service at an ice cream parlor in downtown São Paulo. It was this incident that spurred Arinos to action. The incident itself is discussed in the introduction to the congressional records of the bill, which was approved in December 1950. See *Diario do Congresso Nacional,* Junto 1950, Ano. 4/115. Also see the *Estado de São Paulo,* 14 May 1978, 74. Much thanks to Anani Dzidzienyo for leading me to this explanation. It is possible that the two events, one involving a U.S. African-American dancer, the other involving an Afro-Brazilian, could have both impacted upon the formulation of the Afonso Arinos Law.

16. Author's interview with Raul dos Santos, São Paulo, 1989.

17. *Residual*, as employed here, alludes to Raymond Williams's explication of a cultural form that lies embedded in dominant cultural practices. See "Dominant, Residual and Emergent Cultures," in his *Marxism and Literature* (New York: Oxford University Press, 1977).

18. Diana De G. Brown and Mario Bick. "Religion, Class, and Context: Continuities and Discontinuities in Brazilian Umbanda," *American Ethnologist*, 14, no. 1 (February 1987): 83.

19. Peter Fry, *Para ingles ver* (Rio de Janeiro: Zahar, 1982), 15.

20. Author's interview with Filo, Rio de Janeiro, 1989.

21. Lena Frias provided the first extensive media coverage of the Black Soul phenomenon in "O orgulho (importado) de ser negro no Brasil," *Jornal do Brasil*, 17 July 1976.

22. Quoted in Robert Pierce, "Brazil: Where Force Fails," chap. 2 in *Keeping the Flame: Media and Government in Latin America* (New York: Communication Arts Books, 1979), 37.

23. Ibid., 33.

24. Pedro de Toledo Pizza, then Secretary of Tourism, quoted in "Turismo ve so comercio no Black Rio," in *Jornal do Brasil*, Rio de Janeiro, 15 May 1977.

25. Julio Medaglia, quoted in Antonieta Santo, " 'Black Rio' assusta maestro Julio Medaglia," *Folha de São Paulo*, 10 June 1977.

26. Gilberto Freyre, "Atenção Brasileiros" in *Diario de Pernambuco* (Recife), "Opiniao" section, A-13, 15 May 1977.

27. Interview with SNI official (name withheld), Rio de Janeiro, 1989. Although both Filo and Mr. Funk stated during their interviews that they never experienced, nor knew of, overt actions taken by the military (shutting down of parties, for example), Filo stated he was kidnapped for several hours in Rio de Janeiro by several men who first placed a hood over his head so that he could not identify anyone. While being held against his will, Filo stated he was asked several times to explain why the CIA had given him $1 million to create the Black Soul movement in Brazil. While this may appear far-fetched upon first reading, it is useful to remember that scare tactics like these were used during this period by the military. It could also have been, however, assuming it occurred, done by others interested in Black Soul's demise.

28. Ironically, Negritude—as it was originally conceived by Leopold Senghor, Leon Damas, and Aime Cesaire—was a blend of Pan-Africanism, socialism, and psychoanalysis, and so in this sense both Freyre and mild followers of negritude in Brazil were both off the mark in their separation of negritude from a political and social movement. Aime Cesaire, incidentally, was a member of the Communist party in Martinique at the time of his declaration of negritude, in an attempt to reconcile Marxism and socialist praxis with issues of cultural and racial identity.

29. Monsieur Lima quoted in B. Caderno, "O soul, do grito negro a caderneta de poupança," *Jornal do Brasil* (Rio de Janeiro), 8 March 1976.

30. In an anthropological study of the "Funk" music and dance phenomena in Rio de Janeiro, Hermano Vianna notes both the nonpoliticized nature of the "Funk" craze, in contrast to Black Soul, as well as the noted absence of criminality in Funk and Black Soul epochs. See *O mundo funk Carioca*, ed. Jorge Zahar (Rio de Janeiro: 1988).

31. Carlos Benedito Rodrigues da Silva, "Black Soul: Aglutinação espontanea

ou identidade etnica," in *Movimentos soçiais, urbanos, minorias etnicas e outros estudos,* ed. L. A. Silva et al. (Brasilia, ANPOCS, 1983), 245–62.

32. The relative absence of ethnic or political dimensions to the current Funk and Charme phenomenons is briefly discussed in Vianna's anthropological study of Funk in Rio de Janeiro, *O mundo funk Carioca.*

33. Raymond Williams, *Marxism and Literature* (New York: Oxford University Press, 1977), 113.

34. Maria Ercilia do Nascimento, "A estrategia da desigualdade: O movimento negro dos anos '70" (master's thesis, Ponticifica universidade catholica, 1989), 94.

35. "Movimento Negro e o culturalismo" in *SINBA* 3, no. 4 (Rio de Janeiro, March, 1980): 3.

36. Interview with Paulo Roberto (n.d.) in Lelia Gonzalez and Carlos Hasenbalg, *Lugar do negro* (Rio de Janeiro: Editora Marlo Zero, 1985), 37–38.

37. "Discussions with Trotsky," an excerpt of the discussions between Trotsky and C. L. R. James, can be found in a collection of James's speeches and essays entitled *At the Rendezvous of Victory* (London: Allison and Busby, 1984).

38. For an analysis of the range of Afro-Brazilian literature and journals produced during this time and their political implications, see James Kennedy's "Political Liberalization, Black Consciousness and recent Afro-Brazilian Literature," *Phylon* 3, no. 47 (1986): 199–209.

39. This was taken from an untitled essay presumably composed by the entire "Afro-Latino America" staff ("equipe Afro-Latino America") in support of an eventual PT political party and against, as a matter of principle, the creation of a social-democratic party. See "Afro-Latino-America," final page, *Versus*, March–April, 1978.

40. Tensions between the *Versus* and Afro-Latino contingents emerged in other ways as well, some negative, some positive. Hamilton Cardoso recalled in an interview with the author that some staff members regarded their preoccupation with phenomena such as Black Soul as superstructural, and were quite content with the "Afro-Latino America" team so long as its members did not seek positions of power and leadership within the Convergence and on the *Versus* staff. On the other hand, Cardoso stated that he and other staff members learned to write through *Versus.* "We did not know much about writing in those days," Cardoso stated during an interview, "and at first when editors would criticize my writing I would say, 'You just don't understand that this is a *black* way of writing.' The editor told me, 'there isn't a black or white way of writing. You either know how to write, or you don't.' "

41. The origins of the organizational title has an interesting history by itself, with comparative implications. Abdias do Nascimento, the eminence grise of the black movement, suggested that the word *Negro* (black) be included in the new group's name, in order to rescue it from its normally pejorative denotations, and to give dark-skinned Brazilians a positive symbolic relation to blackness. Later, other groups within the movimento negro would do the same, such as Instituto de Pesquisa das Culturas Negras in Rio de Janeiro (IPCN). Name changing as a political choice of self-identification has been a phenomenon in several multiethnic polities with a racially conscious population of people of African descent. Gilroy (1987), notes the increasing identification with "blackness" and U.S. black

expressions of cultural distinctiveness among Anglo–West Indian youth in Great Britain. In the United States, there is a long history of correlation within black communities between name changing and shifts in social struggle. For the United States, see Michael Hanchard, "Identity, Meaning and the African-American" *Social Text* 8, no. 24 (1990): 31–42.

42. Manifesto read at the steps of O Teatro Municipal, São Paulo, 7 July 1978. Original document, from personal archive of Rafael Pinto, whom I thank for sharing this, as well as other materials from this period.

43. For a more detailed account of the formation and evolution of various black organizations, including MNU, in the 1970s, see Lelia Gonzalez, "Experiênias e tentativas," in Gonzalez and Carlos Hasenbalg, *Lugar do negro* (Rio de Janeiro: Editoria Marco Zero, 1982), 21–65. For more specific material on MNU, see Movimento Negro Unificado, *1978–1988: 10 anos de luta contra o racismo* (São Paulo: MNU-Seção Bahia, 1988); Movimento Negro Unificado, *Programa de ação: Negros protestam em praça publica*, (São Paulo: MNU, ca. 1984).

44. Movimento Negro Unificado Contra Discriminação Racial, *Boletim Informativo* (São Paulo: MNUCDR, September 1979), 11.

45. Gilberto Freyre, "Racismo no Brasil?" *Folha de São Paulo*, 6 May 1979.

46. As reported and commented upon in "Neder teme surgimento de Hitler negro" *O Globo*, 22 March 1979, Rio de Janeiro.

47. *SINBA*, April 1979, 6, had an editorial about Neder's speech.

48. Aldon Morris, *The Origins of the Civil Rights Movement* (New York: Free Press, 1984), 279.

49. Isidorio, former head of CECAN, recounted during his interview his refusal to accept funding from an outside grant institution because of CECAN'S organizational sloppiness. He noted the organization's inability to turn a profit with its newspaper sales at a point in the late 1970s when the newspaper was selling well. "How could we keep account of thousands of dollars when we could not even count for the sale of our newspapers?" he asked in explanation of his refusal of the grant.

50. For Brazil, see Sonia Alvarez, *Engendering Democracy in Brazil*, (Princeton: Princeton University Press, 1990); and Jane S. Jaquette, *The Women's Movements in Latin America* (Boston: Unwin and Hyman, 1984).

51. Author's interview with Francisco Marcos Dias, São Paulo, 1988.

52. One Rio de Janeiro meeting at the home of a white Brazilian feminist attended by Robin Morgan of *Ms.* magazine in the 1980s attests to the difficulties of this alliance. In separate interviews, Morgan and Joselina da Silva recounted how several middle-class white feminists were brought to tears at the suggestion that they were benefiting from racial divisions of labor at the same time that they were advocates for women's equality. The denial of this contradiction by several women at the meeting was thwarted by the presence of black female maidservants who silently brought in food and drinks while the discussions were taking place. This particular incident, according to Morgan and da Silva, radically altered the perspectives of several women present (author's telephone interview with Robin Morgan, 1993).

53. John Rex and David Mason, *Theories of Race and Ethnic Relations* (Cambridge: Cambridge University Press, 1986).

54. First National Conference of Black Women, Rio de Janeiro, December 1988.

55. Witnessed during third debate of black candidates, sponsored by IPCN, October 1989.

56. Decreto no. 22.184, Estado de São Paulo, which created the council. Signed into law on 11 May 1984 by Franco Montoro, then governor of the state of São Paulo.

57. There was debate among black and white *petistas*, and within the black nucleus of PT, over the dissolution of this council. Some claimed that with Erundina in office, there was no longer a contradiction between state and societal interest, and so the council should remain. Others argued that the council was not an outgrowth of a popular group but a governmental administration. While the administration's life had expired, part of its structure remained in the form of the municipal council. This was the position taken by Congresswomen Benedita da Silva and Luiza Erundina as justification for the municipal council's dismantling, and for the creation of *conselhos populares* (popular councils) for all marginalized groups.

58. Author's interview with Paulo Roberto, Instituto Palmares, Rio de Janeiro, 1989.

59. Paragraph 42 of Article 5 was one of the many instances where its first draft was more punitive than its final, constitutional version. The principal criticism by black activists of the final version was its nondefinitional character, the absence of a clear statement on what, precisely, racial discrimination is. The criticisms, however, were not directed at Benedita, for it was believed that the congresswoman had fulfilled her stated commitment to the black community and pushed for the inclusion of such a law within both the consensual framework of the constituent assembly and the constitutional document itself.

CHAPTER SIX
RACIAL POLITICS AND NATIONAL COMMEMORATIONS:
THE STRUGGLE FOR HEGEMONY

1. Jose Sarney's 13 May 1988 address was carried over all major mass media and reported the following day in several newspapers.

2. Lilia K. Moritz Schwarcz, *De festa tambem se vive: Reflexoes sobre o centenario da Abolição em São Paulo* (Rio de Janeiro: CIEC, UFRJ, 1989), 12.

3. See Michael Hanchard, "Raça, hegemonia e subordinação na cultura popular," in *Estudos Afro-Asiaticos* 21 (December 1991): 5–26.

4. Palmares (1601–1665) was the most significant runaway slave society (*quilombo*) in the history of Brazilian slavery. Located in Northeast Brazil, the quilombo of Palmares, at its most powerful, contained approximately twenty thousand runaway slaves. Zumbi, the last leader of Palmares and nephew of its founder, Ganga-Zumba, was killed in the final battle of Palmares, when mercenaries sponsored by the Portuguese government conquered Palmares in 1665.

5. Hanchard, "Raça, hegemonia e subordinação."

6. *Veja* magazine, São Paulo, 11 May 1989, 34.

7. Editorial, João Pedro Baresi "Um seculo depois," in *Sem Fronteras* 159 (São

Paulo, May 1988): 3. This magazine is a publication of a more liberal segment of the Brazilian Catholic church. This particular edition was devoted to the 1988 centennial commemoration, and was in fact one of the more progressive commentaries published on the event.

8. *Catálogo: Centenario da Abolição* (Rio de Janeiro, CIEC–Nucleo de Cor–UFRJ, 1989), 13–14.

9. Ibid., annex.

10. Ibid., annex.

11. Ibid., 14.

12. Ibid., 22, annex.

13. Ibid.

14. Schwarcz, "Festa," 18.

15. *Jornal do Brasil*, Rio de Janeiro, 14 May 1988.

16. Caetana Damasceno and Sonia Giacomini, "Nada Muda: Vamos Mudar" mimeograph, Rio De Janeiro, n.d., 1.

17. *O Globo*, Rio de Janeiro, 12 May 1988, 12.

18. "Treva contra Treva," in *Veja*, 18 May 1988.

19. *O Globo*, Rio de Janeiro, 12 May 1988.

20. *Jornal do Comercio*, Rio de Janeiro, 12 May 1988.

21. Sheldon Wolin, "Injustice and Collective Memory," in his *The Presence of the Past* (Baltimore: Johns Hopkins University Press, 1989), 33.

22. Michael Omi and Howard Winant, *Racial Formation in the United States* (New York: Routledge, 1986), 72.

23. Alfred Stepan, *Rethinking Military Politics* (Princeton University Press, 1988), 4.

24. "Neto da princesa critica lideres do movimento negro," *Folha de São Paulo*, 11 May 1988.

25. See "PM acusados de discrminação e agressão," *O Dia*, Rio de Janeiro, 17 May 1988.

CHAPTER SEVEN
CONCLUSION

1. The voluminous literature on "new" social movements in Western Europe has largely ignored racial politics, which is startling given the intense debates over race, ethnicity, and immigration in that region of the world. See, for example, in Jurgen Habermas, *Reason and Rationalization of Society*, vol. 2 of *Theory of Communicative Action* (Boston: Beacon Press, 1984); Alberto Melucci, "The New Social Movements: A Theoretical Approach," *Social Science*, no. 19 (1980): 199–226; Claus Offe, "Reflections on the Institutional Self-Transformation of the Movement Politics: A Tentative Stage Model," in *Challenging the Political Order*, ed. by Russell J. Dalton and Manfred Kuechler (London: Oxford University Press, 1990), 232–50; and Alain Touraine, *The Voice and the Eye: An Analysis of Social Movements* (Cambridge: Cambridge University Press 1981).

2. See Rusell Dalton and Manfred Kuechler, eds. *Challenging the Political Order* (New York: Oxford University Press, 1990).

3. Jurgen Habermas, *Life-World and System: A Critique of Functionalist Rea-*

son, vol. 2 of *Theory of Communicative Action* (Boston: Beacon Press, 1987), 393.

4. The tendency toward recipes for political action and consciousness has led to modes of analysis that ultimately distort histories of counterhegemonic formations in Africa, the Caribbean, and the United States. One example that comes dangerously close to a "cookbook" approach to the study of colonial hegemonies in the African diaspora is Manning Marable's *African and Caribbean Politics: From Kwame Nkrumah to Maurice Bishop* (London: Verso, 1987), in which Manning posits that "the central, missing element in most national independence movements in the African Diaspora—the lack of strong Marxist parties or cadre-style organizations—was decisive in pushing the Black petty-bourgeoisie towards varieties of anti-Marxist 'socialism'" (81). In the next sentence he states that "another contributing factor," to be examined "briefly," "was the contradictory and sometimes backward role of Communist parties in critical areas of the periphery in the 1950s and 1960s." One must assume from Marable's reading of the "central missing element" of African and Caribbean politics that if we were to infuse the counterfactual, namely, the *ingredient* of strong Marxist parties, the national independence movements would have fared much better than they had. The principal flaw, as I see it, with this type of counterfactual deduction is that it is ultimately ahistorical. By reversing the sequence of Marable's logic, in other words, beginning with the historical reality of "contradictory" and "sometimes backward" parties of the so-called Third World, we could very well understand why petit-bourgeois blacks (and other blacks, for that matter) would be resistant to Marxist parties *as they were historically constructed* and did not see the need to bother with a party formation that had historically been as apathetic or resistant to black culture and political mobilization as the more "reactionary," "right wing" political and economic formations. This doctrinaire reasoning cripples an otherwise sophisticated and far-reaching explication of African and Caribbean politics.

5. Antonio Gramsci, *Selections from the Prison Notebooks of Antonio Gramsci*, trans. and ed. Quentin Hoare and Geoffrey Nowell Smith (New York: International Publishers), 366.

6. Gramsci, *Prison Notebooks*, 365

7. Craig N. Murphy, "Freezing the North-South Bloc(k)," *Socialist Review* 20, no. 3 (July–September 1990): 30.

8. Gramsci, *Prison Notebooks*, 349.

9. Note Gramsci's use of the word *reform* in the previous citation. Its usage, as opposed to, say, *transform* or *revolutionize*, provides linguistic consistency within his formulation of hegemony. To reform modes of consciousness and knowledge suggests a process of reshaping (re-forming) consciousness and knowledge out of forms that already exist. The process of re-forming consciousness and knowledge would, therefore, by necessity precede any transformation or revolution of "structures" and "superstructures" in a given social totality.

10. This need for critical intervention in the thought and praxis of the movimento negro recalls Hannah Arendt's reading of Walter Benjamin, in which she comments metaphorically on Benjamin's poetics, his distinction between fragments and wholes in historical interpretation:

"Like a pearl diver who descends to the bottom of the sea, not to excavate the bottom and bring it to light but to pry loose the rich and the strange, the pearls and the coral in the depths, and to carry them to the surface, this thinking delves into the depths of the past—but not in order to resuscitate it the way it was and to contribute to the renewal of extinct ages. What guides this thinking is the conviction that although the living is subject to the ruin of time, the process of decay is at the same time a process of crystallization, that in the depth of the sea, into which sinks and is dissolved what once was alive, some things 'suffer a sea-change' and survive in new crystallized forms and shapes that remain immune to the elements, as though they waited only for the pearl diver who one day will come down to them and bring them up into the world of the living." Hannah Arendt, "Introduction," in *Illuminations*, by Walter Benjamin (New York: Schocken Books, 1969), 50–51.

11. "Neto da Princesa Critica Lideres do Movimento Negro," *Folha de São Paulo*, 11 May 1988.

12. Black History Month in the United States is paradigmatic of these consequences, as numerous heroes and heroines are lined up on a calendar in the effort to represent black achievement. Martin Luther King, the most exploited symbol during the month of February, is presented as a pacifist whose politics and vision of social change culminated with the "I Have a Dream" speech during the March on Washington in 1963. The later, more radical shift in his political stances on U.S. imperialism abroad and internal colonialism at home are rarely ever encountered in mass media presentations of him. King, like many others in the parade of static figures, become frozen in a time deemed most (politically) appropriate for presentation, i.e., a time that least disturbs the status quo.

APPENDIX

INTERVIEWS 1988–1989

Rio de Janeiro

Jurema Batista
Carlos Alberto Cão
Regina Coeli
Frei David Raimundo dos Santos
Helio dos Santos
Ivanir dos Santos
Joel Rufino dos Santos
Manuel Faustino
Orlando Fernandes
Yedo Ferreira
Oliveira Filho "Filo"'
Januario Garcia
Lelia Gonzalez
Togo Ioruba
Gerson Martins
Carlos Alberto Medeiros

Abdias do Nascimento
Sebastio Oliveira
Jengyra de Paula Assis
Juca Ribeiro
Paulo Roberto
João Marcos Romao
Edson Santos
Osseas Santos
Sylvia Schunemann
Ele Semog
Benedito Sergio
Benedita da Silva
Joselina Da Silva
Luis Carlos de Souza
Julio Cesar Tavares

São Paulo

João Antonio Alves
Antonio Carlos Arruda
Aristedes Barbosa
Milton Barbosa
João Batista de Jesus Felix
Padre Batista Laurindo
Adalberto Camargo
Hamilton Cardoso
Sueli Carneiro
Flavio Carranca
Nice Carranca Tudras
Celso Chagas
Roberto Cruz
Deborah Sylvia dos Santos

Raul dos Santos
Padre Luis Fernando
Isidorio
Antonio Leite
Luis Paulo Lima
Ronaldo Lima
Vanderlei Jose Maria
Francisco Marcos Dias
Rafael Pinto
Divaldo Rosa
Nilza Santos
Theresa Santos
Percy da Silva
Maria Aparecida Teixeira da Silva

CONFERENCES, DEBATES, AND MEETINGS OF THE MOVIMENTO NEGRO, 1988–1989

Rio de Janeiro

Candidatos de Prefeito (Clube Renascenca), 1988.
Candidatos Negros Frente a Frente (IPCN, municipal elections), 17, 21, and 24 Oct. 1988.
Maioria Falante (CEAP, various meetings), 1988, 1989.
Encontro Nacional da Mulher Negra, 1988 (attended by Gisele Audrey Mills).
IPCN (various meetings), 1988, 1989.
Cultura Negra nas Escolas, 1988.
Raça e Differenca, 1989.
Instituto Palmares (inaugural meeting), 1989.

São Paulo

Kizomba, 1988.
O Negro e Sindicalismo (CUT), 1988.
Julgamento do Seculo: Tribunal Winne Mandela, 1988.
Encontro do Movimento Negro Sul-Sudeste, 1989.
Encontro Estadual dos Estudantes Negros, 1989.

BIBLIOGRAPHY

BOOKS AND JOURNAL ARTICLES

"Afro-Latino America," in *Versus*, March/April, 1978. São Paulo.

Alvarez, Sonia. *Engendering Democracy in Brazil*. Princeton: Princeton University Press, 1990.

Anderson, Benedict. *Imagined Communities*. London: Verso, 1983.

Anderson, Perry. "The Antinomies of Antonio Gramsci." *New Left Review* (special hundredth issue) no. 100 (November 1976–January 1977): 5–80.

———. "Portugal and the End of Ultra-Colonialism." *New Left Review*, no. 15 (May–June 1962): 83–102.

Andrews, George Reid. *The Afro-Argentines of Buenos Aires*. Madison: University of Wisconsin Press, 1980.

———. "Black Workers and White: São Paulo, Brazil 1888–1928." *Hispanic American Historical Review* 68, no. 3 (August 1988): 491–524.

———. *Blacks and Whites in São Paulo, Brazil, 1888–1988*. Madison: University of Wisconsin Press, 1991.

Arendt, Hannah. "Introduction." In *Illuminations*, by Walter Benjamin. New York: Schocken Books, 1969.

Aronowitz, Stanley. *The Crisis in Historical Materialism*. New York: Praeger, 1981.

Azevedo, Thales de. *Democracia Racial: Ideología é Realidade*. Petropolis: Editora Vozes, 1975.

Bachrach, Peter, and Morton Baratz. *Power and Poverty*. New York: Oxford University Press, 1970.

Balandier, Georges. *Political Anthropology*. New York: Random House, 1970.

Barthes, Roland. *Mythologies*. New York: Hill and Wang, 1972.

Bastide, Roger. *The African Religions of Brazil*. Baltimore: Johns Hopkins Press, 1978.

———. "The Development of Race Relations in Brazil." In *Industrialisation and Race Relations*, edited by Guy Hunter, 9–29. London: Oxford University Press, 1965.

———. "Estereotipos de negros atraves da literatura brasiliera." In *Estudos Afro-Brasileiros*, 113–28. São Paulo: Perspectiva, 1973.

Bender, Gerald. *Angola Under the Portuguese*. Berkeley: University of California Press, 1978.

Berriel, Maria Maia Oliveira. "A identidade fragmentada—As muitas maneiras de ser negro." São Paulo: USP, tese de mestrado, 1988.

Bienen, Henry. *Political Conflict and Economic Change in Nigeria*. London and Totowa, N.J.: F. Cass, 1985.

Bogle, Donald. *Brown Sugar: Eighty Years of American's Black Female Superstars*. New York: Harmony Books, 1980.

Bourdieu, Pierre. *Outline of a Theory of Practice*. London: Cambridge University Press, 1977.

Braga, Julio. "Candomblé: Força e resistência." *Afro-Asia* (Bahia), no. 15 (1992): 13–17.

Branch, Taylor. *Parting the Waters: America During the King Years, 1954–1963.* New York: Simon and Schuster, 1988.

Brasil: Nunca Mais. Petropolis: Vozes, 1985.

Brookshaw, David. *Raça e cor na literatura brasileira.* Porto Alegre: Mercado Aberto, 1983.

Brown, Diana De G., and Mario Bick. "Religion, Class and Context: Continuities and Discontinuities in Brazilian Umbanda." *American Ethnologist* 14, no. 1 (February 1987): 73–93.

Burleigh, Michael, and Wolfgang Wipperman. *The Racial State: Germany 1933–1945.* New York: Cambridge University Press, 1992.

Campello de Souza, Maria do Carmo. "The New Brazilian Republic: Under the Sword of Damocles." In *Democratizing Brazil,* edited by Alfred Stepan, New York: Oxford University Press, 1989, 351–83.

Casa-Grande e Senzala: 50 anos depois, um encontro com Gilberto Freyre. Rio de Janeiro: FUNARTE, 1985.

Catálogo: Centenario da Abolição. Rio de Janeiro: CIEC–Nucleo de Cor–UFRJ, 1989.

Catálogo de entidades de movimento negro no Brasil. Communicacoes do ISER no. 29. Rio de Janeiro: ISER, 1988.

Clifford, James. *Writing Culture.* Berkeley: University of California Press, 1986.

Collins, Patricia Hill. *Black Feminist Thought.* New York: Routledge, 1991.

Conrad, Robert Edgar. *Children of God's Fire.* Princeton: Princeton University Press, 1983.

———. *The Destruction of Brazilian Slavery, 1850–88.* Berkeley: University of California Press, 1972.

Couceiro, Solange M. *O negro na televisão de São Paulo: Um estudo de relaçoes raciais.* São Paulo: FFLCH-USP, 1983.

Coutinho, Carlos Nelson, and Marco Aurelio Nogueira. *Gramsci e a América Latina.* São Paulo: Paz é Terra, 1985.

Cox, Oliver C. *Caste, Class and Race.* New York: Monthly Review Press, 1948.

Cunha, Henrique, Jr. "A indecisão dos pais faça a percepção da discriminação racial na escola pela criança." *Cadernos de Pesquisa* (São Paulo) 63 (November 1987): 51–53.

———. "Os movimentos negros no Brasil." *Jornal do Leitura* (São Paulo) 7, no. 74 (July 1988): 6–7.

Dalton, Rusell J., and Manfred Kuechler, eds. *Challenging the Political Order.* New York: Oxford University Press, 1990.

DaMatta, Roberto. *Relativizando.* 4th ed. Petropolis: Vozes, 1984.

Dean, Warren. *Rio Claro: A Brazilian Plantation System, 1820–1920.* Palo Alto: Stanford University Press, 1976.

Degler, Carl. *Neither Black nor White: Slavery and Race Relations in the United States and Brazil.* New York: Macmillan, 1971.

Diaz-Polanco, Hector. *Etnia, nación y política.* Mexico City: J. Pablos, 1987.

Dionysos: Teatro Experimental do Negro. No. 28. Rio de Janeiro: minC FUNDACEN, 1988.

DuBois, W.E.B. *Black Reconstruction in America, 1860–1880*. Cleveland: World Publishers, 1969.

Dzidzienyo, Anani. *The Position of Blacks in Brazilian Society*. London: Minority Rights Group, 1971.

Enloe, Cynthia. *Ethnic Conflict and Political Development*. Boston: Little, Brown and Company, 1973.

Fernandes, Florestan. *The Negro In Brazilian Society*. New York: Columbia University Press, 1969.

————. *Significado do Protesto Negro*. Coleção polemicas do nosso tempo, vol. 33. São Paulo: Cortez: Autores Associados, 1989.

Figueira, Vera. "Preconceito racial: Diffusão e manutencão na escola." *Intercambio* (SESC, Rio de Janeiro) 1, no. 1 (January–April 1988): 37–46.

————. "O preconceito racial na escola." *Estudos Afro-Asiaticos* (Rio de Janeiro: Centro de Estudos Afro-Asiaticos) 18 (May 1990): 63–72.

Fischer, Michael M. J. "Ethnicity and the Post-Modern Arts of Memory." In *Writing Culture*, edited by James Clifford, 194–233. Berkeley: University of California Press, 1986.

Fontaine, Pierre-Michel. *Race, Class and Power in Brazil*. Los Angeles: Center for Afro-American Studies, UCLA, 1985.

————. "Research in the Political Economy of Afro-Latino America." *Latin American Research Review* 15, no. 2 (1980): 111–42.

Franklin, John Hope. *Reconstruction After the Civil War*. Chicago: University of Chicago, 1961.

Frazier, E. Franklin. *Black Bourgeoisie*. New York: Collier, 1962.

Freyre, Gilberto. *The Masters and the Slaves*. New York: Alfred A. Knopf, 1946.

————. *Sobrados e Macumbos*. 3d. ed. São Paulo: J. Olympia, 1951.

Fry, Peter. *Para ingles ver*. Rio de Janeiro: Zahar, 1982.

Garrow, David J. *Bearing the Cross: Martin Luther King Jr. and the Southern Christian Leadership Conference*. New York: H. Morrow, 1986.

Geertz, Clifford. *The Interpretation of Cultures*. New York: Basic Books, 1970.

Genovese, Eugene. *Roll, Jordan, Roll: The World the Slaves Made*. New York, Vintage Books, 1976.

Gilroy, Paul. *There Ain't No Black in the Union Jack*. London: Hutchinson, 1987.

Glazer, Nathan, and Moynihan, Daniel P., eds. *Beyond the Melting Pot*. 2d ed. Cambridge: MIT Press, 1970.

————. *Ethnicity: Theory and Experience*. Cambridge: Harvard University Press, 1975.

Gonzalez, Lelia, and Carlos Hasenbalg. *Lugar do negro*. Rio de Janeiro: Editoria Marco Zero, 1985.

Graham, Richard, ed. *The Idea of Race in Latin America*. Austin: University of Texas Press, 1990.

Gramsci, Antonio. *Selections from the Prison Notebooks of Antonio Gramsci*, translated and edited by Quintin Hoare and Geoffrey Nowell Smith. New York: International Publishers, 1971.

Greenberg, Stanley. *Race, State, and Captialist Development*. New Haven: Yale University Press, 1980.

Guha, Ranajit, and Gayatri Chakravorty Spivak. *Selected Subaltern Studies.* New York: Oxford University Press, 1988.

Habermas, Jurgen. *Reason and the Rationalization of Society.* Vol. 2 of *The Theory of Communicative Action.* Boston: Beacon Press, 1984.

Hall, Stuart. "Gramsci's Relevance for the Study of Race and Ethnicity." *Journal of Communication Inquiry* 10, no. 2 (Summer 1986): 5–27.

———. "Race, Culture and Communications: Looking Backward and Forward at Cultural Studies." *Rethinking Marxism* 5, no. 1 (Spring 1992): 10–18.

Hanchard, Michael. "Identity, Meaning and the African-American." *Social Text* 8, no. 24 (1990): 31–42.

———. "Raça, hegemonia e subordinação na cultura popular." *Estudos Afro-Asiáticos* (Rio de Janeiro: Centro de Estudos Afro-Asiáticos, Conjunto Universitario Candido Mendes) 21 (December 1991): 5–26. 1991.

———. "Racial Consciousness and Afro-Diasporic Experiences: Antonio Gramsci Reconsidered." *Socialism and Democracy* 7, no. 14 (Fall 1991): 83–106.

Harris, Marvin. *Patterns of Race in the Americas.* New York: Walker, 1964.

Hartz, Louis. *The Liberal Tradition in America.* New York: Harcourt, Brace and World, 1955.

Hasenbalg, Carlos. *Discriminação e Desigualdades Raciais no Brasil.* Rio de Janeiro: Graal, 1979.

———. "Race and Socioeconomic Inequalities in Brazil." In *Race, Class and Power in Brazil,* edited by Pierre-Michel Fontaine, 25–41. Los Angeles: UCLA, Center for Afro-American Studies, 1985.

Hasenbalg, Carlos, and Nelson do Valle Silva. *Estructura Social, Mobilidade e Raça.* São Paulo: Vertice e IUPERJ, 1988.

Hellwig, David. *African-American Reflections on Brazil's Racial Paradise.* Philadelphia: Temple University Press, 1992.

———. "Racial Paradise or Run-around? Afro-North American Views of Race Relations in Brazil." *American Studies* 31 (Fall 1990): 43–60.

Hobsbawm, Eric. *Banditry.* New York: Pantheon, 1969.

Hobsbawm, Eric, and Terence Ranger, eds. *The Invention of Tradition.* Cambridge: Cambridge University Press, 1984.

Hoetink, Harold. *Caribbean Race Relations.* London: Oxford University Press, 1967.

Holanda Barbosa, Livia Neves de. "O jeitinho, ou a arte de ser mais igual que os outros." *Ciência Hoje* (São Paulo: Sociedade Brasileira Para o Progresso da Ciencia) 7, no. 42 (May 1988): 50–56.

Hunter, Guy, ed. *Industrialisation and Race Relations,* London: Oxford University Press, 1965.

Ianni, Octavio. "Race and Class in Brazil." in *Presence Africaine* (English ed. Paris: Presence Africaine) 25, no. 53 (1965).

James, C. L. R. *At the Rendezvous of Victory.* London: Allison and Busby, 1984.

Jameson, Frederic. *The Political Unconscious.* Ithaca: Cornell University Press, 1981.

Jaquette, Jane S., ed. *The Women's Movement in Latin America.* Boston: Unwin and Hyman, 1989.

Jimenez, Michael F. "Class, Gender, and Peasant Resistance in Central Colombia,

1900–1930." In *Everyday Forms of Peasant Resistance*, edited by Forrest Colburn, 122–50. New York: M. E. Sharpe, 1989.

Johnson, Pauline. *Marxist Aesthetics*. London: Routledge & Kegan Paul, 1984.

Johnson, Randal. *Cinema Novo*. Austin: University of Texas Press, 1984.

Johnson, Randal, and Robert Stam, eds. *Brazilian Cinema*. Rutherford, N.J., and London: Fairleigh Dickinson University Press and Associated University Press, 1982.

Katznelson, Ira. *Black Men, White Cities*. London: Oxford University Press, 1973.

Kennedy, James. "Political Liberalization, Black Consciousness, and Recent Afro-Brazilian Literature." *Phylon* 3, no. 47 (1986): 199–209.

Knight, Alan. "Racism, Revolution and *Indigenismo*: Mexico, 1910–1940." In *The Idea of Race in Latin America*, 227–63. Austin: University of Texas Press, 1990.

Laitin, David. *Hegemony and Culture*. Chicago: University of Chicago Press, 1986.

Leite, José Correia and Cuti. . . . *E disse o velho militante José Correia*. São Paulo: Seçretaria Municipal de Cultura, 1992.

Levine, Robert M. "The First Afro-Brazilian Congress: Opportunities for the Study of Race in the Brazilian Northeast." *Race* 2, no. 15 (1973): 185–93. London: Centre for Race Relations, 1973.

———. *The Vargas Regime: The Critical Years, 1934–1938*. New York: Columbia University Press, 1970.

Lewis, Oscar. "The Culture of Poverty." *Scientific American* 215, no. 4 (October 1966): 14–25.

Lovell, Peggy. "Development and Racial Inequality in Brazil: Wage Discrimination in Urban Labor Markets, 1960–1980." Paper presented at The Peopling of the Americas Conference, Veracruz, Mexico, 1992.

Lovel, Peggy, ed. *Desigualdade racial no brasil contemporâneo*. Belo Horizonte: MGSP Editores Ltda., 1991.

Lukes, Steven. *Power: A Radical View*. London: Macmillan, 1974.

Maggie, Yvonne. "O que se cala quando se fala do negro no Brasil." Mimeo, June 1988.

Marable, Manning. *African and Caribbean Politics: From Kwame Nkrumah to Maurice Bishop*. London: Verso, 1987.

Maram, Sheldon. "Labor and the Left in Brazil, 1890–1921: A Movement Aborted." *Hispanic American Historical Review* 57, no. 2 (1977): 254–72.

Marti, Jose. *On Education*, edited by Phillip S. Foner. New York: Monthly Review Press, 1979.

Martinez-Alier, Verena. *Marriage, Class and Colour in Nineteenth Century Cuba: A Study of Racial Attitudes and Sexual Values in a Slave Society*. London: Cambridge University Press, 1974.

Maues, Maria Angelica de Motta. "Entre o branqueamento e a negritude: O TEN e o debate da questão racial." In *Dionysos: Teatro Experimental do Negro*. No. 28. Rio de Janeiro: minC FUNDACEN, 1988.

———. "Negro sobre negro: A questão racial no pensamento das elites negras brasileiras." Paper presented at the ANPOCS conference, Brazil, 1987.

McAdam, Doug, *Political Process and the Development of Black Insurgency, 1930–1970.* Chicago: University of Chicago Press. 1981.

"Mesa Redonda: Materialismo Historico e Questão Racial." *Estudos Afro-Asiáticos* (Rio de Janeiro: Centro de Estudos Afro-Asiaticos), no. 12 (August 1986): 31–35.

Mintz, Sidney. "Currency Problems in Eighteenth Century Jamaica and Gresham's Law." In *Process and Pattern in Culture: Essays in Honor of Julian H. Steward,* edited by Robert Manners, 264–85. Chicago: Aldine Publishing, 1964.

Mitchell, Michael. "Racial Consciousness and the Political Attitudes and Behavior of Blacks in São Paulo, Brazil." Ph.D. diss., University of Michigan, 1977.

Moore, Barrington. *The Social Origins of Dictatorship and Democracy.* Boston: Beacon Press, 1966.

Morris, Aldon. *The Origins of the Civil Rights Movement.* New York: Free Press, 1984.

Moura, Clovis. *Quilombos, resistencia ao escravismo.* São Paulo: Atica, 1987.

———. *Sociologa do negro brasiliero.* São Paulo: Atica, 1988.

"Movimento negro e o culturalismo." *SINBA* (Rio de Janeiro: Marco) 3, no. 4 (1980): 3.

Movimento Negro Unificado. *1978–1988: 10 Anos de luta contra o racismo.* São Paulo: MNU—Seção Bahia, 1988.

———. *Programa de ação: Negros protestam em praca publica.* São Paulo: MNU, ca. 1984.

Movimento Negro Unificado Contra Discriminação Racial. *Boletim informativo.* São Paulo: MNUCDR, September 1979.

———. "O papel do aparato policial do Estado no processo de dominação do Negro e a Anistia." Paper presented before National Amnesty Congress, São Paulo, 1978.

Murphy, Craig N. "Freezing the North-South Bloc(k)." *Socialist Review* 20, no. 3 (July-September 1990): 25–46.

Nascimento, Abdias do. *Mixture or Massacre: Essays in the Genocide of a Black People.* Buffalo: Afrodiaspora, 1979.

Nascimento, Maria Ercilia do. "A estrategia da desigualdade: O movimento negro dos anos '70." Master's thesis, Pontifica Universidade Catolica, 1989.

Negros no Brasil, dados da realidade. Petropolis: VOZES, Instituto Brasileiro de Analises Sociais e Economicas, 1989.

Nogueira, Oracy. "Preconceito de Marca e preconceito racial de origem." In *Anais do XXXI Congresso Internacional de Americanistas,* 409–34. São Paulo: Editors Anhembi, 1955.

Offe, Claus, "Reflections on the Institutional Self-Transformation of Movement Politics: A Tentative Stage Model," in *Challenging the Political Order,* edited by Russel J. Dalton and Manfred Kuechler, 232–50. London: (Oxford University Press, 1990).

Omi, Michael, and Howard Winant. *Racial Formation in the United States.* New York: Routledge, 1986.

Patterson, Orlando. "Context and Choice in Ethnic Allegiance: A Theoretical Framework and Caribbean Case Study." In *Ethnicity: Theory and Experience,* edited by Nathan Glazer and Daniel P. Moynihan, 305–50. Cambridge: Harvard University Press, 1975.

Pereira, João Baptista Borges. "Aspectos do comportamento politico do negro em São Paulo." *Ciência e Cultura* (São Paulo: FFLCH/USP) 34, no. 10 (October 1982): 1286–94.

Perlman, Janice. *The Myth of Marginality*. Berkeley: University of California, 1976.

Pierce, Robert. *Keeping the Flame: Media and Government in Latin America*. New York: Communication Arts Books, 1979.

Pierson, Donald. *Negroes in Brazil: A Study of Race Conflict in Bahia*. Carbondale: Southern Illinois University Press, 1967.

Pinto, R. P. "A representação do negro em livros didaticos de leitura." *Cadernos de Pesquisa* (São Paulo) 63 (November 1987): 88–92.

Piven, Frances Fox, and Richard A. Cloward. *Poor Peoples Movements*. New York: Pantheon, 1977.

Poggi, Gianfranco. *The Development of the Modern State*. Palo Alto: Stanford University Press, 1978.

Prandi, Reginaldo. *Os candomblés de São Paulo*. São Paulo: Editora HUCITEC, 1991.

"Raça negra e educação." *Cadernos de pesquisa* (São Paulo: Fundação Carlos Chagas), no. 63 (November 1987).

Rafael, Alison. "Samba and Social Control." Ph.D. diss., Columbia University, 1981.

Ramos, Guerreiro. *Introdução critica a sociedade brasileira*. Rio de Janerio: Editora Andes, 1957.

Reis, João Jose, ed. *Escravidão e Invenção da Liberdade*. São Paulo: Editora Brasiliense, 1988.

Rex, John, and David Mason. *Theories of Race and Ethnic Relations*. Cambridge: Cambridge University Press, 1986.

Robinson, Cedric. *Black Marxism*. London: Zed, 1983.

Rolnik, Raquel. "Territorios negros nas cidades brasileiras (Ethnicidade e cidade em São Paulo e no Rio de Janeiro)." *Estudos Afro-Asiáticos* (Rio de Janeiro: Conjunto Universitario Candido Mendes), no. 17 (1989): 29–41.

Rodrigues da Silva, Carlos Benedito. "Black Soul: Aglutinaçao espontanea ou identidade etnica." In *Movimentos sociais, urbanos, minorias etnicas e outros estudos*, edited by L. A. Silva, et al., 245–62. Brasilia: ANPOCS, 1983.

Rosemberg, Fluvia. "Discriminaçoes etnico-raciais na literatura infanto-juvenil brasileira." *Rev. Bras., Bibliotecon. Doc.* (São Paulo) 12, nos. 3–4 (July –December 1979): 155–66.

Rouquie, Alain. "Demilitarization and the Institutionalization of Military Dominated Polities in Latin America." In *Transitions from Authoritarian Rule*, edited by Guillermo O'Donnell, Phillipe Schmitter, and Laurence Whitehead, 108–36. Baltimore: Johns Hopkins University Press, 1988.

Russell-Wood, A. J. R. *The Black Man in Slavery and Freedom in Colonial Brazil*. New York: St. Martin's Press, 1982.

Sandoval, Salvador. "The Mechanisms of Race Discrimination in the Labor Market: The Case of Urban Brazil." Paper presented at the Fifteenth International

Meeting of the Latin American Studies Association, San Juan, Puerto Rico, 21–23 Sept. 1989.

Santos, Joel Rufino dos. "O movimento negro é a crise brasileira," in *Politica é Administração* (Rio de Janeiro) 2, no. 2 (July-September 1985): 287–307.

Schwarcz, Lilia K. Moritz. *De festa tambem se vive: Reflexoes sobre o centenario da Abolição em São Paulo.* Rio de Janeiro: CIEC—UFRJ, 1989.

Schwarcz, Lilia Morita K. *Retrato em branco e negro: Escravos e cidadoes em São Paulo no seculo XIX.* São Paulo: Companhia das Letras, 1987.

Scott, James. *Domination and the Arts of Resistance.* New Haven: Yale University Press, 1990.

———. *Weapons of the Weak.* New Haven: Yale University Press, 1985.

Seyferth, Giralda. "As ciências sociais no Brasil e a questão racial." In *Cateiro e Liberdade,* 11–31. Rio de Janeiro: Instituto de Filosofia e Ciências Humanas (IFCH-UERG), 1989.

Skidmore, Thomas. "Bi-Racial U.S. v. Multi-Racial Brazil: Is the Contrast Still Valid?" Paper presented at the Conference on Racism and Race Relations in the Countries of the African Diaspora, Rio de Janiero, 6–10 Apr. 1992.

———. *Black Into White.* New York: Oxford University Press, 1974.

———. *The Politics of Military Rule in Brazil, 1964–1985.* New York: Oxford University Press, 1988.

Skocpol, Theda. *States and Social Revolutions.* New York: Cambridge University Press, 1979.

Spickard, Paul R. *Mixed Blood: Intermarriage and Ethnic Identity in Twentieth Century America.* Madison: University of Wisconsin Press, 1989.

Spivak, Gayatri. *In Other Worlds.* London: Routledge & Kegan Paul, 1988.

Sombart, Werner. *Why Is There No Socialism in the United States?* London: Macmillan, 1976.

Stampp, Kenneth. *The Era of Reconstruction 1865–1877.* New York: Vintage, 1965.

Stepan, Alfred. *Rethinking Military Politics.* Princeton: Princeton University Press, 1988.

———. *The State and Society: Peru in Comparative Perspective.* Princeton: Princeton University Press, 1978.

Stepan, Alfred, ed. *Democratizing Brazil: Problems of Transition and Consolidation.* New York: Oxford University Press, 1989.

Stepan, Nancy Leys. *The Hour of Eugenics.* Ithaca: Cornell University Press, 1991.

Stolcke, Verena. *Cafeicultura: Homens, mulheres e capital.* São Paulo: Editora Brasilense, 1986.

Tannenbaum, Frank. "The Destiny of the Negro in the Western Hemisphere." *Political Science Quarterly* 61, no. 1 (March 1946).

———. *Slave and Citizen.* New York: Alfred A. Knopf, 1947.

Telles, Edward. "Residential Segregation by Skin Color in Brazil." *American Sociological Review* 57 (1992): 186–97.

Toms, Coons, Mulattoes, Mammies and Bucks: An Interpretive History of Blacks in American Films (New York: Viking, 1973.)

Toplin, Robert Brent. "Abolition and the Issue of the Black Freedman's Future in Brazil." In *Slavery and Race Relations in Latin America,* edited by Robert Brent Toplin, 253–76. Westport, Conn.: Greenwood Press, 1974.

Touraine, Alain. *The Voice and the Eye: An Analysis of Social Movements.*. Cambridge: Cambridge University Press, 1981.

Tucci Carneiro, Maria Luiza. *O anti-Semitismo na era Vargas.* São Paulo: Editora Brasilense, 1988.

———. *Preconceito racial no Brasil-colônia.* São Paulo: Editora Brasilense, 1983.

Vainer, Carlos B. "Estado e raça no Brasil: Notas exploratorias." *Estudos Afro-Asiaticos,* no. 18 (1990): 103–17.

Van den Berghe, Pierre. *Race and Ethnicity.* New York: Basic Books, 1970.

Valente, Ana Lucia E. F. *Politica e relaçoes raciais: Os negros e as eleiçoes Paulistas de 1982.* São Paulo: FFLCH-USP1, 1986.

Valle Silva, Nelson do. "The High Cost of Not Being White in Brazil." In *Race, Class and Power in Brazil,* edited by Pierre-Michel Fontaine, 42–55. Los Angeles: Center for Afro-American Studies, UCLA, 1985.

Vianna, Hermano. *O mundo funk Carioca,* Rio de Janeiro: Jorge Zahar, 1988.

Viotti, Emilia da Costa. *The Brazilian Empire: Myths and Histories.* Chicago: University of Chicago Press, 1985.

Wagley, Charles. *Race and Class in Rural Brazil.* 2d. ed. Paris: UNESCO, 1963.

Warren, Kay. *The Symbolism of Subordination.* Austin: University of Texas Press, 1978.

West, Cornel. "Marxist Theory and the Specificity of Afro-American Oppression," in *Marxism and the Interpretation of Culture,* edited by Cary Nelson and Lawrence Grossberg. Urbana and Chicago: University of Illinois Press, 1988.

Williams, Raymond. *Marxism and Literature.* New York: Oxford University Press, 1977.

Winant, Howard. *Racial Conditions: Theories, Politics and Comparisons.* Minneapolis: University of Minnesota Press, 1994.

Wolf, Eric. *Peasant Wars of the 20th Century.* New York: Harper and Row, 1969.

Wolin, Sheldon. "Contract and Birthright." In *The Presense of the Past,* 137–50. Baltimore: Johns Hopkins University Press, 1989.

Wood, Charles. "Categorias censitarias é classificaçãos subjectivas de paca no Brasil." In *Desigualdade racial no Brasil contemporaneo,* edited by Peggy A. Lovell. Belo Horizonte: CEDEALAR, 1991.

Woodward, C. Vann. *The Strange Career of Jim Crow.* New York: Harper and Row, 1969.

Wright, Winthrop R. *Café con Leche: Race, Class and National Image in Venezuela.* Austin: University of Texas Press, 1990.

Young, Crawford. *The Politics of Cultural Pluralism.* Madison: University of Wisconsin Press, 1976.

NEWSPAPER ARTICLES

"'Black Rio' assusta maestro Julio Medaglia." *Folha de São Paulo.* 10 June 1977.

"Divergencias marcam festa da Abolição na capital paulista," *Jornal do Brasil.* Rio de Janeiro, 14 May 1988.

Freyre, Gilberto. "Atenção, brasileiros!" *Diario de Pernambuco,* Recife, 15 May 1977.

———. "Racismo no Brasil?" *Folha de São Paulo.* 6 May 1979.

"Neder teme surgimento de Hitler negro." *O Globo*, Rio de Janeiro, 22 March 1979.

"Neto da princesa critica lideres do movimento negro." *Folha de São Paulo*, 11 May 1988.

"O soul, do grito negro a caderneta de poupança." *Jornal do Brasil*, Rio de Janeiro, 8 Mar. 1976.

"PMs acusados de discriminação e agressão." *O Dia*. Rio de Janeiro, 17 May 1988.

"Policiais impedem marcha de movimento negro pelo Centro." *Jornal do Comercio*, Rio de Janeiro, 12 May 1988.

"Quatro mil negros saem em passeata contra o 13 de Maio." *O Globo*. Rio de Janeiro, 12 May 1988.

"Treva Contra Treva." *Veja*, Rio de Janeiro, 18 May 1988.

"Turismo ve só comercio no black Rio," in *Jornal Do Brasil*. Rio de Janeiro, 15 May 1977.

INDEX